Stealing History

Stealing History

GERALD STERN

TRINITY UNIVERSITY PRESS
SAN ANTONIO

Published by Trinity University Press
San Antonio, Texas 78212

Copyright © 2012 by Gerald Stern

Cover design by Nicole Hayward
Book design by BookMatters, Berkeley
Cover photograph by Gerald Zörner

Some of the pieces in this book have appeared or will appear in the following journals. *Organica*, "Trip to New York with Poet Potter"; *American Poetry Review*, "Park Bench," "Etheridge Knight," "Neighbors III," and "Port Authority Bus Terminal."

Trinity University Press strives to produce its books using methods and materials in an environmentally sensitive manner. We favor working with manufacturers that practice sustainable management of all natural resources, produce paper using recycled stock, and manage forests with the best possible practices for people, biodiversity, and sustainability. The press is a member of the Green Press Initiative, a nonprofit program dedicated to supporting publishers in their efforts to reduce their impacts on endangered forests, climate change, and forest-dependent communities.

The paper used in this publication meets the minimum requirements of the American National Standard for Information Sciences—Permanence of Paper for Printed Library Materials, ANSI 39.48-1992.

Library of Congress Cataloging-in-Publication Data

Stern, Gerald, 1925–
    Stealing history / Gerald Stern.
      p.   cm.
SUMMARY: "Stern reflects with wit, pathos, rage, and tenderness on eighty-five years of life, much of it spent engaged with literature and learning—as a major American poet, a longtime teacher at the University of Iowa Writers' Workshop, an insatiably broad reader, and a devoted friend to artists and writers"—*Provided by publisher.*
ISBN 978-1-59534-114-3 (hardcover : alk. paper)
ISBN 978-1-59534-141-9 (paperback : alk. paper)
    1. Stern, Gerald, 1925– 2. Poets, American—20th century—Biography. I. Title.
PS3569.T3888Z46   2012
811'.54—dc23 [B]   2011043734

16   15   14   13   12   5   4   3   2   1

Contents

1 Park Bench

When I was as young as twenty-five or six, part of me was exhausted from the difficult life I was leading as a young writer and the absurd responsibilities that were already coming my way and though I anticipated at least another half-century of it, I was thinking (already) of "the stillness after," taking some classical form of, well, giving away all my earthly goods and living in a tent or a hut somewhere—maybe a small cheap hotel room with a bathroom in the hall, though I had to remind myself that—at that time—I had very few earthly goods and could probably squeeze everything, including my responsibilities, into a cardboard or canvas suitcase of some sort.

I had already picked out a dream place for the stillness after, a park bench in Pittsburgh directly in front of the main Carnegie library, parking spaces in the cement square behind me, and a lovely old bridge to one side, leading directly into Schenley Park and, I might add, the beautiful old Forbes Field a little beyond the parking where, as a boy, I would sometimes pay a dime, on Boys' Day, to watch the Waner brothers and Al Todd and Arky Vaughn play against the Cubs or the Cardinals, though mostly I snuck in, taking advantage of a loose board and a gulley and a large shadow that covered the crime, even if the joy was not so much in saving ten cents—though that counted—but the pleasure of a free ride, a burdenless existence, a liberation into the heaven of free baseball, say forever.

Why I chose a park bench instead of a sling chair under a tree, or a rocky hillside, or a dark and silent cellar, or a seashore, or a cave— for there were caves—I don't know. A park bench is very little like a mountain, but you never can tell. It was Bernard Baruch, famous advisor to presidents who, like me, sat on a bench. He actually had two benches, one in Lafayette Park across from the White House and one in Central Park, New York. I checked, *en passant*, with a friend of mine, a novelist, in her early seventies, or late sixties, to see if his was a familiar name to her and, to my amazement, it wasn't, so I have to assume that Baruch is likewise not to the thousands younger than her who even bother to read a little or even—like her—write a dozen or so brilliant books.

Baruch was a famous financier and statesman. He made millions buying and selling stocks and devoted much of his time to advising politicians, particularly Woodrow Wilson and Franklin D. Roosevelt, on economic matters. He certainly was—for them—the wise Jew of mystic tradition, a Joseph to their Pharaoh, a Mordecai to their Ahasuerus, with or without a famous cousin, certainly with a bowler on his head and a stiff white collar on his neck. Encyclopedias tell us that he amassed a fortune before the age of thirty via speculation in the sugar market, that his father, Simon Baruch, was a surgeon on the staff of General Robert E. Lee during the Civil War, and that he not only accompanied President Wilson to Versailles but was a member of FDR's "Brain Trust." He entered City College at the age of fourteen, and it was he, not Winston Churchill or Walter Lippmann, who originated the term "Cold War." He had a 17,500-acre winter residence on the coast of South Carolina that presidents visited, yet Bulldog Hoover kept tabs on him. There is a statue of him sitting on the famous bench inside the entrance to Baruch College in New York that I sat beside once, wiping his stone tears. I don't know anything about his wife, his children, his mistress, and his dog, nor do I have the time to find out. I do know that his mother counseled him "to be kind to the negroes in (your) care," referring to the descendants of the enslaved African Americans on Hobcaw Plantation, his happy hunting grounds. He did provide beds for "negroes" in the hospital he built in Georgetown County, South Carolina, and he did give money for scholarships to Negro colleges. He was, therefore, more or less, a liberal southerner, somewhere at the lower end of the ladder.

I of course resent him for his park benches and his co-option. And that he used a sacred place for charm's sake. And that he used the bench to labor, not to refresh himself or take stock or change his life or give up. Though, I must admit—for charity's sake—that he might have been doing some of those things. And I am a little insistent. But for me the park bench was, or is, for the stillness after, though I might, if pressured, give a little counsel, even if it was more for squirrels and pigeons than for presidents and the like. One time, when I was actually sitting, someone asked me a question, but they were looking for directions, not direction, and no one, thanks God, ever asked me what the secret of life was, or how many angels it would take to change a lightbulb, or should they study law or write poetry, or could a fullback show compassion and did he have to pray before the game and did he have to pat or slap his teammate's ass, and, if so, before or after the whistle.

The truth is I don't know if that park bench is still there, for everything changes, as Ovid—and Heraclites—observed. But there are many other benches and many parks, and the issue anyhow is not the bench but the mind's location, or the heart's, and one may have to transfer his thoughts and his affects to someplace else. I wrote a while ago about a bald Chinese poet in the fifteenth century, standing on a cliff top looking at the sky. There were some clouds below on one side and hints of a pine forest on the other. His hut was in the midst of the pine forest. He was wearing a loose robe and holding a long stick in his left hand and tightening a sash around his waist. There was a mountain, a kind of smudge, tower-, ing in the distance. He was thinking of his wife and the poem that he had composed for her years ago. The subject was separation. The grief. Now he was *thinking* of the grief. He remembers the T'ang era and wishes it was he who broke away from the elegance. He weeps when he remembers the poem of the grass hovel, "Not even a tattered blanket to sleep on," "No coals in the house." And he wonders what he should do when the rain starts. He tries to remember the name of his last supervisor—at the office of metal-lurgy and naval procurement—but, for the life of him, he can't. He is in a good place, for he, the bald one with the fringe, is discon-nected somewhere on that mountain. He has lost his anger, maybe his desire, certainly his greed. Or his *former* greed. He may seem selfish to us, unworried about his family's welfare, but surely he did some things before he left his former home, *n'est-ce pas?* Surpris-ingly, he is no longer in exile, even if his mountain is called exile. Even if he is alone. He may even have forgotten the name of his absurd outpost, where he slaved away all those years, caught up in ritual, politics, and repetitive acts. He calls what he does remember "the larger things," and he calls where he lived "the lower world," but he doesn't do that with contempt. And he is amused by the simultaneity of the literal and the figurative, how a mountain is a mountain and yet more than a mountain, and he doesn't give a damn if the romantic sublime is in fashion or not.

What my Chinese poet may have done diurnally, where he got his food, how he passed his time, I don't know—but I could guess. Where I would sleep when I left that park bench, likewise. For a year or so, when I and my former wife were unbearably poor, we lived on dried lima beans. We boiled them, with a touch of onion, and poured ketchup over them—the cheapest possible dish, twice a day. When I lived in New York in the very late 1940s, studying for a degree at Columbia, I lived on the G.I. Bill, seventy-five dollars a month, which gave me maybe a dollar fifty a day for food. But I had ways to cope. I went hungry, I ate only two meals a day, and sometimes I made a sandwich in one of the superettes on Broadway, cheese and ham, a roll, all retrieved from the cases and the bins. Even mayonnaise. Not only did I have no guilt, but I wasn't worried about the Law since I was consuming the food *in* the store. I doubt if that could be called larceny, and, anyhow, I swallowed the crime. Though in no way was I either righteous or revengeful. I didn't think the world owed me a living because of my insane devotion to a certain part of the brain. The act was, as far as I can tell, nonpolitical.

The bald poet was, of course, a civil servant of a certain grade and probably had an excellent retirement income, for all we know, superior to today's plan, say in Georgia or Indiana or even New Jersey. I imagine he gave 80 percent to his wife and children and kept two books, a quill, a cloak, a small mattress, a chair, and a pot, all of which he conceivably pushed—or pulled—up the mountain. I imagine also that he wrote one letter a year to his wife and one to his oldest son. Maybe he took a brush too as well as a quill, and some colored ink. If he had worked there in the lower world for twenty-five or even thirty years, he would be in his early fifties. Already a little old. Certainly he wasn't yet sixty-five, the absurd and arbitrary age when we theoretically stop working, at which point social security, in all its compassion, kicks in. Lately, I have discovered cabbage and onions, sautéed to perfection, which I eat either with a hard-boiled egg or a little bit of cottage cheese. But I'm mostly still in the lower world and spend a hundred dollars or so for supper for my partner, Anne Marie, and me, may God forgive me.

I was just getting started in my fifties, so it's ridiculous to think I might have retired at that time. And I'm so involved with "the things" and so little prepared to leave them that I am less inclined now than I was, say, thirty, forty years ago to journey to my bench, my cave, or my mountain. It may be that I won't leave my "things"; most people don't. If I made an inventory, it would stretch like an oversized rug, from wall to wall, then up one side and down the other. Terrifying to think of; even with the eighty or so oversize boxes Stephanie and I organized into an archive and sold or gave away. Under other hands, that, and cataloged, but does it not weigh something? About forty years ago, my dearest friend and his wife, along with the two of us, my wife and I—and the children, theirs and ours—were vacationing on the Jersey shore, and at a certain point, on a clear and sunny day, the two of *us*—the breadwinners—were walking in the sand with our hands behind us, talking earnestly, picking up mussels and scattering sandpipers when we decided we had done enough and were now going to *retire*. We were in our early forties. Our wives, when they heard the news, screamed with laughter. For five minutes. We had about a dime between us. But I'm not sure that that was exactly the point. We hadn't yet finished our work. We were weighed down with not only boxes. My friend, Robert Summers, hung himself a year or so later, for which I never stop mourning. The issue was work, of course, not boxes. And, I might add that living Thoreau-like or Diogenes-like, say in silence at the bottom of a well somewhere in Greece or Morocco, and eating poisonous soup or subsisting on celery, doesn't necessarily give you a foot up, even if your myth sustains you a little. The same money, the same boxes, the same—even better—narcissism, for the water is clear down there. And even if it's not a bad thing to live in the imagination, you have to be careful for you could bump into a hydrant or trip on a broken sidewalk as you went dreaming by at a fast and inattentive pace. I sat on my park bench once in the middle of the winter with heavy flakes of snow falling on my hat and clouding over my glasses. A mountain, surely, and a seashore. And though I tried hard, all I could think about was the joy of my next labor. Hercules, you could say.

2 Dragonfly, Famous Deaths

"What we cannot speak about," Wittgenstein said, "we must pass over in silence," though he actually said, "Wovon man nicht sprechen kann, darüber muß man schweigen." I think it has implications in the German that are not present in English, but I respectfully request that I be freed from *that* lecture. Although I will say that the reference is not only to the unspeakable, that is, that which can't be spoken of since the true words aren't there, but that which is frightful or hideous beyond imagination, as we say, the "inspeakable." Death is unspeakable. The name of God is unspeakable; the truly restricted, the orthodox, call God "the name," thus checking Wittgenstein. We could even, in today's lingo, call him "whatever." I mean God, not Wittgenstein. Although we don't call death "whatever." We are too respectful, too terrified.

Death came to me in my ten-year-old Honda the last month or so in the form of a dead dragonfly who first lay on my dashboard as if still alive and ready to hover and bite, then, growing smaller by the day, or seeming to do so, his, or her, body folding, her abdomen withering, her legs collapsing! Dead as she was, she seemed to have a life, especially since she assumed new postures and even changed locations, whenever I looked. The wind, the swerving of the car, the very chemical change in her, had much to do with this, as well as my own unintentional and unconscious movements, the placing of a pen or a cup of coffee, or a bag of grapes at my side. One day she was lying on her back, her delicate wings under her, her complicated and shriveled abdomen helpless in the air, and one day she disappeared altogether, only to reappear later on the seat beside me, right side up, as if we were taking a little ride together, for ice cream maybe, or to see an old covered bridge or sunset. I became very sensitive to the issue of her location, her *place*, and when she would disappear from time to time, causing me great regret and sadness, I felt more alone than I normally do, only to rejoice almost as she appeared, very much there, in the cup holder, one of her four wings and two of her many legs mischievously and coyly reaching up and out as if to get more air or fume or light, as if to flirt there.

For decades I have avoided killing insects, stepping nimbly and gingerly around them. I don't wash them down the sink, and I try to help them escape. I observe my own sentimentality and stupidity when I do this. I only protest when they get into my eyes or ears or on my food. That's reflex. I knew a woman once who lived in an old deranged stone house deep in the countryside in Perry County, Pennsylvania, above Harrisburg and Carlyle in a giant ten-acre tract full of small plants, grasses and trees, all untended. She was my landlady. I rented an old Norwegian-style lodge from her, built maybe in the seventeenth century when the Norse came up from Baltimore to populate central Pennsylvania. I had to drive my car up a narrow road through her property to pay my rent or to complain, and when I did she gave me strict instructions to drive less than ten miles an hour so as not to disturb the insects too much, crawling, flying, jumping, buzzing, and humming on that ten acres. She wore gauze over her mouth and nose so as not to breathe in some innocent victim, as if she were living in Bengal and following the strictures of some Jain or other. She rode a bicycle and had a wooden leg and was all set to sell me the lodge—a huge porch, a covered bridge, a trout stream, outbuildings, fences, and for twenty thousand (1990)—when the Dutch moved up from Lancaster to start a pig farm next to her (imagine!) and she was forced to move to the lodge, away from the smell of putrid flesh and the noise and the killing and the Deutsch humming *partout*.

Insects are supposed to die, by the hundreds and the thousands. That's why they copulate in the air and underwater and on the bottom of leaves by weird and ridiculously efficient means and lay billions of eggs anywhere and everywhere, according to some natural—or divine—scheme. They eat everything, including each other, and vie in their modes—their tongues, their teeth, yea their noses, as if there were a gigantic show and there were prizes, say, for clumsiness, for cruelty, for ripping and tearing, for chewing, and for shock, involving suffocation, dismemberment, and even affection.

The dragonfly eats mosquitoes by the pound. And he eats butterflies, gnats, midges, damselflies, swarming ants, and dozens of other flying insects. He also eats other dragonflies, for he is a born cannibal. He, she, is ravenous, though he seems to disdain vegetation, delicious grass and the like. He seems to typify the insect world, and perhaps ours as well, seen in its brutal, unadorned and nonmythic reality—he eats and fucks, and if he can hover or fly backward or glide or protect his "property" and fight ferociously or show off the most gorgeous colors, it's just because he eats and fucks, that's what he does—with amazing efficiency.

It's been my experience that the very orthodox among us, the fundamentalists, as we call them, object strenuously to comparing humans to any "lesser" animals, certainly great apes and the Lucys, but my god, insects? I think the very best secularist, the humanists, even those who are horrified at slicing up cooked mammals and birds, might swat a fly, or a mosquito. We all have our standards. I don't wear the gauze, but I am careful not to walk on an ant, even if he would delightedly walk over my sugary body and tickle and nibble from time to time. Me, I remember with fascination the torture systems in the Tarzan movies and comic strips. A prisoner, an enemy, was tied down to stakes in the ground, on his back, his arms and legs stretched out. He wore a filthy loincloth, and he was sweating in fear, as well as from the heat, as they rubbed his body in a sweet-smelling sticky substance, certainly honey. He begged, in some unknown African tongue, to be freed and he would tell all, where the leopard steaks are buried, who has the diamonds, what the secret of life is, and, most of all, what the map says, folded up and creased, barely legible in some lost alphabet read upside down and backward in an older version of what the language might be—if it's a language at all; and if it's the first map or the second. Tarzan is tied to a tree, thinking in upper-class English, and the Caucasian goons, with their own troop of African mercenaries, the ones who applied the honey, speak in a kind of German, for the war is on and they are Nazis and the implications are far beyond gold and diamonds, maybe the secret metal, as yet only ore, that will arm one side or the other invincibly, and Tarzan knows all; and he will not give in. Not even if Jane is imprisoned with a hungry lion; not even if Cheetah himself is dipped. But ants are ants, and they do ants' work, only more diverse, complicated, and indirect, though still automatic, unthinking, we could say.

The argument over ethics is seventh-grade stuff. "Resolved the insect must be treated ethically," regardless of what he is or does. Toss a coin, take either side. Something like the argument over socialized medicine, the words always loaded. No question what Heidegger's position would be—or Hitler's—but Nietzsche might surprise you. A nagging issue. Certainly it would be better to argue about horses, or blue jays. I am guessing that the Talmud would instruct us to be kind, no matter what, but to take precautions and not forget yellow fever, and the like. It might also emphasize that the insects—finally—are there for our benefit, as the other lower orders are, which takes us back all the way to Genesis. God knows it's finally for His benefit—I guess—though the insects must have a large amount of the ungodly, for some reason or other, as we cruel humans certainly do.

I'm feeling a little silly about it, for a dog is a dog is a dog. And a dragonfly, I think, doesn't weep over the loss of a beloved. And I'm not doing anyone any harm if I point out that, whatever cruel things insects do, from eating their lovers after the deed is done to eating a limb or so from time to time from a warehoused prey, they, after all, only have a class system and only have slaves and only drain the fat from a fellow insect after beheading him and only do war and only live in superior quarters and only beat servants on the back of their heads—thus murdering them for the sake of having the same servants in the next world—if, and *only* if, these things are predetermined and genetically programmed; as I say, "natural." It's humans who do these things, with their huge brains. Not even the largemouth carp, which is destroying all fish life on its furious journey up the Mississippi into Lake Michigan and the lakes beyond, does this—only humans. Humans, mind you, who are mindful and show compassion and meditate silently and who resist greed and anger and are not confused by suffering; these. Who do not mix meat with milk, who honor their parents, who refrain from pig; these. And who listen to the Sermon on the Hill with head bowed and tears streaming. And stop running once a week. And light candles once a year. Who give watches and wear socks. Who adore emptiness. These. And those who slip on ice, who rub the dog with a thick towel. These.

The dragonfly doesn't live in delusion—unless everything, including eating and fucking, is delusion. At William Matthews's funeral, that fine poet, his fiancé sat in the front row a foot or two in front of the speakers. When it was my turn, I looked at her with pity, fear, and embarrassment, and either addressed half my words to her or avoided her altogether. I don't know what she said to the other speakers, or if she talked to them at all, but to me she spoke as if there were just the two of us in the room and, as if it were a mantra she was repeating, she kept saying "it's a dream, it's a dream." One thinks of Shakespeare here—*Hamlet*—and other plays as well, and one thinks of the *layers:* was life itself a dream, or *just* a dream, and she was passing through it (as through a cloud) and exquisitely aware of her state; was it a dream, that which happened to her, her luck, her joy; was death a dream or *the* dream, and was his (Bill

Matthews's) death such a dream, a *passing* dream we might say—or, really, the true defining dream beside which the others were almost fraudulent; and was she not the victim of a giant complicated game, or ritual; or, most of all, to reiterate the first, was she given privy knowledge—which we all ultimately get—of the absurdity, the senselessness, the nonsubstantiality, the merely symbolic, the hideously comic narrative; or something else? Somewhere I read—probably everybody has—what some of the famous said at the great moment, Tolstoy, Henry James, Oscar Wilde. The words are mostly either a little pretentious or a little cute, as if they were rehearsed and, like evil, somewhat banal. Did Oscar Wilde really say, "I am in a duel to the death with this wallpaper. One of us must go"? Did Beethoven say, "I shall hear in heaven!'"? Or W. C. Fields, "Goddamn the whole fucking world and everyone in it"? What did Reagan say—from what movie? Will Kissinger do it in German or English? What if no one's in the room? I like the Jewish joke: the *alter* is on his deathbed and, in a faint voice with a slightly Yiddish accent, he asks for his children. Is Becky here? Jacob, Rivka, Benjamin, etc. Then he almost raises himself on his elbow and asks in an almost ringing, almost demanding tone, "Who's watching the store?" It was one of my father's terrible, boring jokes. I cringed with embarrassment, say, at fifteen. Now I tell the same jokes. And the young treat me with kindness—tolerance—and roll their eyes, only a little. But they will all be telling bad jokes! It's only a question of time. Everything is. Or space. The holy boys were gathered around the death bed, waiting for the rebbe's last words. "Life is a fountain"; maybe it was "mountain." Maybe he said "Bounty," thinking of the different thicknesses, the designs, the water retention, or the goats on his uncle's farm. "Life is a bounty!" There were sixteen men there, of all ages, corresponding to a certain sixteen Hebrew letters, I either can't tell you which, or I don't know. The words spread, secretly, from ear to ear. They moved around the room; in some cases there was a humming or a buzzing or a shrill ringing because of the hearing aids, "Life is a bounty," "Life is a fountain." Faintly declaimed. By the time it reached the last letter it may have said, "Life is a Zebra," or "Speak in Hebrew," or "Your wife is a mountain," or even, the puzzled, or disappointed, last one said, or more properly asked, in a loud voice, "Life is a *fountain?*" To which the *alter*, blessed be him, responded, in a *very* faint voice: "Oh, is it your position that life is *not* a fountain?" Not even a joke! Not even a bad joke! Not one of my father's anyhow, blessed be him.

If there is ever a time that life, not only our lives but existence itself, seems, or might seem, a dream, it is at that mortal moment. I suspect that we are too busy, too occupied, too embroiled at other times. There is no stopping. Unless, somehow, in meditation, in reading, in art, or in religion. Does this—the mortal moment—make life itself richer, or poorer? More, or less, meaningful? Do we feel cheated? Elated? Disconnected? Dizzy? At peace? Were we always at peace and didn't know it? Are all questions the same question? Am I being sucked into the joke? Then there is also the moment that another kind of disconnection occurs. The moment of anxiety, of terror, a consciousness of being so much "out of" life, its hum, that Being itself is unbearable. The hum is no hum. This state can be "realized" naturally (it's called mental illness) or through drugs. I have—personally—had the joy of achieving it both ways. I used to be an expert. I suppose the two kinds of disconnections— should we call them the happy and the sad?—are cousins, maybe close ones. The hum is there at all times. But hearing it can be a great pleasure or a great torture. Neither way, though, is evidence of the existence or nonexistence of anything. And I might add that, one, I don't have tinnitus, and two, I am not speaking metaphorically. Just today Linda Gregg told me that Jack Gilbert, who has dementia and is in assisted living in Berkeley, California, asked her, when she was about to take a cab to Oakland for a red-eye back to New York, whether his life would continue after she left. A strange question that one in his (sad) condition might ask. Did he mean would the meals continue and would his room still be his, and would they take him to the doctor and pick him up when he fell down; or did he mean that when she disappeared, he would too and the life he had? Is it cruel to make the words of the demented especially significant or symbolic or full of otherwise unavailable information or knowledge? Are the demented among us avatars of wisdom, holy fools and the like? What did Ginsberg's Naomi know, whose self-portrait in crayons I have on my wall?

The dragonfly seems never to be demented, or confused or kind. He eats and fucks. His eyes alone are huge and ferocious beyond belief. He does not boast or discriminate or entertain the *noumenon*. If he brings benefit to the world, it is not volitional. He does not judge between right and wrong. He is not peaceful or merciful or happy. He doesn't know moderation. If he is jealous, it is dragonfly jealousy. He walks over death and he has no delusions. Or beliefs. He doesn't live in a dream world. He is a horrible Buddhist.

I can't find the last words of William James among the famous others, though his brother Henry said, "At last, the great good thing," or something of the sort. My memory tells me that he (William) was sitting in his office at Harvard and when death came he was able to write down words like, "What can we conclude?" "What is to conclude in regard to what . . . ?" In short, a philosophic conundrum. More or less unbelievable, with the possible exception of a dedicated figure like William James, a mystic, a Protestant, a democrat, so unlike his brother Henry, a fastidious penniless snob, according to Bertrand Russell. If I were having a heart attack or a stroke, I would crawl for help, or lie down somewhere in terror, though I have acted weird enough the one or two times I was in true danger, singing, giving the surgeons directions and the like. But what James wrote, William James, lies this side of the mortal moment—it is not that sense of disconnection I wrote about, it is not being transferred to another world, a new one, if only its duration is but for a moment. It is the building of a tent, a continuation, a cultural and civilized act, obedient to law. Yet bless him for it and for his work, he who was Gertrude Stein's teacher and George Santayana's, the one he disliked for his "rotten" aesthetic theories, particularly his take on Christianity, summed up so perfectly in Robert Lowell's single line in his poem about Santayana: "There is no God, and Mary is his mother," a Catholic aestheticism which has many lateral roots all over Europe and America, which enthroned beauty and enshrined Christian "myth" at the expense of either belief or morality. James was a New England Protestant, if heretical. A puritan in the "Hebrew" tradition, who believed that "good conduct," ethical behavior, was the issue—the supreme issue—in religion. Thus, a practice that was purely aesthetic—symbolic—from the offering of body and blood to the mystic blessings of the Mater would be—by William—perceived at the very least as immoral, especially, as is generally the case, when the privileged beauticians are either content—or demand—that the others, the unprivileged, should engage in right practice and, indeed, belief. Which means, as Russell pointed out in 1945, that there was "one truth for philosophers and another for the vulgar."

One could argue that Beauty was one of the entrances, but I feel Beauty is a dangerous god, especially maybe for "nonbelievers," like Jews. Though Jews, we Jews, have our own doors in. One for women, one for men, one for beauticians. When I go into the old Romanian synagogue on Rivington Street—in New York—or the old schul in Prague, or even the Beth This or Beth That, especially when the bimah is in the center, I am sucked in; almost sucked in. But you can get away with anything in my religion, and you don't have to really swallow anything. At least now. "All artificiality is false and the person whose life is dominated by artifice cannot be a true man—he is alienated from himself," says the Taoist Chuang Tzu. I like reading him, though my detractors (there are three, I think) insist I have my own artificialities and, as I approach one hundred, I am becoming more traditional, which happens to all ex-romantics. Spinoza I love, and Eugene Debs, to pick two out of a hat. And Woodrow Wilson I do *not* love, to pick one. I don't know what any of their final words were, though the Romanian schul, I just learned, is no longer there.

3 Chance Writing, Saints

Chance writing and capricious writing are a little different from each other, but they both relate to a kind of relaxation of the mind and an invitation to something else. Relaxation of mind, not absence—and the lamp on so you can read what you wrote, and ginger ale your strongest substance.

As it turns out, I was passing the bookcase where religion and philosophy are stored, and reaching out, in the dark hall, with my left hand, quick as a three-foot tongue, I retrieved, first, Matthew Fox's translation of Meister Eckhart's sermons—thirty of them—and, second, *Studies in Judaism* (third series) by S. Schechter, M.A., Litt.D., 1924, one in the morning and one in the afternoon, only the tongue was less than three feet, more like two.

Whether or not I was being directed by a power inside or out, or it was just an accident, a case of capriciousness, was one thing; and whether or not I was taking direction from the books themselves and so arranged my mind, so to speak, was another; but, in the case of Schechter, I opened the book to page eleven—an essay called "Jewish Saints in Medieval Germany"—and found a description of my own methodology in writing and in thinking; and in the case of Fox, I found the Christian, albeit mystic, description of justice, in sermon thirty-three, as well as a sermon (number five) on how all creatures share an equality of being, two things—two sermons— I had been looking for—waiting for—to help me on my journey, like a bike rider climbing an alp and getting from a bystander a sip of the marvelous, bottled water.

It says, in Schechter, that Luzzatto (a famous Venetian rabbi) remarked that it was rarely given to the Jew to write a systematic piece of work reproducing all his thought in a methodical way. Rather, the strength of the Jew lay, according to him, in occasional notes and stray remarks and abrupt flashes of thought. An exaggeration, says Schechter, but I feel comfortable with it myself since it describes my own style of writing. He (Schechter) compares the Ashkenazi school with the Sephardic, and juxtaposes the methodology of Maimonides, the great Sephardic scholar—who brought Aristotelian order to the rabbinical chaos by producing a systematic code—with that of the Ashkenazis, who knew nothing about Aristotle and did not need to reconcile the Hebrew Bible with Greek philosophy, thus harmonizing contradictory views. The saints of Germany, Schechter tells us, were in the habit of weighing and counting the very words of the prayers and benedictions. This may be seen, in our time, as a compulsive disorder, but the close attention, for them, had its place in the extensive commentaries on the liturgy. If I were to be disgracefully cynical, I would say it gave the men in black something to (endlessly) do; and I would refer to my friend Peter Feldstein's compulsive habit of checking the legs of every piece of furniture in his bedroom—the bed, the dresser, the fat-legged cupboards, before he allows himself to fall asleep; or to myself counting stairs wherever I go—and repeating the numbers endlessly in Anne Marie's house and my own, even though they are carved in my heart. We should remember that these "saints" experienced for four centuries the crusaders traveling through their towns and killing Jews by the thousands on their way to some absurd murderous destination, and yet they taught us to "Be ever careful to feed the poultry in thy house before thou takest thy meal" and to "Be careful never to cheat a non-Jew or to deceive anybody in any way for such things are worse than eating pork"; and "Never keep back thy mercy and compassion from anything which the Holy One, blessed be He, created in this world, be it even a dog or a cat or a creeping thing, or even a fly or a wasp"; and "Never put to shame thy man-servant or thy maid-servant"; and "Keep thyself supplied with the various fruits which the Lord has created, so that thou mayest praise him for every particular kind. For indeed, man will give account and reckoning for everything which he saw and did not taste, if permitted to him." We are talking eleventh, twelfth, thirteenth, fourteenth centuries. Keep fruit in the house, pears and grapes. Don't fast too much. I must acknowledge that one saint in the fourteenth century reminds us not to speak what is superfluous. But he may have been tired. I like their names: Judah Hasid, Eliezer ha-Kohen, R. Solomon Yitzhaki (Rashi). One of the saints says: "If thou hast a guest, never speak to him about learned matters unless thou knowest he is able to partake in the conversation." I am feeling the pull of that warning in writing about relatively obscure things in "abrupt flashes of thought," and I beg my guest not to hate me, or throw my book into a wooden or plastic basket. I believe profoundly in clarity and hate obscurity, though our minds, in our day, go a hundred different ways and some of them tend to be personal, if not private, and (madly) solipsistic.

It would be utterly "capricious," and more than "chance" if I would allow my pen to go where it wants to go, for there is much debris, both in the world and in my head, even if I do govern myself more than a little. If you want to know the truth, there are two— I am counting only two—stray images that, this morning, tend to awkwardly, willy-nilly, hopelessly, and determinedly enter or interrupt the Stream—or the flood—in my case. One is that of a cow standing on a white door, the brass doorknob intact, floating past my house in 1973, down the swollen and strong-smelling river; the other is Mahmoud Ahmadinejad's head spiked on top of an iron fence, the skin and veins hanging down in loose bloody threads as if in a medieval Flemish painting. As far as the cow, it was black and white and no longer mooing, just trying to keep its balance on the door. As far as Ahmadinejad, when I saw his rat's face in a magazine recently, I must confess I spit on it, almost involuntarily, suddenly and without thinking. It was a shocking thing to do—I felt shocked by what my mouth did. And I wondered if in some cultures there's more spitting on faces than in others, or whether it's a gender issue. No one has ever spit in—or on—my face, though images of me may have been doused. I don't think I have ever truly spit at anybody, or a photo of anybody before. Like an angry monkey. Why don't girls spit like boys, women like men? One day Joe Tolochko's beautiful sister walked a few blocks with me on our way to school. I was fourteen or fifteen and she was probably seventeen. I was embarrassed and awkward and I spit several times, for which she chided me. Dear Joe, a walk-on, like me, on the freshman football team at Pitt, in 1942. A superb end. We called them hockers. Clams.

Eckhart will wait till later.

4 The Lamb

Dean Young begins a poem by invoking the "slain lamb," and even though he incorporates unexpected, or bizarre, images in his poetry, the lamb, and indeed the "slain" lamb, is quite familiar. The name of the poem is "Procession":

> They're carrying toward you now
> the single yellow flower.
> They're carrying toward you
> the lamb that has been slain.

If the lamb is Jesus, or another sacrificed victim or a nation or merely a lamb, one of the eternally killed and eaten—always over prayers—in the Middle East and elsewhere, the poor thing is "slain," indicating his sacrificial nature, and destiny. I myself wrote about the lamb, but quite late. My lamb—my lamb—took an odd turn, if I can put it that way. They were, for example, themselves meat-eating and oddly aggressive and frightening. Wherever that comes from. For my first decades I thought very little of the Lamb for there was nothing in either Beth-El or Beth-Shalom (House of God, House of Peace) concerning that dumb animal, no lambs on the bimah, none on the walls, nor did I know that Jesus was a lamb, not really till I went to Ghent and saw the Adoration (although the Lamb did play a significant part in the Pesach feast and in Jewish metaphor, I realized later, as I started to pay closer attention). The shank bone is one of the items on the Seder Plate, the lamb's shank bone, along with a hard-boiled egg, bitter herbs, *charoses*, *karpas*, and *chazeret*. I use the Hebrew words or all the mystery is gone. Who cares about romaine—or fresh horseradish?

Maxwell House, the Family of Coffees, tells us in its famous Passover Haggadah that the Paschal Lamb was eaten because the Angel of Death (blessed be Him) "passed over" the houses of our ancestors in Egypt and that the lamb's blood was sprinkled on the lintels and doorposts of their houses to guide Him on his deadly journey to smite the firstborn (sons) of the Egyptians. I guess "our ancestors" used some kind of brush or rag to apply the blood. It is confusing because the blood itself represented a sacrifice, yet it was the Egyptians who were sacrificed. Maxwell House suggests that it was in revenge (in memory?) of Pharaoh killing the male children of the Israelites lest one of them (Moses) lead a rebellion against him. It was called "our sorrow," and the whipping of the poor bricklayers was called "our oppression."

I'm not making fun of it—I just don't feel the awe. Yet I love the memory, the rebellion of the young, the homemade Haggadahs of the 1960s celebrating civil rights and hating the war in Vietnam, the hunger, the boredom, the battles over Palestine, the bad poems, the guitars, the satin pillows, the family arguments, the learned (irrelevant) lectures by the detached (male) intellectuals about medieval Spain, the rights of labor, the Sabbath, and God knows what else.

In 1965 we had a seder in our house in Indiana, Pennsylvania, near Pittsburgh. I was teaching then at IUP, Indiana University of Pennsylvania, and my mother and father drove up from Pittsburgh—fifty miles—for the occasion. We had put a cup of wine, as was the custom, outside the door—for Elijah—who, you never know, might just surprise us by announcing the messianic age and, lo, at the (holy) moment, as I invoked his name, there was a loud pounding on the front door; it was my friend, Karl Stirner, who was coming back to Philadelphia with his wife, Heather, and their three children, after an extended stay in Mexico—where he was digging in caves for pre-Columbian artifacts—and decided to visit us in Indiana on the way home.

Elijah was a ninth-century BCE prophet who called fire from the heavens and bawled out dishonest and apostate kings. He was revered by the other prophets and holds a tender place in Jewish memory. He performed miracles and was so identified with the messianic role that some Christians believe he was an earlier incarnation of John the Baptist or that he was present at the transfiguration, and Jews believed—believe—he was the harbinger of the age to come and even of the Messiah. (Blessed be Him.) The truth was he looked like Karl Stirner, or Stirner like him (Stirner was in his early forties in 1967)—or so I thought then, for I was convinced immediately that Elijah was well over six feet tall, had a rough beard beginning to turn gray, was immensely strong, severe, opinionated, carried a huge stick and dressed if not in rags then raggedly. Karl made his children fly through the air like birds, turned his fingers into burning candles, changed animals into metal, confronted nothingness, and would have flown around the house himself like a giant bat, but the ceilings were too low. He and his family left the next morning in their converted U.S. mail truck, complete with bunks, a stove, a heater, storage space, and secret compartments for the Mexican loot. I don't remember if it ascended like an airplane or hobbled off like a farting dray horse, but there was a certain emptiness in the house when they left.

In this mind-filled space I have entered there is little distinction between young and old and rich and poor. I would call it timeless if it were not so pompous to do so. I would realize that around the hundreds of tables, thousands really, the cut-glass wine glasses—and the paper cups—were brimful with a moment of peace—and joy—in the face of the common misery; and I was in the center—I felt—of a deathless space where I could ask the four questions and answer them simultaneously, and I could ask after the Egyptians and even the Canaanites and thank them for the riches they gave us. And thank those stubborn heads for a three-thousand-year-old holiday that combines in its way the Fourth of July and Thanksgiving and for its ideas of liberation and redemption, the Easter of our babies.

Which brings us to the Last Supper, the best-known seder of all, depicted by Da Vinci and dozens of others in caves, and on walls and sidewalks, in chalk and in oil. Though it conceivably could be not a seder but a celebratory meal in keeping with the many celebratory meals Jews—and Greeks—held; for the Jews, witnesses tell us, a kind of foretaste for the life to come, as if this were the supreme joy and they were meant, hopefully, to spend eternity this way, accompanied of course with sharp readings of the Torah, recitations from the prophets, and reinterpretation upon reinterpretation of the sacred events. Though, given the season and the date, Pesach and the spirit of Pesach had to be present at the long table. There were over a hundred thousand pilgrims in Jerusalem, staying in tents, outbuildings, and rented rooms. Tension and debate were in the air and Jesus, a master of psychology, had to have used the occasion for symbolic action and for transformative ideas. It could even have been a mock seder—and I don't say this out of disrespect—or the seder could have been a layer or a metaphor. Me, I wonder why women and children were not present and why there wasn't an abundance of food on the table and where the servers were. But I'm just asking. I'm sure there was a shank bone and I'm sure they consumed a lamb and a bit at that table and the bread was very, very thin, but, that Jesus himself, teacher, visionary, upturner of other tables, was not yet, himself, a lamb. That would come later.

I have respect for the Passion, even wonder, though I'm tired of the Baptists and Catholics, of all sorts, stealing history, and even if every religion, every culture, endlessly steals, none has been so relentless, so murderously affectionate as they, let time, culture, historical complexity, and poetic metaphor be damned. The madness is that the baby religion believes so insistently, so wildly, in the miracles, but that the daddy religion—with some black-clad exceptions—no longer insists. The madness is that the babies must, or *think* they must. It may be that Moses thought he was talking to God on the windy mountain. So what? It doesn't matter and it doesn't—for me—change anything. I'm embarrassed to have to be saying this—I sound like a turn-of-the-*last*-century scoffer, a Bertrand Russell (blessed be him), a Danish liberal, or a Reformed Sunday school teacher who forgets that one end of the see-saw is as boring as the other, Thomas Jefferson vs. Paul, George Bernard Shaw vs. Luke, and that both eventually lose their footing.

It's on the cross that Jesus finally becomes a lamb, though there is foreknowledge at the seder, and even before, of the Suffering to come, even taking into account interpolation and *ex post facto* rewriting, though the Lamb was not docile and not a nibbler. He spoke authoritatively, he warned, he scolded, he taught, he predicted, sometimes lovingly, but he was more shepherd than sheep; and he filled the room in such a way that the disciples seemed a little stupid; as in Plato, as in Paul; or he was, in an amazing way, like the Zen master—for all things meet—who insulted and even beat *his* disciples. Those strange rationalists among us, linguists, historians, anthropologists, astronomers, Phoenicians, the lowest of the low, like to point out that there were dozens of others, some Lambs, some Goats, all with wild hair and long nails, which may be so, but the one who survived and was celebrated and, finally, worshipped may have had the hair and the nails, but he was filled with love for the afflicted and powerless, and though he spoke and acted like the others, there was something new, certainly that love, mixed as it was with magic, intelligence, presence, and power.

Today, December 16, 2009, I read Mark again and I was reminded of the stiff discolored paperback New Testament that I read in the guardhouse—read jail—at Aberdeen Proving Grounds in Maryland where, as I wrote elsewhere, I was being held on seven or eight charges, and where, though I was found not guilty of everything, I suffered nonetheless at the hands of a sadistic provost-sergeant who, as I wrote, hated me because I was a Jew, an intellectual (of sorts), and a northerner, and was forced to chop rocks with a twelve-pound sledgehammer twelve or thirteen hours a day, including on both my Sabbath and his, for five or six months, waiting for trial. It was a good place to read a gospel or two, late at night under a dim bulb, for some of those early Christians had chopped a little too. I wrote that everyone else there—the other prisoners—were, without exception, African American, and they understood and sympathized with my situation and squirreled away food and comic books for me and thought I was a preacher because of the stiff book I was reading and came to me for advice and wished me luck, all of them, when I went up to Baltimore for my two-day trial at Camp Holabird where I was found not guilty, on all counts.

I like the Gospel of Mark because it is the shortest, and the narrative never strays. But it is a cruel narrative, in many ways pre-prophetic in its speaking of demons and Satan, and it reflects the people's fears and superstitions and is rampant with the kind of healing that the farmers and fishermen might understand, which, though Mark said it came of faith, came also with primitive touching and even the application (again) of spit, God's spit. The Yeshua of Mark is a busy healer—we hear endlessly about disease and cures and unclean spirits, not to mention unforgiving condemnations, retributions, and such, which seem somewhat distant from love and compassion. And there is a lot of magic and spiritual whispering. Most of all, it is the Yeshua of power and knowledge and secrecy, superior to, even aloof from, his disciples. Who are sometimes, I am sorry to say, like Shakespearean bumpkins, living in another world from him and he from them. Though there is a point, a little over halfway through, where things begin to change somewhat. It was, it is, as if he were becoming more fully *himself.* And though he continued his healing, and continued to identify it with *belief*, with faith, he more and more showed the tenderness we know him for, even if it was coupled with his fury: "Whoever causes one of these little ones [read poor, helpless, afflicted] to stumble, it would be better for him if a millstone were hung around his neck, and he were thrown into the sea." Or "It is better for you to enter the kingdom of God with one eye [the other is plucked out] rather than having two eyes, to be cast into hell fire." And tenderness such as "If you have anything against anyone, forgive him, that your Father in heaven may also forgive you . . ." and "Let the little children come to Me, and do not forbid them; for of such is the kingdom of God."

Mark (blessed be Him) as an eschatologist, a lover—and predictor—of final things, should make our current crop of end-worshippers in the various Disney spaces quite happy as they presume in their movies and books and music to treat what were deadly serious and indeed holy things to a small nation of dreaming perfectionists in a frivolous—and literal—manner. Mark says there will be tribulations, and the sun will be darkened, and brother will betray brother unto death. We will all be lambs then, even the scribes and the elders. My own heart goes out to the scribes for I could have been one, though my handwriting is unworthy and I am of the awkward sort; and my heart goes out to the elders—they may even have been as old as sixty, some of them. I say this who will be eighty-five in a few months. That lamb of the Adoration— was it lamb or was it sheep? Think of the difference. Think of Blake. "Little sheep, who made thee?" "I a sheep and you a sheep." Think of how different a goat is and how "goat" works—for its purpose—and "kid" doesn't—how it is the very opposite. And how I felt in Greece when my landlady came up the road carrying one of the two kids, the black one, in her arms, screaming. And when I asked her—in German—what she was doing she made the sign of the knife across her throat, for she was taking that little goat to his bloody altar, a wooden table in the shed, where he would be killed, then cut up and cooked—with herbs—and served with rice, for the Easter feast, twenty-two and a half years ago in Samos, the Turks nearby.

We live in ignorance and sometimes we are helped by a small book or a map or maybe a letter. I was lucky enough to spend eight days or so in the Low Countries while waiting for a slow-moving Dutch freighter to take me from Antwerp back to Hoboken, the New Jersey city I had left from a little over a year earlier, and I was saved from helpless and ignorant wandering from place to place by some abbreviated Baedeker I found in a church or a bar or sticking out of some garbage can, designed to help a poor pilgrim like me move somewhat intelligently through the six or seven marvelous cities in that flat little heaven. Two heavens. I remember I went to the Hague on a Sunday and I remember I slept on a pool table in Amsterdam for several nights and I remember a shave—in a barbershop—cost four cents American, given the exchange, and I remember the good sandwiches and I recall Bruges vividly but most of all I remember the altarpiece in Ghent and how shocked, how overwhelmed I was by it. I kept going back to the church, the cathedral, and though I eventually took in the various panels and began to understand the general aesthetic, it was the Lamb on his platform, with the angels worshipping him, that moved me. Though the lamb was (here too) more like a sheep, muscular and alert, as if the artist, though he could say it and think it, could not truly *picture* it—a tiny, say kneeling, lamb—and make it worthy of his worship for, no mistake, the lamb [the sheep whom we *called* lamb] was itself being worshipped, standing as it was on that platform, isolated, powerful, enigmatic, lonely, radiant, thus an idol. Though it did come to be a symbol of Yeshua himself, He who— *by the way*—would have been horrified by the idea, He whose first thought was Thou Should Have No Other Gods. Though far be it for me to be so foolish, boring, and maudlin as to mention it.

5 Christ

Today, December 28, 2009, I read the shocking last line and a half of Fanny Howe's poem "A Hymn" in *Poetry:* "Like fish in a secular city // flipping through sewers for a flash of Christ." It is a long poem—seven pages—which speaks of those ancient things, mercy and justice (I forget which comes first), through the lens of novels and films, more or less. (More comes first.) It's where "scripture meets fictions," she says in her opening line; the good cynic would say "where fiction meets fiction," but I'm going to refrain. The end reconsiders Orson Welles's *The Third Man,* produced right after World War II, and concentrates on the famous relationship (in the film) of Orson Welles (Harry Lime) and Joseph Cotten (Holly

Martins). The two of them are on a Ferris wheel in an amusement park in Vienna, a place where one is ". . . forever / stuck in the fog and iron," and Lime, ". . . a mix between Paul Celan and Oscar Levant," is offering his famous diatribe against Switzerland: "All they gave the world is cuckoo clocks," just before he is pursued in the sewers and finally killed by Martins for "poisoning babies for profit" (diluting black-market penicillin).

The line that bespeaks the impossible refers to a "flash of Christ" in the sewer, which is apparently what you get in a "secular city." I have seen that movie many times but I never saw that flash. "Christ"—or a glint of him—is there because Fanny Howe says he is, and the authority is the beauty of her metaphor plus the history of the word "Christ," its constant centuries-old use. I guess the "fish" refer to early Christians, also underground, although there was reference earlier to some long-ago light "pulsating in a trout's heart / on a laboratory dish" and how the light "enters all holes / no matter how small." Oscar Levant was a popular pianist and light-weight comedian who was in many 1940s movies. My dear stepson Jeremy's Blackberry tells him—and me—that Christ is "Jesus of Nazareth, held by Christians to be the fulfillment of prophesies in the Old Testament regarding the eventual coming of the Messiah." The Hebrew and Aramaic word is *Meshiya*, but neither Messiah nor Meshiya resonate like the word "Christ." "Messiah" doesn't make you shiver or gasp; "Christ" does, or can:

> O Western wind, when wilt thou blow
> that the small rain down can rain?
> Christ, that my love were in my arms
> and I in my bed again.

Almost used as a curse here. A far cry anywhere, anyhow, from the Lamb.

If "Christ" ("Christos") were Greek for "Messiah," it finally

came to mean more—or other—than "Messiah," if "Messiah" tra-
ditionally meant "the anointed one," a high priest maybe, a com-
ing king, conqueror, hero, ideal ruler, in whose time God would
establish a perfect and permanent reign on earth characterized by
peace, prosperity, and justice; even as it came sometimes—or some-
time later—to mean the Servant of the Lord who bears our sins and
intercedes. But it never truly meant "God" or God's eternal son
or a mystical confusion of the two. Nor did God's name become
"Messiah" as God's name became "Christ." Though many branches
sprang up in the wild, early centuries before—and after—the Event.

John (the last Gospel) takes us radically in the new direction.
The Lamb is only mentioned once, and Jesus is divine; he is not of
this world; he is the son of God; he came into this world for judg-
ment; before Abraham was, he was; all who came before him were
thieves and bandits; he gives eternal life to those who believe in
him; those who hate life in this world will keep it for the later life;
he is God's *equal*. He—John—endlessly attacks the Jews, not just the
Pharisees, but the Jews. It is a moot point to say his writing came out
of the mad Jewish imagination of the time, or that it represents the
conflict between a particular Christian community and synagogue
authorities, and that the community was probably composed of Jew-
ish Christians. But I almost admire the violence, the ferocity, and
the insistence on a certain kind of belief—or faith—and I admire
the meditation on "the word," and the teaching of light, whether it
came from Egypt, Persia, or just some hill in Judea; though I miss the
tenderness and the wisdom of the other hill, called "The Mount."

I read about a theoretical lamb once that could occupy an entire
block and feed a city. The crazy scientists said they could indeed do
it but it would probably be *politically* unacceptable. They used that
word, not "socially" or "morally." I don't know how much they
spelled it out at the time, what biological modification would be
necessary, issues of bone growth and such, but they were serious.

I couldn't imagine such a lamb standing up or even being alive. I saw him—or her—as already murdered and lying on her side. It was too horrible to think of it as trimmed, drained of blood, and ready for cutting. Too hideous to think of the entire skin removed and the reddish brown carcass with the empty eye sockets and slightly snarling mouth lying on the ground, maybe in a cement playground or a specially prepared grass enclosure, with a wire fence around it and guards wearing gas masks against the smell. I couldn't help wondering what the taste would be, what kind of ladders or platforms—scaffolding—the butchers would use for their cutting, what the cuts would be, how big a chop was, how they would do the wrapping, how fast they'd have to distribute it, who would set the price and make the profit, how long the lines would be, would the beast have a name, whether there would be protests—and whether they would be Christian, vegan, anarchist, left of center or right. What the *Daily News*, the *Times*, or Larry King would say.

In Revelation (Apocalypse), Yeshua is no longer a bleeding white lamb whom we can pity and weep over but a fierce, violent, and vengeful judge, who is merciless and exact. Someplace else I said he was both the butcher and the thing butchered, but I think he was more one than the other. I have no rights here, nor am I making judgment myself; I'm merely making a point. As Willis Barnstone says in his *Restored New Testament*, ". . . Yeshua as a force is not the itinerant rabbi wandering the villages of Galilee or Judea but a cosmic God, interchangeable with YHWH, with eyes of fire and a two-edged sword." Yet he is still called "The Lamb" in a strange reversal of meaning where the great power of the writing— for it is one of the world's great books—not just seduces but overwhelms the reader into accepting—believing—what the author wants him to believe. Anticipatory—I almost said "reminiscent"— of the hideous, violent, insane thing called The Rapture, by which the "worthy" are saved and the others sent to some boiling lake or other. I guess my dear father, who escaped the Germans and their pet Ukrainians by going to another continent, and my grandson Dylan—now five years old and learning the law of thermodynamics on his little skis—will swim in the boiling lake or bake in the fires because they have sinned by having some secular habits or because they haven't read *The Late Great Planet Earth* and will not have the pleasure of meeting Yeshua in the air immediately preceding his second coming (according to one version). I don't know where this or that fits on the tribulation table but I think I'm to wait (dead or alive) until the Israelis build another temple before *I'm* boiled. And I want to point out that my father was already dead and my little Dylan not yet born when Hal Lindsey wrote his best seller. I was delighted to see (in the *New York Times* on January 2, 2010) that the news had spread, and the ayatollah who leads the Guardian Council in Iran called protesters against his fascist government "flagrant examples of the corrupt on Earth" and urged that they be executed as "in the early days of the revolution." The deputy chief of judiciary said that those detained (protesters) would be charged with *moharib*, meaning enemies of God, a charge punishable by death. The biblical poets have extensive and hairy attachments, don't they?

It is interesting that "a few" of the chosen "walk in white because they're worthy," and that "the victorious, like them, will be clothed in white clothing"—as it says in Revelation—and that their names "will never be obliterated from the book of life." White is forever the color of purity, and purity (sexual comes to mind) is demanded. Though often, on my uncle's—and my grandfather's—farms, they who were clothed in white, those sheep, were often less than white, even filthy—poor things.

It was "the hour of trial / about to come upon the entire world," and the Lamb was judge, that simple. Twenty-two chapters, filled with white horses and mystic seals and dragons and beasts of the deep and scorpions and thrones and fire and bejeweled descending

cities, and through it all a lamb sitting on a throne with the book
open and the finger wagging and the voice raging, one of many
many visionary books of the time, perhaps the greatest. The author,
this Yohanan or that, to take his place with John Milton and Wil-
liam Blake and Walt Whitman—or they with him.

> And when the lamb opened the fifth seal,
> I saw under the altar the souls of those
> Who were slaughtered for the word of God.

> They were told not to kill them but to torture them
> For five months, and their torture should equal
> The scorpion's torture when it strikes a person.
> And in such days the people will seek death
> But not find it, and they will desire to die
> But they won't fall into escape to death.

> Then I saw, and look, the lamb standing on
> Mount Zion and with him 144
> Thousand who had his name and the name of
> His father written on their foreheads.

> . . . they will be tormented
> In fire and in sulfur before the holy angels
> And before the lamb.

Myself, I read and try to understand where I do have rights. I am
as cynical as they come, and as believing. I believe in Moses talking
to God, the grandness and the dignity, whatever spell he (Moses)
was under, whatever he ate to get there, or he (the actual author)
with his hungry imagination, some other Moses. And I'm embar-
rassed, to say the least, about the ridiculous drunk Noah and his two
of a kind and about the gratuitous cruelty. I have to call some of my
Orthodox cousins to see how literal their belief is. I love cities fall-
ing from the sky and combustible water and demons with shining
copper eyes and brass shoulders and fish who talk and flying legs and
God himself resting in a cloud after his tiresome day on a throne,

but I hate it when these things are put to stupid or repressive uses. And I must add that I hate purity—except sometimes in language— Jewish purity, Christian purity, Muslim purity. And though I like a white shirt occasionally, I don't mistake it for a sheep.

· On January 2, 2010, I read—again—in the *New York Times* that the London Jewish Museum of Art had just bought a small Chagall called *Apocalypse in Lilac: Capriccio*, a depiction, the *Times* said, of the Holocaust. It shows Jesus on a cross as in *The White Crucifixion*, only all sweetness and decoration is gone. This Jesus is not wearing a prayer shawl to hide his nakedness and though there is a ladder, as in the other, it is solid, less vague and functional. More than ever before, Jesus is a metaphor for persecuted Jewry. It is brutal. A Nazi storm trooper, with legs like an animal—and a tail sticking out of his uniform—is bent over at the foot of the ladder. He has a backward swastika on his arm and—like Hitler—a black moustache. Jesus looks down on him with hatred and contempt. An upside-down clock is falling from the sky and the margins are filled with sad figures—mothers protecting infants, animals, violinists, and Jewish peasants hugging Torahs. Those who want to can compare the German animal with his Roman forebear. For a Jew like myself, who was beaten up on his way to his first day of kindergarten for killing Christ and has listened to the shit for more than eighty years, it is finally not just dumb but utterly boring.

The time of the Lamb was the in-between time—four hundred yearswhen we lived in chaos or in a dream and were obsessed by the invisible and thought to remake ourselves. While in the other worlds most humans were merely eating, sleeping, and slaughtering, in a small coastal strip on the Mediterranean, strangely learned people were furiously arguing over the future. If they had had weapons they would have slaughtered each other—which they later did, some of them, when they did have the weapons. Two hundred years before the Event and two hundred years after. Sacrifice

was the issue, and wearing out the knees. What to ingest, when to
contemplate, what to wear, where to live, how to live, and how to
speak and what and how not to speak. No one will believe it, but
I based my own life on sacrifice and denial and deferral. The only
ascetic practice I still believe in is "the flight to a wilderness." But
my wilderness. There I will wear out my own knees—I have—and
will show whatever love I have to whatever comes my way. I am
grateful. And I wish I could remove just one bloody spike from his
palm, from his ankle—one hard rusted twelve-inch screwed angry
unjust painful spike.

6 Diary of the Mind

What I'm doing, I suppose, is writing a kind of diary of the mind,
a record of what I'm thinking about over a certain period of time,
what passes by, what stays, complicated by where I am, or where
I just happen to be, what I'm reading (high or low), what drifts in
and, like a wild and obstinate dog, attaches itself to me and keeps
whining until I finally reach down and stroke its bony grateful
head, which means getting up—sometimes from my bed—find-
ing a pen and something to write on, usually in the dark, until I'm
finally free to lie there on my back listening to him, her, snore and
drifting off myself, or dropping my pen and starting my own heavy
breathing, whatever bed or country or city I'm in.

I am writing this in Italy, a month before my eighty-fifth birth-
day, and I am full now of Italian memories. I am in Rome—we are
in Rome, Anne Marie and I—and I am sitting at a cafe in the Piazza
del Popolo, near where we're staying, at the Hotel Locarno on via
della Penna. We're on the terrace, though it's January, and to our
right are the vomiting lions and the Egyptian obelisk and the statue
of Neptune—in the northwest corner; and beyond that, the old
northern gateway into the city, the Porta del Popolo and the beau-

tiful church, Santa Maria del Popolo, built on the site where an ear-
lier church was erected to combat the demons that were hovering
over Nero's grave, demons with fiddles and flutes. The café is called
Canova and it faces the twin baroque churches at the southern end
of the square, a little over half a mile from the Piazzi di Spagna and
the Spanish Steps. There are two Caravaggios in Santa Maria del
Popolo, one the *Crucifixion of St. Peter* and the other the *Conversion
of St. Paul on the Road to Damascus.* I saw Larry Levis lurking there,
he who so loved Caravaggio. I saw him holding onto the cross in
one painting and under the horse's belly in the other. He was Paul
as Caravaggio was, swallowing his own tongue in confusion and
derangement. Or maybe he was the horse itself, brown and white,
his mane, long and wild, his veins engorged, one shoe showing.
Larry with a pen in his hand, his mind bursting with knowledge.

7 Dogs

A woman I loved once told me I wrote too much about birds. She
was actually furious and lectured me about the greed, stupidity, and
viciousness of birds, of their evolutionary relationship to snakes, of
their desperation in the wind and the snow, their inadequacy as a
symbol of escape from the primal bonds, and of the foolish indul-
gence of poets—more than anyone else—in using them as emblems
of freedom, something poets are apparently particularly interested
in. She led me back to my books and to counting my birds, the way
my stepson Luke does in the annual bird counts in the swamps and
meadows of southern New Jersey, and she so terrorized me that, fif-
teen years later, when I was on a ridiculous panel at the annual AWP
conference, I think in Austin, on "Birds and Poetry," I remembered
her fury and—for my portion—sang World War II songs about
swallows and bluebirds instead of lecturing the packed and over-
heated room, though I was directed that way more than a little by

the boring presentations before me, one in particular. But it's dogs I'm interested in, not birds, at least for now, or by now, not only for the joy, sadness, or fear of the encounter but for the emblematic value as well, and I think I have written as much about dogs as birds.

It may be, since we're in Italy now, that my mind goes back to the strange canine experience Pat Stern and I had—in 1954—on the Amalfi Coast, a few hundred miles south of where I am just now—at a small outdoor table, swooning in the bright winter sun. We were staying at a youth hostel a mile or so in the sky above Priano, just north of disgraceful Positano where women bared their breasts on the rocks; and the owner's dog was determined, against all pleas, to follow us through the woods and down the steep hill to the Gulf of Sorrento. That dog certainly had many hidden bones and an attentive master but insisted on staying with us though I threw many sticks, and stones, back up the hill, and once even tied him with a shoelace or a length of twine to a tree, which he was able to break away from easily and continue to follow us. I didn't have much respect for that dog, partly because of his disloyalty and partly because of his short legs, which I never much respected in dogs. I don't mean that he was small and thereby had small legs— he was a kind of German Shepherd, with tan hair for a covering and a huge head and upper body attached to inappropriate legs, a weird mixture of something, which gave him a slightly comic yet frightening look. He followed us all the way down to the house of Papa Luigi in Praiano, listed (incorrectly) in some book or other we were referencing as a youth hostel. Papa Luigi's wife, Josefina, answered the door and screamed, *"Lupe, lupe"* when she saw the dog, but Luigi was more world-wise and gracious when he saw the animal—and us. It took us a whole afternoon to reach the owner by telephone—in the only hotel in town and the only public phone— and when he drove the half-hour or so it took to find us he was neither kind nor grateful but assumed we had stolen the dog and coaxed him down the mountain. I wore out a pair of cheap shoes on that trek and developed such blisters on my feet that we stayed in Praiano—with Luigi—for most of a week till the skin had healed before we continued our travels.

That's where I sang for hours with the drunken Welshmen and that's where I had the encounter with the German woman (second telling) who argued with me about who bombed whom first and explained to me—in English—how it was terrible what der Führer did but the Jews did constitute an international conspiracy and we Americans were too innocent to understand that, and who broke down when I told her—in German—that I was a Jew and begged my forgiveness in the middle of the night overlooking the Mediterranean in what had to be a full moon and tried to kiss my hand. I have forgiven her a hundred times and hope she's still alive; and I'm sorry her husband died while on leave from the Wehrmacht in Hamburg when we fire-bombed it, burning the throats and cutting off the air of three hundred thousand people. We never did—by the way—give that dog a name, though we were his faithful slaves for half a day or more. I think I'll call him Charlot (after Charlie Chaplin).

Now I am remembering another ferocious dog with a huge mouth and grotesquely short legs. I even remember *his* name, Baskie—or Basky—but I can't remember his owner's name, though he was a kind of friend, and Pat and I occasionally visited him and his wife, Patty. They lived near Broadway and 120th Street—I remember climbing the hill below the Satter Gates singing and staggering in a disgraceful way, Pat beside me, helpless. Seamus—I recall his name now, Seamus Daly—and I walked Baskie one late afternoon in Riverside Park. His cover was a lighter tan than Charlot, but otherwise they looked remarkably alike, and both refused to listen to their "owners," which could be, in a dog, either stupidity, stubbornness, or genius. When we got on the elevator to go down to the lobby we were joined by a Hungarian, a small man

who spoke a broken but intelligent English and who was carrying
a quiet little white dog in his arms. Baskie immediately tried to
attack the small dog while Seamus held him by the leash, shouting
"Heel, heel!" Twenty minutes, a half-hour later, Baskie, who was
loose by this time—in the park—met up again with small white and
grabbed him by the throat, causing blood to pour down his white
chest. The owner, probably a recent refugee, half asleep while the
dog played near him, was terrified and shouting in German while
Seamus, still with his "Heel, heel!" put his hand inside Baskie's
mouth, trying to pull him away. Seamus later had to have stitches—
I remember twelve—but what happened to small white I never
found out, though I'm sure Seamus knocked on doors, expressed
regret, and offered to pay—or Patty did. Seamus was in advertising
and worked in the green building on 57th Street. He went to Pea-
body High School in Pittsburgh, but I only met him later in New
York. He died, in his late fifties, overweight and forlorn. When I
look at the TV program called *Mad Men*, a series about ad men in
New York in the 1950s and '60s, I think of Seamus, the false labor
he did and the novel he never wrote.

Where I live, in Lambertville, New Jersey, the dogs have *long*
legs. Many of them are greyhounds, their racing days over, saved
from early slaughter by the good citizens of my city. Technically,
legally, it's a city, though small for such a designation. Just before we
drove to JFK for the flight to Rome, I saw one of those long-legged
greyhounds following after its mistress, but only on three legs since
one, the front right, was missing. He was half-hopping and half-
walking. Greyhounds are always serious and worried, so you don't
know just how much his demeanor had to do with his missing leg.
And you wanted to ask the owner where, how, and when, but you
didn't. Out of respect for that dark greyhound.

I want to write about other dogs now: Dolly, the only family dog
we ever had—for six months maybe—and stolen, or for all I know

given away, for I was only five—an Eskimo spitz; or the collie pup
my father brought home one Saturday night, causing a long, loud,
and violent argument between him and my dog-fearing mother,
which I heard from my bed upstairs—I was eight or nine—and
which also disappeared the next morning before I got up, nor was
I permitted even to mention it, I was so trained. White and black,
with a little brown probably. Or the other Dolly, owned by Peter
and Josephine Feldstein of Iowa City, eerily also a spitz and a per-
fect likeness of the first, whom Peter photographed with me to
accompany a dog poem I wrote when the editor of an anthology in
which the poem was to appear requested a photo; or the rottweiler
in Nashville, who belonged to a friend's gun-packing brother and
threatened me in an isolated third-floor hallway; or Louise Fish-
man's tiny curly-haired dog with the large eyes that was murdered
in one second by a vicious pit bull, the dog Louise carried in her
bag in and out of restaurants, Louise, my student in ancient Phila-
delphia, now a world-renowned painter; and the black Labrador my
next-door neighbor gave me, oh, thirty-five years ago, who went
into and out of the Pennsylvania canal at the back of my house and
the (Delaware) river in front, but was not allowed into the house,
for fear of her shaking water or sniffing crotches, that I kept and
cared for about two weeks before I gave her back. Cats, though, we
had ten or twelve of them over the years, a whole history there of
broken legs and smashed jaws and death by car, the only one I ever
wrote about—the one that jumped on Bob Summer's bony thigh
when he was struggling with his aphasia, dreaming, it so happened,
that he himself was a paralyzed dog, struggling on the floor.

The rottweiler, my friend's brother told us, had an amazing bite,
something about pounds and jaws by which such things are mea-
sured; and he was used in the German concentration camps as a
guard and attack dog, along with the shepherds, he proudly added,
something I already knew. I was climbing the stairs with a paper

cup of hot coffee in my hand on my way to the third-floor sitting room when we encountered each other. I could hear the loud voices behind the closed door but they couldn't possibly hear me. The dog—surprised and angry—crouched down and started to growl. My hand shook and I spilled hot coffee on his nose, at which he howled and ran as fast as his claws could take him over the wooden floor and down the steps. A cosmic victory, involving Auschwitz and Confederate flags.

8 Tyler School of Art

Louise Fishman studied art at Tyler, a part of Temple University, where I taught from 1956 to 1963. It had a separate campus then—in Cheltenham, Pennsylvania, just outside the city, and I was, for years, the one-man English Department, providing the art students with enough composition, literature, and madness to give them a minor in English, if they so chose. I was actually exiled from the main campus on Broad Street either for having an idea, or for leg wrestling with Allen Jackson on the floor of the faculty lounge during an English Department party, or for wearing wide-wale corduroys, or for correcting Temple's president at a public meeting. Jackson, who changed his name later to Myles Dearborn, was a defensive end for Michigan about ten years earlier and played in the Rose Bowl. He wrote an article attacking college football, which was reprinted in *Reader's Digest,* and he was hired sight unseen by Ernest Earnest, the chair of the department. He always beat me in leg wrestling, but I took him easily in arm wrestling. He was fired, after two or three years, I think, for throwing a heavy briefcase at me—from the hall door at the start of my evening class in creative writing, which hit one of my students and knocked her down, if not out. One night he and I experimented on a reel-to-reel tape recorder in imaginary spontaneous interviews—one of former King Farouk of Egypt, for

example, in a nudist colony from his exile in Nice. It was the end of
the 1950s, and our radical satire was very effective. We appeared on
a live radio show and were highly praised and applauded. But sud-
denly Al wanted us—to my horror—to have names and write out a
script and memorize it. To make matters worse, I had already made
contact, through a friend of mine, Hermione Basnight, with her
cousin who was a senior executive at MCA, and Al and I were due
to go to New York for an interview with him. I thought he would
hate our pieces, but to my shock, and Allen's joy, he liked them and
proposed that we make an appearance on the *Jack Paar Show*, which
I thought was the kiss-off till he told us he was Paar's agent and sug-
gested we arrange to do a few of our pieces in a Philadelphia café to
prepare ourselves. When we went down the elevator, I was abso-
lutely dismayed, but Al kept pounding me on the back with his big
calloused hands and insisted we eat spaghetti to celebrate and buy
stools at once in a store he knew in Chinatown (Philadelphia) in
preparation for getting our show ready. We practiced for a week or
so, but I couldn't memorize my part. I couldn't even say, "Uh, huh,
and then?" Finally, after a pathetic rehearsal at my house, I phoned
him—he lived on Fawn Street off of Pine—and told him I quit! It
was no surprise to his dear wife, Lisa. We had already found a café
and he went on with the show, engaging Hadyn Goldberg (from
Maine), a colleague of ours, to take my place—as Dr. Twiggs. The
show wasn't a great success, nor did they ever appear on *Jack Paar*.

I did see Paar on television one night at a nearby bar on Lime-
kiln Pike, when we lived on West Oak Lane. I could hardly believe
how boring and artificial it was and vowed never to own a televi-
sion set in this life. Till Al Barber, a former student, who was legally
blind in Pennsylvania, sold me his for twenty-five dollars, in time
for Kennedy's election. Al Jackson wrote me two or three times
over the years to see if I still had the tapes and asked if we couldn't
start over. I last saw him ten years ago in Hoboken where he was

the night manager at the YMCA and lived there, in a small room. He was writing a novel then and had previously managed a taxi company. He saw a book of mine in a bookstore and called me up. We went to dinner and when I tried to pay the bill, he said, "I pay my own way." The tapes are in the library at Pitt, with my papers. I hope he's still alive. He was an important person in my life, and I remember him with affection.

I got waylaid about Louise. And about Tyler Art School. Her class, and the one before it and after it, was full of brilliant anti-authoritarian students, who hated—and deeply enjoyed—their decade, the 1950s. I taught them Stein, Beckett, Camus, Lawrence, Woolf, Joyce, Faulkner, Orwell, Malamud, Bellow, Henry Miller, Isherwood, Rilke, Dickinson, Sartre. And the Spanish and Chilean poets. And Auden, Eliot, Pound, Hart Crane, Dylan Thomas, Robert Lowell, Hugh MacDiarmid, Blake, Yeats, Swift, Coleridge, Melville, and Whitman. I was ten years older than them—in a few cases, the same age. I drove a gigantic 1953 Plymouth station wagon, which I bought for junk price (fifteen dollars) and with the help of my friend Karl Stirner, who owned an identical car, got it in running condition after a few trips to the junk yard. Karl (Elijah) taught metal sculpture and jewelry making at Tyler and lived across the street from me with his aging mother. They spoke a singsong mountain German that sounded a lot like Yiddish. I could understand most of it.

Boris Blai was the founder of Tyler. Probably born Blavatsky. He had been one of Rodin's gophers; he probably brought in clay and might have met Rilke. I heard about Blai's early years from the owner of the Albany Fruit Market in New Brunswick, New Jersey, now probably part of a J&J building—when Dave Burrows and I rented the huge upstairs rooms as studios, me writing, him doing photography. We taught together at Douglass College, part of Rutgers University. They—the fruit man and Blai—had roomed together in the late 1920s in center city, Philadelphia. Blai, he told me, slept in the bathtub. Later, maybe in the 1940s or late '30s, Blai and his wife, an opera singer, had a studio where Blai was doing some primitive kind of art therapy—through drawing and sculpture. One day the doorbell rang and a badly scarred, acne-ridden woman showed up to appeal to him for help. "I cannot help you," Blai said in his heavy Russian accent. His wife—the opera singer—kept pointing out the window and when Blai looked he saw two Rolls Royces below, at which point he said, "I vill help you"—and help her he did, teaching her to sculpt and curing her acne. For which she ceded him one of her estates, which he turned into a school and named after her, the Stella Elkins Tyler School of Fine Arts (think Elkins Park, PA). Later, Blai sold—or deeded—the property to Temple University, which in turn appointed him dean—for life, I guess.

He was a delightful tyrant, about five-foot-five and over two hundred pounds. "Mister five-by-five." He terrorized his small faculty, forced them to eat lunch with him, and lectured on politics and art, nonstop. It was the late 1950s. Myself, he couldn't touch for I reported to Ernest Earnest, the English Department chair. Anyhow he liked, even loved me, and when he retired he wanted to start a college of sorts on Long Beach Island—in Loveladies, New Jersey—where he had a beautiful home a few feet from the ocean, but the hurricane of '63 destroyed his home—and that dream. I was to be in charge of literature and such. His cohort. With a real salary. He couldn't read too well in English but was more than proficient in Russian and French.

In a burst of loyalty, he made a slightly smaller than life-size statue relating the myth or legend that underlay Temple University, the "Johnny Ring story." Johnny was a drummer boy and messenger in the Civil War, who went back over a bombed-out bridge to retrieve his mother's Bible, which saved his life when it deflected a bullet. As a consequence, the general in charge, Russell Conwell, a notorious scoffer, became a sudden believer and, after the war, a renowned Baptist minister. He delivered a famous three-minute sermon about "finding riches in your own backyard" and became very wealthy traveling from city to city delivering it (the sermon was called "Acres of Diamonds"). He used the money to found Temple in the 1880s. Blai's statue, which was prominently displayed outside the main building at Tyler, had one spelling of Johnny on the plinth and another (Johnnie) on the pediment. When I pointed this out to him he went immediately into his office and fired his secretary who was, presumably, responsible for the discrepancy. Her name was Joan. She was six feet tall, blonde and beautiful. She left in tears. When I returned to give a reading, maybe fifteen years later, I found the statue in a small remote garden, on the Broad Street campus, overrun with plants and weeds, and the discrepancy still there.

Louise lives in Chelsea, near her gallery on 24th Street. In a world of dumb little moments in the arts she remains a painter of profound and complex personal feeling and endless formal ideas, richly and amazingly unified, shockingly beautiful, and more and more her very own self as she moves into her seventies. She and I spoke together at Dartmouth College a year or so ago, where she was, at the time, the painter-in-residence. We were hosted by Colleen Randall, the painter, and Susanna Heschel, the Reconstructionist scholar. Our subject was the 1950s in art, the radical changes in America, and our relationship as teacher and student.

9 Rome and the Jews

But I should be writing about the Church, shouldn't I, now that I'm in Rome, or at the very least about the Romans and the stark transition, or the beginning, clouded partly in myth and partly in mythic history? Maybe about the Jewish presence throughout the

centuries, or the persecution, or the Italian version of the Final
Solution, or Pius XII and what he did and what he did *not* do con-
cerning the Jews—and Germany—during the war, or the Ghetto
and the closing of the gates under Paul IV, or the arguments over
the hidden documents and the excuses, revisions, and rationaliza-
tions or—at the very, very least—I should write about the Jewish
food at Pipernos. I don't want to be a nasty Protestant attacking
Mariology, and making wry comments on Joseph's halo-ridden
horns. Or a Popogynist, indignant at the fifty kinds of corruption,
compromise, interference, abuse, hypocrisy, con artistry, deceit,
delusion, jugglery, cross-dressing, gluttony, duplicity, indifference,
nepotism, murder, and such. Pride, secrecy, bribery, greed, pom-
posity. Anyhow, everyone knows it, and it's not just popes; think
of the priests of Egypt, not to mention Judea; and weren't there
good popes who built not for themselves but for the Lamb and
who grudgingly put on the big hat and the purple coat and maybe
would have rather fed the poor but felt they had to sustain the insti-
tution even if burdensome? And anyhow I was only a guest here,
and a guest should shut his mouth. That's rule two, after the rule
of stinking fish. Furthermore, it's Poli Sci 101, and the pope is head
of a state. And he has to compromise, and make phone calls, and
entertain fools, and learn the rules of snooker, or he wouldn't be
there in the first place. Can you imagine the Lamb as pope, any-
thing so ridiculous? Or Paul who wrote the letters? Or Peter with
his sardines? Poor Peter and his bones. Furthermore, if the world
wasn't going to come to an end, at least for a while, one had to man-
age things. There had to be a *system*, and a systematic way of doing
things. This is true even in running a shoe store, or a shoemaker's
store, with matching tickets and the dear smell of oil. If the cross-
ing and the kneeling and the dead music gives comfort to some and
ecstasy to others, what's the harm? Except maybe for the interfer-
ence. Except maybe to meddlers like me.

I'll leave it alone. What would I have done anyway if Jews were not an issue—would I not have said, ah, it's another system of stolen beliefs, as all systems are, or "borrowed," as we say, composed partly of this, partly of that; interesting how they combined gods, how there was no embarrassment, how what they had once trampled upon is what they worship, how uninformed and intolerant they are. But I'll leave it alone, the humiliation, the enclosures, the entrapments, the ignorance, the restrictions; the mockery, the rewriting. Did you know that on the façade of a church facing the Ghetto there was an inscription, in Latin and in Hebrew, from Isaiah 65 (third Isaiah) that said, "I have spread out my hands all the day unto a rebellious people, which walketh in a way that was not good, after their own thoughts; a people that provoketh me to anger continually to my face"—referring in this case to Jews who refused to convert to Christianity. And who were forced to attend mass on Sunday and listen to the sermons. And out of rebelliousness put wax in their ears. Their own Isaiah used to condemn *them*. Something out of Stalin.

Ah, what a Jew I have become in my old age. Even the bad Jewish jokes are coming back. In Rome our bathroom is like an echo-chamber. So I sing and roar with laughter. I'm sure everyone on the floor hears me. I sing of Rosita who met one young fellow (the moon was mellow), I put my notebook—so it won't get wet—on the bidet. I experiment with the lights. I try to shave in the magnifying mirror. I forgive the saints. I am grateful beyond words for the great luck of having met and talked to Dorothy Day the few times I did. And her lover, or co-worker, Peter Maurin—whom I met in Bill Basnight's apartment on Spruce Street in Philadelphia—and his outfit, mismatched corduroy pants and jacket, a flannel shirt and wool tie I imitated and wore for twenty years. The jacket with pleats. Basnight with whom I spent the long hour in Seattle just before he died. And Jack Lindemann—is he still here, who lost his hearing in the Battle

of the Bulge and picked the poems for *The Catholic Worker?* In Fleet-
wood, Pennsylvania, now—or gone. Dust, or slime—water, in his
case. His own magazine was called *Whetstone* and he published often
in *Poetry*. His dog was also deaf, the two of them hopeless.

10 The Living Presence

I'm reading *The Winter Sun*, by Fanny Howe, collecting informa-
tion, as I do, for I know not what. I don't know if I prefer the suc-
cinct moving narratives more or the meditative paragraphs where
she broods on language and feeling as if she were writing proverbs.
It is a familiar book, in its physical organization and in its subject
matter, yet it is strange in many ways—or I find it so—because of
the wildly different worlds the two of us grew up in. There is a
difference in age, too—she is almost seventy, I am almost eighty-
five, and in her case, mine too, age and the specifics of our history
are absolutely telling, crucial I might say, not only in the events
themselves, not only in tone, but in the perceived order of things,
as if each person had a divine privilege, a number, a print, like no
other, and his or her telling of the experience, whatever it was, or
even the feeling thereof, could only be fully understood by *that*
person, never by another. I think I understand her seventy years—
the historical, not the personal part, and I know *more*, even as she
shall know more after. But the attitude, say to the "hot radio," to
the particular voices, is different since our divine privileges, our
prints, are different, and Pittsburgh is so different from Cambridge,
then *and* now, and our families, our houses, our sofas, our religions,
what adheres, so different.

   On page 20 Fanny describes a "living presence" that she secretly
calls God that came from the sun falling onto the walk of an Epis-
copal convent she saw from her window. "Whether it was cold,
yellow, white, warm, orange, or a spread of violet, that light was

my surrounding other," she says and compares it to the *geistige*, the ghostliness that, she says, Edith Stein described as being always present to consciousness. "It refused to go away, and it refused to be located." Fanny says, "I sensed it as a light with an intention infusing it, a presence that had no attributes, not even love." "I breathed it," she says, "and it made images emerge from inside me to meet the ones on the outside. Its attachment to me came because of my being young, and from what I could tell, it would disappear with age."

I read the passage several times, it struck such a chord; not that I had had that image—though I'm as Zoroastric as the rest—but that there was, for more than a few years as I remember now, a ghostly experience *I* had, though when it happened I would have described it as a kind of dizziness, of being filled with a deep pleasantness, a pleasure in which I was *overcome* and held onto the brick wall of a building beside me. I seem to remember I was always going slightly downhill, and it was my right hand I held against the wall—and it lasted for maybe ten, fifteen seconds—I think longer—and it was delicious, and there was absolutely no fear in it, and I walked normally and happily immediately after, and I never much thought about it betweentimes and never told anyone about it. Were I to discuss it later, with a psychologist, say, I might ascribe it to a physical condition, some slight aberration, but the truth is I saw it as—not so much *secret* as *personal*—and too difficult to describe and, well, quickly forgotten as I moved on. Her "light" reminds me of that, though I didn't think of it then as a religious experience in any sense of the word, unless, as I see it now, becoming "overcome" is just that. The feelings of awe I had at that time were all related to something else—to the huge sky and to sudden openness and to brilliant colors. Magnificences I saw in rivers and, of course, in mountains; but that was *nature*, it was what produced poesy. The second, maybe the third poem I wrote was at the peak of Mt. Chicora, after the long haul up. I tended to run up then, at least in the beginning, and

I'm sure the awe was as much from oxygen deprivation as it was from scenery. But sky, especially when it was filled with color, was beyond that. I saw it over and over again in the great space where the Schenley oval was, and I saw it years later in Indiana and Iowa when I stopped my car on a back road. That, as much as anything else, was one of the blessings in going to teach out there with the corn and the pigs.

11 "Christians" in Haiti

This week is the atrocious news that a group of "Christians" went to Haiti just after the earthquake (in January 2010) to steal some children, thirty-three, I think, and bring them, as I understand it, to America through the Dominican Republic. One of them—the leader—in plain Idaho English, said that God "spoke" to her. God, who is interested in child-trafficking and kidnapping. She seemed surprised, even indignant, at any suggestion that they were breaking the law, a good Christian law-abiding Republican. It's true they didn't have documents, but do they have such things in Haiti? It's true they were taking the children to a place where there were swimming pools—and toys—and, anyhow, God knows what's best for the black children—at least their Idaho God does, and if one or two of the children themselves scream that they are *not* orphans and want their mamas, well, who knows what's best for whom, and if there's not enough water or food or clothing on the bus, well, it's better than they're used to anyhow, as Mama Bush said of the African Americans from New Orleans, crowded into the crazy stadium. Just think of them all holding hands somewhere—the Haitians and their white kidnappers and breaking out into nasal song. And God prefers English to French. It's called *lingua inglese*. Rhymes with *chiese*. Moreover, it must not be forgotten that these children, raised certainly on Roman Catholic and Voodoo beliefs, will not only have swimming pools but will be housed in a "loving Christian homelike environment"—I guess in the Dominican Republic—and will eventually be eligible for adoption through agencies in the United States. I love the phrase "loving Christian homelike environment." God knows the un-Christian loveless environments they lived in before. (The lack of swimming pools, for example.) It reminds me of the "home-cooking" signs you get in bad diners.

The state of Florida, I read, has—remarkably—accepted five hundred critically wounded Haitians into hospitals. But why not five thousand—why not take over the hotels in South Beach—as the government did in World War II—turn them into hospitals, and bring resident physicians down from Boston and Philadelphia? Forget love, the big thing, show some mercy, try a little tenderness, as the schnozzola proposed. Are we, are they, afraid that the doubly cursed Haitians will stay in Florida? Not just black, but Creole-speaking. It would be an honor for them to stay, if they chose, if *some* of them chose. They would be not just cab drivers, not just eating hot chicken in an open field cooked in a trash can, but poets and painters and politicians and doctors. Even, *hélas*, accountants. Doctors Without Borders, yes, the Red Cross, yes, battleships, parachute drops, but also they should be welcome in our cities, especially after our century of interference, manipulation, and exploitation. We have some penance to do. Wouldn't it have been nice to build a whole new city for them, a city of a hundred thousand, or one such city in Florida and one in upstate New York, say? That's what is meant by hospitality, by shelter. Maybe a little of it would even rub off on Louisiana.

The Nation, our bellwether and Johnny-on-the-spot, has two short articles in its February 8, 2010, issue calling attention to the misunderstandings about Haiti and the enormous prejudice against Haitians, often by armchair commentators who continue to pass on hostile and unloving views in which deforestation, flimsy construction, and laziness—an eternal characteristic of the very poor—are mostly responsible for the earthquake, not to mention, as several famous millionaire fundamentalists have, that the quake was God's punishment for incorrect belief—devil pacts—for example. That was certainly true a century or so ago in San Francisco, a few centuries earlier in Lisbon, and, God knows, the case in Sicily, not to mention the biblical flood.

12 Education of the Poet

Fanny Howe says that "For many years, as one who could not stand historical injustice, I spent my time trying to prove to myself that I was wrong to sense that this injustice was also eternal, fatal." It was as if, as a child of the sixties (she was born in 1940), she believed for a while that humans—Americans, say—could overcome the greed, violence, and indifference that marked, that absolutely characterized, our lives, and create a truly just world—as the prophets imagined. There were hundreds like her who, in the face of fire hoses, attack dogs, lying governments, and lying corporations, not to mention sheer stupidity, chaos, and maliciousness, had this vision. Myself, I was always a kind of activist—a very minor prophet— but mainly in regard to the issues, the injustices, that *came my way*, nor did I ever have *their* beautiful belief, nor was I conflicted in the matter of the temporal (the historical) and the eternal, for which I want to say "alas." As much as anything else, it had to do with the kind of poetry I was writing and the *state* of my poetry at the time. It was almost as if poetry then, my poetry, was in conflict with my other, my political self, and it would take me a while to combine— to coalesce—the two.

The fact was that by the mid-1960s I was turning forty and struggling with my invisibility, the onslaught of age, and an enormous sense of loss and waste involving the "wrong" choices I had made. I couldn't give birth to myself—I'll put it that way. It was the longest lasting cocoon in literary history. I read till I was blind but I consulted no one, and isolated myself more and more. Though it was a kind of pleasure when I found out—later—that I was not the only one doing this, and if I have committed myself, with ferocity, to unearthing, and encouraging—by water, by dirt, by love—the other lost plants, it was because of the pity I had for their struggle against fences and among rocks. I took agonizing walks in my late thirties, only then I was pitying myself, a strange plant with juicy and hairy roots but only a few dry leaves and the very occasional bloom.

Gilbert, Dick Hazley, and I were all alike in this, Pittsburgh gophers I would say, hardly ever inquisitive rats, digging holes for themselves and storing their stems and roots and tubers—in our case, our secret knowledge—in the pockets and shallow burrows of our hearts. Sentimental gophers. We hid our tubers. We sniffed the air instead and shared it grandly. Hazley knew the most and developed the earliest but never truly continued, for he lacked the will, if not the madness. Gilbert put "poet" for profession in his passport, though he had never written a line, and would hold on to a mediocre four-line lyric—his only production—for years. The change in him occurred suddenly—maybe ten or twelve years later, over a period of days as it always does—in Oregon maybe, or the Haight. In the late 1940s we met practically every night in the dining room of the Webster Hall Hotel on Fifth near Bellfield. We treated the dining room—a rather upscale place—as if it were a European coffeehouse and, as much as possible, sat at a table in the far corner. We got there about eight and generally closed the facility at ten or ten-thirty, quite late for a hotel restaurant at the time. We ordered small plates of potato salad or tea or olives—sometimes coffee. The waitress was patient but not amused. I'm sure we tipped her, but not liberally.

When I think of the "wrong choices," when I *used* to think of the wrong choices, I thought of two things: the first was not staying

in Europe after my year in France in 1949–50, taking advantage of
a teaching offer in Toulouse, and spending five or six years on the
continent; and the second was not going to the West Coast, meet-
ing Robert Duncan and ending up in Seattle with Roethke, whose
poetry I loved, though wrong choices also had to do with econom-
ics and sexual freedom, the male poet's adolescent reverie. But of
course I didn't have to go to California. I could have just moved to
the East Village and lived on two beans and a grain of rice a day. My
issue was not geography; and it was not money, or schools of poesy.
It was finding a way of living—breathing—fully, maximally, and
engaging *all* my passions, but essentially my central one, poetry,
and not letting the whiffs from the past—dragons, I'll call them—
overcome me, or make me lift my pencil from the ragged page;
dragons, four or five of them that always hid in drawers, bookcases,
beds, bathrooms, kitchen tables, and in cellars and trees, each with
ferocious cardboard teeth and, if you looked closely, no spine at all.

The Henry Miller School of Abandonment doesn't move me.
It's too simplistic and too narcissistic to leave wife and job (or not
to have wife and job) and to devote yourself just to Balzac or to a
hill outside of town in Greece or Morocco where you can either
eat poisonous fish or eat without paying—in any way—with your
friends (read patrons), a different night of the week for each one.
Then you can devote yourself freely to your high moral or aesthetic
vision, no one there either to listen or—since they are so lowly—to
object. It cost the prophets a lot to do what they did, it cost Miller
nothing. Nothing cost him anything. He loved his "poverty."

13　Straddling

Finally though, it was not really the dragons at all, it was the atti-
tude I took to the arts, and to the artist; how—and what—I learned,
processed as they say; nor was it a question of "straddling," as I used

to think, say, "playing it safe," with a job in one room and poetry in the other; nor was it a question of "finding my voice," that idiotic thing, for finding your voice is really finding yourself, so it's more finding your *self*, being born, if I can borrow a metaphor from the dippers. Maybe it's two stages. It's grandiose—and pompous—to say it, but I molted, at a very early age, though I needed a couple of decades to find my wings, and I was born with odd eyes and an odd heart. What I had to do was accept those eyes and that heart. My own weird combination. Which I am amazed one introducer or another gets right from time to time. So that I can learn from him or her what it is I am, and do! I love when it's that and they don't just read from my bio. I don't even care if they get it wrong.

I guess I'm threading the same needle over and over, odd Sisyphusism. Anyhow, you never get it right in prose—that's why you write poetry. That way you avoid the pitfalls. Just as you create others. I want to say, though, that it was never economics itself, even if I thought it was. In my late forties I was writing poem after poem, throwing very few away, yet at the same time I was teaching four or five sections at a community college, chairing the English Department, heading the college union (A.F.T.), heading the state union (New Jersey), fighting the administration there with its cutthroat pedagogical system, negotiating huge raises, leading strikes and—at the same time—heading the Poets-in-the-Schools program in Pennsylvania (I lived in that state, across the border), and hired, trained, and evaluated over forty poets, for all sixty-two counties, and gave out grants from my perch in Harrisburg or the one in Easton and—at the same time—taught graduate courses in poetry writing at Sarah Lawrence College and Columbia University as well as a writing class at the 92nd Street Y. In consideration of which, I would like to suggest that younger poets shouldn't pity themselves too much about their "load." I would like to give them, if I could, free room and board forever—in Palermo, maybe—or

Fez. At the same time, I ask them to remember that Philip Levine was still teaching composition courses at Fresno State in his sixties. And, at the same time, writing his magnificent poetry.

Enfin, maybe my admirers will leave me alone and stop praising me for "publishing late." Damned with dumb praise (as two people today, when I told each of them I was eighty-five, looked at me with wonder and said, each one, "I hope I'm still as active—lively—as you when I'm eighty-five"). Meaning: can an eighty-five-year-old still stand up?

What if I told you—for I love fiction—that I wrote my first book of poems when I was twelve and won the Chatterton Prize for it, the same year that I learned to stand on my head? The judge was Kenneth Burke, who may have been influenced because we both went roller skating on Craig Street in Pittsburgh, though at different times. We talked for hours once in western New Jersey about the importance of the skate key and which pocket you should put it in when you're racing downhill, and how to jump over the cracks, and what you can do even on one skate when the other is dangling, and what it was like at Schenley High School, where he studied advanced Greek; and in Taylor Allderdice High School where we carried homemade blackjacks inside our shirts.

Two weasels sat under a redwood tree having an argument.

14 My Mother and Father

My mother was forty-nine when I left the first time for Europe—by bus to Hoboken and freighter to Antwerp. She was a year younger than my daughter is now. My footlocker was packed—mostly with books of poetry—and sitting, open, on the floor beside the front door. I remember the key to the lock was called a T-44 and one T-44 was the same as the next so there really wasn't a lock. My mother was in the bedroom, twelve or so feet away, lying on her bed and, presumably, dying from a heart attack, her second or third. My father was either at the pool hall or the drugstore with the gossips. When her doctor arrived—I remember his name was Frieberg—he stopped to chat with me for five or ten minutes before he went in to see her. He looked at my books and my underwear and remembered lovingly his own *wanderyahr*. When he returned he told me there was nothing wrong with her heart, she had a little anxiety about me leaving, and it would be good medicine if I stayed a few days and took a later boat, but I left the next day, hoisting my small trunk into the Greyhound, the side where they put the suitcases, the motor running. We never mentioned that particular night again, my mother and I, the forty-five years she lived after that.

My father I saw briefly the next morning. We shook hands and he seemed to be sad but admiring, if surprised, that I was going to another continent for a year. He had come the other way when he was eight and never wanted to go back. He must have thought of his oldest brother, who stayed in Ruzhin (Ukraine)—already dead though my father didn't know it—and his nephews, older than him, if they were still alive. I was driven by beauty, cheap living, the French language, and the pieces in *Look* magazine and *Life*. I suspect I was more tied to his grief than to hers. It may have been, however, my sister Sylvia's death that caused my grief as much as their golden expectations—that Harry and Ida. How I longed to have three older brothers and one or two living sisters. How I wanted to be the useless one. How I envied this or that poet whose father was dead, whose mother was illiterate, whose brothers were plumbers and carpenters. The only demand on them that they stay out of jail. For a while I was a kind of captive, even if I was allowed the yard.

There is a photograph of my mother and father, taken in the early 1950s, of them and their store in Detroit on Woodward Avenue. They are standing two or three feet apart, my mother on the left, my father on the right, in front of the tables, their salesmen, four or five of them, in rows behind them. Shirts, sweaters, and pants are piled up on the tables with large hand-painted signs everywhere announcing the (astounding) prices of sport coats, sweaters, and suits. Everyone is perfectly still and more or less at attention. My mother, stout, beautiful, and dazed, beads at her throat, is the only woman there. My father is thirty years younger than I am now but still seems older. It is one of four or five stores, in Detroit, Akron, Cincinnati, that my father owns with his two partners; one a man-ufacturer named Jack Wolk and one a goyische financier, Norbert Sterne. They are in the going-out-of-business business, liquidation and bankruptcy, and the sign at the back of the store says "Factory Outlet of Surplus Stock." The sport shirts are $2.69, three for $7.00. A "sport-coat" is $19.95. I am, at the same time, in Smithtown, Long Island, teaching at a private school, my first full-time job: French, English, history, typewriting. Or it's a year later or so and I'm back in Europe, teaching high school in Glasgow, the first year of an extended stay in Britain, France, and Italy, though this time married—to Pat Stern—and living a more settled life than I did on my first trip. It's the store—the one in the picture—they wanted me to manage, five floors, men's and women's clothing, furniture, dry goods. I would have been rich in five years but I turned it down to work in Scotland for twenty-eight dollars a week (second or third telling). Isn't it amazing that the two of them, standing at attention there, should have even the smallest claim on me, and that, because of them, I caused myself such pain?

15 The Train Station

Throughout history men and women have found a certain peace in that strange place we call *sky*. It was, and is, the source of vision, memory, hope, ideals, and even historical connections. All we know is there in the sky. Not in the planets, the stars, the formations—I love that too, but I think mostly of sky—a daytime sky—with clouds and sun and water—and the colors. It is the upper regions of the air, it is the heavens, the celestial region. Heaven itself, the foolish place. And sometimes the entire sky every which way you look is covered with clouds, from the ground up, it seems, as if it were a tent of white, a Mongolian tent, enormous and round and here and there a hole, a blue hole, in the fabric so the blue dust can get in or so we can see out, oh here and there into the great expanse, what they call firmament. Though sometimes, in a great cave, in a cathedral, in a huge train station, there is a simulacrum of this sky and once in the silence of the main hall of the Pennsylvania Railroad, in Pittsburgh, ten or eleven at night, I was caught in the endless space. The roof was so distant it was almost invisible. And there was nothing there but three wagons, one broken, two waiting to be pulled. For a second I was alone. We had not yet loaded the wagons and attached ourselves like mules, pulling the boxes and loading the freight cars for our eight hours, from five p.m. to one in the morning, the smell of sulfur our drug. There was no happiness like that. There was only obedience to the heft, and if our heads were often bent forward to assist our shoulders and arms, it was the slight wind and the hard rubber on the concrete and the mysterious cog in the heart of the wagon that helped us. Though sometimes we were aided by the leftover straw from a previous load, and sometimes we swore we were going downhill. There was no motor and no pneumatic inflated tires. If there was deep attention, there was no divine assistance; and sometimes there were two of us, and sometimes one, and sometimes we were overtaken by the weight of things and our forward momentum. If there was grace we hardly knew it and if there was joy it was when the first box—or carton—was lifted up over the steel rim; it was when the wagon ceased to be that huge and menacing—and we found nothing lurking there invisible to our touch. And the weight of the boxes increasing as we reached bottom. The return so fast we ran.

16 Athletes

I forget about my back when I'm sitting, and I'm generally sitting when I write—and read—but I'm standing a lot over tables and counters recently, either reading or writing. The pain, when it comes, is mysterious. From time to time I read from my copy of *Healing Back Pain*, which claims more or less that it is "emotional," but when I can barely stand from the tightness, the stiffness, and the burning, Sarno's book seems somewhat quaint, and even ridiculous. I am told that I have spinal stenosis, a condition that commonly comes with age and is a building up of debris, causing pressure on a nerve—something like that—that causes the pain. In my case, it's often not *pain* but a loss of feeling in my right foot, or "pins and needles," or a stiffness from below the right knee to the ankle that makes me slow down, limp, bend forward, and depend on my cane. I have had the usual tests and I'm told there's nothing wrong with my discs. I'm also told there are two kinds of operations I can have, that injections often work—if temporarily—and that I can take pills (steroids), which obliterated the pain altogether for a week once. In the mornings I can walk without pain for three or four blocks, sometimes more, and I've developed various strategies of leaning against walls or sitting on some, on any, godforsaken semblance of a bench or chair to alleviate the pain. If I sit for, say, even twenty seconds I am ready to go again. In the country, or on college campuses, I relax against trees; in the city, I have come to rely on standpipes, male or female, or even the hoods of cars.

Here in Rome I've been pretty good and have walked some distances, in spite of the rain and the rough sidewalks, even the precarious streets and noisily aggressive motorcycles and speeding cars. But you think eternally here in Rome, at least you go back to your earlier years and their physicality, one decade measured against another, now that eight and then some have passed. I was a fat child who, in keeping with Leviticus, was made to drink my milk *before* I ate my meat, some hideous version of kashruth whereby simultaneously the law was overcome and the holy lactate was permitted ingress into the astonished digestive tract. And when the meat came, and the mashed potatoes (my God, did my mother forget where butter came from?), the quantity was so huge you could easily die from it. My father ate seven or eight burgers, along with the rest, though there was very little in the way of vegetables to soften the onslaught, a canned string bean or two, a lonely pea. When I was fourteen I decided I would change. I learned calories and vitamins, I went on a diet as part of a huge battle with my parents, and I began to exercise—endlessly—pull-ups, push-ups, the horses, the ropes, the standing on my head and hands, swimming, running, weightlifting, basketball, heavy bag. At fifteen I had reached my full height and wore size eleven and a half shoes. I ran the mile, the half-mile, and cross country in high school. I came in third my senior year in the city of Pittsburgh in the mile. Almost every night, in every season, though absolutely no one ran then—outside of a team—I ran at least twice around the old Schenley oval, a mile-and-a-half racetrack from the 1920s or '30s. My father picked me up on his way home from work, or I ran the two miles to our house, our apartment. When I was seventeen I was a walk-on for the University of Pittsburgh football team, a freshman. I was a running back (left halfback in the old single-wing system). But I quit in the late fall because of the endless days of it, with no time for studies—or living. In the army, a few years later, I did some boxing—at 180 pounds—and caused a few concussions, though I was close to blind then. All this because I was a fatty and because I had a stubborn, insistent, uncompromising will. I blossomed out in my twenties and gave myself up to more important pursuits than, say, running, or hitting a bag or rolling around on a ball, though I turned to four-wall handball in the weird place called Indiana, Pennsylvania, in my mid-thirties. Indiana, where Jimmy Stewart once lived on Vinegar Hill and his father displayed the Oscars in the window of Stewart's Hardware. And I walked, I always walked good distances, and I always planned on walking farther. This is what I think about when I limp down a street or look at the old man looking at me, a little bent over, in a mirror in the morning or in one of the *toilettes*—or *bagnos*, whatever they're called—in this city of Piuses and Pauls and Johns and now a Benedetto, talking pope talk. Always corrected the next morning by an aide holding his round head in his hand and murmuring in Judeo-German, "Oi, vey."

I want to be able to walk my hour or so in the morning, even up the steep hill at the edge of town, and throw this silver stick away, on a shelf I mean, on a rack, on a hook, in a stand, in a corner; collecting dust, which I would kiss and kiss again, with my dust-starved lips. Ah, Socrates I spoke to the other day, a slow-speaking Greek, unlike the thirty-something Greek women, twice as fast— and as loud—as their Italian counterparts, sitting at the next table over from us, four of them. "Listen, Jew," Socrates said, "if that grandfather of yours, the clever Jacob, had not left Ruzhin even before the main pogrom had taken place and come to filthy Pittsburgh, of all places, to open a little stogie factory, and if your father, the youngest, had not come a few years later with his reluctant mother, Anna; and if your own mother had not left Bialystock at the age of five and emigrated, or fled, with mother and brothers, and in *her* case, a reluctant father—and they had not settled on Townsend Street, in The Hill, a few blocks from Stern's Cigars and she had not met Aaron, your father, fifteen years later—at a dance, after the basketball game, and you weren't born a year after your sister, three, four years down the road—as we say in Athens—you would be only some dust, or a drop of rain embedded in that black cloud there. Or if you existed in some Mongolian or Canaanite form you would be one of those Ukrainian Jews, like your second cousins or first cousins once removed, who *didn't* flee, and might have been shot or gassed or buried alive or worked to death, whoever the dust your father or the melancholy dust your mother might turn out to be. And you have had such a lucky life, for fortune it is who rules not only those deadly Tarquins and we Athenians but you as well, and don't make me start reciting the names of your dear friends who are dead by now or blind or deaf or crippled—not that absurd thing. Or how the chance you took might have been a lost chance and how I was more than willing to die at seventy and how those Greek girls are just like ours were and I bow down like a cloud myself in love of them, my face wet with desire, even picking up a word or two of their absurd demotic speech, reminiscent of our places and the things we hold dear, though they know it not, actors, actresses, my tongue must say, in your drama, your absurd ill-starred drama."

Truth is I would much rather have heard from a Jewish saint from deep in the south of France or on the Rhine; some Rashi or ben Joseph or a false savior, an Isaac ben Luria, living at last in Turkey like a true heretic, one of *us*, doomed forever (for in Rome you are doomed forever) to read—not Dickens—as in Evelyn Waugh, but Shaw or Mark Twain, who, like me, made fun of St. Agnes's skull, on display in Sant'Agnes in Agone, too small maybe, too bare-boned, as Twain said. St. Agnes, who was nude and "pilloried" and whose hair grew miraculously to cover her body—for shame's sake.

Rashi would ask me, I'm sure of it, how much my coat cost, and what makes a zipper go, and how is the vest—the lining—inserted and what a God we Jews have, he would say, or Isaac from Provence

might have asked how much I bench-pressed or how many min-
utes it took for the half-mile or how long I could stay under water.
I would end up telling him about what a magnificent athlete my
father was, and how he swam like a seal and hit the ball over the
fence every time he had a bat in his hand, or how he ran twenty-five
balls in straight pool, and I was a poor imitation of him; and how
my son David was already beating me at badminton when he was
sixteen, though I think I still took him in sidewalk tennis—because
I had Tourette's and the quick reflexes that go with that famous dis-
ease, like so many athletes and comedians; and how Ross Gay, ball-
player, teacher, and poet-supremo, along with Thomas Pletzinger,
my German translator, also a ballplayer, and prizewinning novelist,
were sitting in Anne Marie's living room watching basketball on
TV and recounting to each other the players they saw on the screen
they had played with in Philadelphia and Berlin, both of them six-
foot-five; and how my friend's father, Ziggie Kahn, had played foot-
ball opposite Jim Thorpe; and how the two brothers, my cousins
the Grossmans, from the Hill, two of eleven children, ten of them
boys, Moses and Jacob, had both fought Fritzie Zivic, welterweight
champion from 1939–45, and how Jack (Jacob) was the only one ever
to knock Zivic down and how Moses beat Zivic in a nontitle fight;
Zivic, dirtiest fighter in history, Pittsburgh's own; and how shortly
after, I think it was then, I became a kind of friend of Billy Conn,
who had come nine minutes away from beating Joe Louis, in 1940, if
he had only stayed away from him the last three rounds, and whom
the Goldstein brothers, who owned him, begged him to, and who
said, "I'll kill the bum" and was floored—forever—by one punch
in the thirteenth; and (who) worked out at the YMHA on Bellfield
Avenue, as I did, smaller than me, really a bloated middleweight
who was scared to death of the rematch in 1946 and whom I had the
absurd honor of sparring with for a few rounds in the ring on the
second floor, thus for a second or two a ridiculous nano-inch away

from the Brown Embalmer; the title of my second book, *Lucky Life*, a version of what Louis said after every fight, his opponent lying in a pool of blood or supporting a loose brain, "Lucky night, lucky night." Billy Conn, who asked Louis why he wouldn't let him be the champ, just for one year, and who replied: "You were the champ for twelve rounds, and blew it"; Louis, who destroyed Schmeling and whom the IRS hounded, who ended up a greeter at a club in Nevada, hunched over and smiling.

17 Jack Gilbert

Jack Gilbert, who has dementia, has ended up in California—in Berkeley—instead of New York City or Northampton, Massachusetts, partly because of the weather and partly because of the close "followers" he had there. Linda fills me in on every detail, including the several facilities he's been in, why he left, how much he weighs, and how he's being treated. His friends, his admirers, all belonged to a workshop Jack led in San Francisco years ago. Of the four I know, one is a retired high school teacher, one a wine salesman, one a lawyer, and one who lives by kindness. It might be demeaning to give the details, how, in the latest facility called Sunrise, the patients spend most of the day sitting in wheelchairs in the hall, or how his shoes were stolen. "I made a mistake about beauty and truth," he told Linda. "I took the wrong side; I should have privileged the truth." His roommate is a 104-year-old Jew named Saul. "Don't tell anyone, but I'm already dead," Jack said.

18 Haiti, the Long History

It's early March 2010 now, but the news about Haiti will continue and the *New York Times* will be the barometer of interest, as it was for Katrina, five years earlier. It will gradually move off the front pages and the columnists will address the issues from time to time, inevitably less and less, but when a new issue or discovery—a corruption, a stupidity, a sad drama—appears it will flash up again, briefly, like a sparkler on the Fourth of July, a sudden light and a sudden disappearance. One day the news was about the foreign doctors who will be haunted by the Haitians they couldn't help, and their references to amputations where hacksaws were used and vodka was relied upon for sterilization. Limbs were sacrificed and lives were lost to injuries that are no longer supposed to be disabling or deadly. These doctors were overwhelmed by conflicting feelings of accomplishment and guilt, practicing, as they did, nineteenth-century medicine, in order to save lives. They will remember the bravery of their patients—and they will come back, with drugs, oxygen, blood, prosthetics. Another day the president, René Préval, will declare a day of mourning and address his nation "like a father blessing his children"; and another day we will hear of the tears that fall, finally, mostly in pity and hopelessness; and another day we will have rage. There will be no *Kanaval*—maybe next year. The songs will be different then, and though the dresses will blaze again with flowers, love will have another key.

And out of the destruction and the grief *some* of Haiti's real history might be revealed. How, in 1809, the slave-state revolted against the French government, and France, acting for the former slave-owners, returned in 1825 with a flotilla of warships and a huge army, demanding that Haiti pay ninety million gold francs, ten times its annual revenue at the time, in a mad agreement whereby former slaves are not paid reparations but are forced themselves to pay the brutal owners for their own freedom. It's as if Lincoln were to award the Confederacy for freeing the slaves—or Israel, say, instead of receiving financial help from Germany, would have to pay room and board for prisoners in Buchenwald and Auschwitz. Gelt gone crazy, reparations turned on its head. Ninety million francs—for three centuries of stolen labor—a debt which, with crippling interest, wasn't paid off until 1947. In addition to which, the Duvalier regimes, U.S. pets and puppets, incurred their own huge debts, estimated, Naomi Klein tells us, at $844 million, half of which was "misappropriated" by the two Docs, which the World Bank and the IMF still are trying—or were trying—to collect, in spite of the fact that most of the money wasn't spent in Haiti. Haiti, which once provided the world with sugar, coffee, cotton, and hardwood. A third of its population killed in the war with France. Ruined by slavery, debt, and war, a massive embargo, isolation, invasion, racism, intervention, poverty, deforestation. From what I know, walking down my canal and yelling at the geese, a follower of I. M. Stone, a reader of *The Nation*.

19 Exploitation

We bought our house in Raubsville, Pennsylvania, six miles south of Easton, on the Delaware River and the Pennsylvania Canal in 1968, and lived there till 1982. One mile south, facing the canal, is a beautiful low-lying stone building that's been empty—as far as I know—since the late 1970s. I knew it as the Structural Pre-Cast Company, but I understand it was formerly the power house for the trolleys, or street cars, that ran from Easton to Philadelphia and Doylestown, capitol of Bucks County, and from Easton to Bethlehem, PA, and back. My next-door neighbor, Stan Barrett, worked at Pre-Cast as a welder for maybe twenty-five years, before the business suddenly closed—without notice, as I understand—just as he was about to retire, whose owners took his—and others'—retirement money with them, leaving the workers, some of whom, like Stan, had invested in a "plan" for twenty-some years, jobless, abandoned, and penniless, already in their sixties, just as rust had entered into the equation in the whole region.

The industry was primarily in the cities, Easton, Allentown, Bethlehem, but there were always smaller, self-contained firms in the countryside or in villages where everything was organized around a single idea or project and the finances could even have been arranged by local banks, borrowing as they probably did, from larger banks in nearby cities, with advice and funding even coming from the metropolitan centers, Philadelphia and New York. For all I know there could have been a loose connection with Bethlehem Steel, but all that doesn't matter—it was Stan Barrett, my next-door neighbor in Raubsville, PA, located on Pennsylvania Route 611, an hour and twenty minutes north of Philadelphia, ten minutes from Easton, PA, and an hour and a half from New York City, who was ruined financially and destroyed emotionally, just as he was about to finally indulge himself with his garden, his old truck, and his music.

What they did at Pre-Cast was fabricate bridge girders, septic tanks, park benches, drainage conduits, and the like. As a welder, Stan made forms and prepared metal bars over which the concrete was poured and which gave it its strength. It was called reinforced concrete. I vaguely remember something about stands in Yankee Stadium, but I'm not sure. There were mounds of coal downhill from the plant, not too pretty a sight for someone walking his dog on the mule path, north and south, in the direction of Easton or Riegelsville.

Stan and his wife, Florence, lived in a bungalow, probably built in the 1930s or '40s, facing, as our house did, old Route 611, a narrow, abandoned highway that had been converted into a local street two or three blocks long, when the new 611—the road from Philadelphia to Easton—was built on the other (western) side of the Pennsylvania Canal. Stan walked to work, either down the towpath or the road, probably carried his lunch in a pail and started and finished the day early. He had a 1952 or '53 Chevy truck in his backyard, which he tended long and lovingly, his head, as often as not, bent down into the motor, wiping things with a rag and making adjustments. I was in his and Florence's house once, maybe twice, and he and she inside mine only once the fourteen years we lived on the river. His basement was finished and there was a long polished bar there, with colored lights where, especially in the earlier days, they and their friends gathered to drink, eat, and play music. Stan played the trumpet beautifully; you could hear the notes come out of the basement and, on occasion, he stood on his front porch, facing the river, and played, as if to the small waves or the brilliant late light on the water or to the maples and the black locusts on the bank, as if they were some leafy audience waiting to applaud and eternally ask for more in the slow way those limbs did, especially when the cold and persistent winds urged them on. In the spring Stan planted his small red flowers, his salvia, at the edge of his parking space across the road. He had room for maybe three cars but I could accommodate seven or eight in our space, and once or twice he asked me, almost angrily, if some of his guests could park there.

Stan and I weren't close—we weren't *friends*—and after we talked, usually a few sentences, something about a bush that bordered our properties, or the age of his shining truck, I felt overcome, as if I were keeping something away from him, or simply that I was intruding. I didn't know if he knew I was a Jew or if he ever thought about it, or just a stranger and newcomer to the river, a "New Yorker," an intellectual, who kept different hours than he and who tubed down the river with his strange friends, half-naked women, loud and bearded men, who drank and picnicked on the river bank, on the grass under the locusts, and sped away as it grew dark in their dirty foreign vehicles.

It never occurred to me then that he might have been shy, or felt inferior, or responded to the gulf between us in a manner that was familiar and comfortable for him, intractability and stiffness, silence, though he may have been—of course he was—just as uncomfortable as I, and just as disturbed. I have to say that I was more at ease with some of the others on my road, a beery garage owner who drove his car one day into the canal and drowned; a former taxicab driver—out of Philadelphia—and her husband, who went to the theater in New York from time to time; the mailman, sort of across the way from us, catty-corner from our property; the owner of the ancient stone hotel, who backed his motorcycle one day over the bank into the river, the water everywhere so beckoning then. Florence, Stan's wife, was more open and more friendly, the women always cutting across class and caste. She was kind and beautiful—in every way—but terribly nervous. She and Stan were very close and you could see how dependent they were on each other.

Stan had his first heart attack shortly after Pre-Cast closed. I was already gone—to Iowa to teach—when he had his second attack and died. What I remember most, and what endeared me to him, was that, after his first bout he asked me if he could use my rowboat for exercise—clearly he was following his doctor's advice—and it gave me pleasure to know that my cheap metal boat, which I had bought for thirty dollars, oars included, somewhere in Easton, would be put to some use after I traveled out to the corn and pigs. It was the only real favor he ever asked of me, and he did it without caution and reserve, which I loved him for.

I know that Stan was still alive in the spring of '73 when the three great river systems in Pennsylvania flooded and the Delaware missed our two houses by only a few inches. Stan and Florence were helpless since, as I said, they lived in a bungalow, but I promised her—and Stan—I would take their furniture, dishes, rugs, pictures, etc., up to my second floor since I had a team of friends waiting (and drinking beer). She was shaking with fear, but we got the news early that the river had crested upstream and we were safe.

That evening, the two of them knocked on our front door to thank us and we invited them in for tea, the one time they came to our house. Florence moved three miles down the river to Riegelsville, Pennsylvania, after Stan's death and remarried. I think of them whenever I drive up 611 on the way to Easton.

20 The Comic

I've been thinking about comedy, and comics, for years now, partly for their own sake and partly for the connection there is with "tragedy," and partly the connection, or the *presence*, in the artist; of course, particularly in poetry. There are some standard texts on the subject, beginning with a Neanderthal joke that made the Cro-Magnons pull their long hair and moan, and there's Aristotle and a few others. Naturally, it's got to do with anger and bitterness. And, in my case, how I went almost unthinking, plunging ahead into any thorns and brambles that lay in my way. And of course sometimes bled. And didn't *prepare*. And didn't *care*. Though I was overly sensitive, really—and subject to hurt feelings. And did this truly from the very beginning; until it became such a habit—more than a habit, a way of being, call it loose, improvisational, tentative, capricious, stubborn, attentive, secret, or very secret. And how you take up comedy or the comic as a way of getting even—at least sometimes. And how you're getting even with yourself, at least at first, for being a prig; for not having the courage; for being Matthew Arnold; for not being Thomas Hardy; for having a tight pen, for being too interested in beauty, and then later for choking on a fish bone, for changing partners while dancing; for lining your dresser drawers with envy; for reading the 1950s newspapers; for not forgiving; for one foot being longer than the other; for letting people die; for letting them die too soon; for being silent for twelve years; for not reading fourteen books; for not reading them over and over.

For the comic is a way of sticking your hand in someone's mouth; or pulling your own teeth with pliers. Or being merciless, or keeping your distance and getting even. Being bewildered. Being low-down. Bullying back. Cruelty, really. Lack of respect. For every day is Carnival; and every wife is exhausted. And Carnival is such that you can spit in anyone's eye, you can break a window—or open it in the snow—or jump on top of a car roof, or shoot an arrow into the sofa, or bark at a dog, or kiss the cleaning woman or the bus driver, or sing in Yiddish, for example, in a French restaurant, or imitate a cripple, say on Broadway or Amsterdam, you with your cane.

Spit is important here. Though spitting in a king's eye is really a metaphor. No one spits in a king's eye. For one thing an eye is hard to find, and spit is mostly not a clear stream. Just throwing a shoe gets you beaten half to death. Carnival is a temporary disruption of the rules, behavior that would get you thrown into jail or drowned, say, or starved or beaten with nail-studded clubs, preferably two-by-fours. For subversion is only temporary and may be just a letting off of steam. And the police are watching, and they are looking at their clocks. And either Carnival (a) helps create a kind of permanent farcical and rebellious attitude among the less powerful and the powerless, or (b) it is a way of reconciling people to their more typical roles, and letting them go back to the office or factory more content, even happier, because of those small moments. Maybe even too obvious to have to say. And, of course, sexual freedom, subversion, masks, liberties, reminiscent of the one or two days or weeks—of freedom and choice—for women in earlier cultures, where horns were tolerated, nay, encouraged, and the husband smiled blandly and slept a little on the train ride home holding his wild wife's hand.

Though I'm moving more to the left (a) even now, for I do think the subversion—and the inversion, the spit in the eye—may be worth something more permanent, may have a lasting and substantial effect, may help build up true resistance almost to the point that the corporations, and the governments, and the churches may begin to feel uneasy and may finally reveal their true nature by openly limiting freedom and privileges if there is too much orneriness and horniness displayed. I may have to read Rabelais again—I *will* read him, but my main point is that the comic, the comedian, is at, is in, a permanent Carnival, a disruptive disastrous state, at least in his mind and his heart if not also in his appurtenances, his clothes, his nose, his rose.

My father was the absolute embodiment of obedience. He got a haircut every ten days, he put on a different suit and a fresh starched shirt every morning, and in forty-five years he never missed one day of work. But one Sunday he, my mother, and I went to a cousin's wedding—at the Schenley Hotel in Pittsburgh—and he drank a bit there and on the way home, backing out of a parking space, he hit a pole behind us and then a fireplug in front and, rather liking it, went back and forth, from pole to plug, deliberately smashing up his shiny Pontiac, my mother screaming "Harry, Harry," my father laughing like a madman. When he got home he dropped his pants and fell into bed. He was wild, subversive, for one hour—and it cost him hundreds. He lived with his older sisters as a boy and was a kind of orphan who had to be good. He was a loving man, embarrassed by "misbehavior" and long hair.

The comedian doesn't seem to get embarrassed. But who knows what his sleep is like—or his dreams. His *going* to sleep. The brim of his hat is always too small and his pants too large. His shoes are a crazy color. If his culture, his country, is terrified of sex, he makes sexual jokes; if it is terrified of government, he makes political jokes. He—she—corrects our lies, our self-deceit. She forces us to laugh at our false behavior. She constantly reminds us that we are animals, and have animal functions, which we constantly deny.

I am in Leipzig, Johann Sebastian Bach's city, for the Leipzig

Book Fair. It is the 325th year of his birth, so they're going to do something special to celebrate the occasion. I remember his 300th and how we celebrated it in Philadelphia in 1985, naming a street for him, singing his praises, playing his music.

In a restaurant last night, after my reading, there were little white clay busts of Bach in a display case but I didn't see anyone buying them. The restaurant was folk-style—the waitresses were dressed in colorful Bavarian costumes, but the mood wasn't festive since it was late and they were tired. We ate, I'm ashamed to say, Sauerbraten, some kind of potato dumpling, and some tasteless skinny carrots. I thought of *apfel* strudel but I resisted. The "country bread" was good, though. A few meters away was the bronze bust of the founder of the restaurant. He was born in 1853 and died in 1927. There wasn't a small sledgehammer around to wound him or change his shape. Before my reading—German and English, with my translator Thomas Pletzinger and my editor Hans Koch, I talked to the audience and asked them about the comic *auf Deutschland*, but they were loath to speak or too embarrassed. It reminded me of classes I had in my early years, pulling teeth, as we say in Lenni Lenape. I talked about Jewish comedians and African American and Irish. I was interested in the German comics, but they didn't have one word to say. Hans suggested that schadenfreude was the typical German humor, a sort of laughing at someone else's pain, and he gave me, as an example, German *soldaten* laughing at the Jews they forced to clean the sidewalks with a toothbrush dipped in soapy water. Hans is eternally furious at the Nazis. He was probably born shortly after the war, maybe 1945, and it's as if he were cheated of a life and forced to do penance for what he was not responsible for.

I read my poem "Roses" at the reading and told the audience— as I always do when I read that poem—how roses are named after famous people, artists, movie stars, millionaires, and I don't know any longer which roses I made up. And when I talked about rose bushes I naturally recalled a certain prick and liar who inhabited the White House for eight ridiculous years and how you should piss on Bushes and how unfortunate it is that women can't, given the nature of the genitals, though a young woman from the U.S. Embassy later told me she *had* pissed on rose bushes and how that laden stream was actually good for the Bush. When I talked about Chancellor Merkel pissing, no one seemed to object, but I was kind to the pope and didn't talk about the dress he wears—or how *he* pisses.

We went, late at night, to the chocolate factory overlooking the Rhine to eat and drink. I sang Heine's song there—to universal applause. (*Ruhig fließt der Rhein. Im Abendsonnenschein.*) My only objection—reservation—about Deutschland is that they treated me with too much respect, even reverence. Partly because of my age, partly because I was a Jew, partly because of the poems. I don't think I was ever applauded as long as I was in both Hamburg and Köln. I was embarrassed. And in Köln they lined up all the way to the door to buy books and talk to me. What if the dumb French and British would have stopped Hitler's army—armed with only wooden guns—in 1936 in the Ruhr? What if *that* were the Final Solution? And Chamberlain—let it rain boiling water on him and his umbrella forever, the wet street he lives on in Hell! Can there be no comedy after the Holocaust? Can there be *only* comedy? Chaplin was too sentimental in *The Great Dictator*, but he knew where—and how—to focus. Though he ended up preaching, didn't he? What could he do after the Camps were discovered? Preaching is always the secret problem for comics. Thanks God they only hurl *numbers* at each other—and check their Bibles at the door.

It's too exhausting, let alone meaningless, to compare the two kinds of Mongolian humor and how the political border between them did and did not matter; or to compare Bob Hope with the

Marx Brothers. Kant himself listened to frog song and condemned the cutting up of pouches. So did Henri Bergson. The Buddha laughs mostly at himself, as Yahweh must, who lost his footing. The historically powerless, including peasants, Kurds, blacks, women, poor people, and immigrants, have a lot to say—a lot of it ironic—when they are allowed to say it. The low-residency MFA program in comedy teaches surprise, scatology, ridicule, slapstick, incongruity, conflict, repetitiveness, sudden glory, the unexpected, satire, hat attire, parody, paradox, as well as screwball, blueball, and taboo. Love is called tripping on the mons and ends up with both of them soaking their feet in hot water. In a *shiksel*, as my grandmother used to say as she rubbed the welts. In the South there was race humor. Also in the North. *The Odyssey* is a comedy.

Just think of Tiger Woods. It wouldn't be quite so funny if there wasn't a Bill Clinton before. One is a parody of the other. The fall of two giants is not a tragedy. A blow job and a car window broken by a golf club are just not tragic. Hélas, Gatorade will probably drop him. Maybe he can endorse Trojans. The best idea since turning ketchup bottles upside down.

Comedy is the most human of all enterprises because of its unexpected, almost magical nature. I want to even say mystical, but that's a weird word to use for the Marx Brothers, those priests of the 1930s. I'm interested, in particular, how my "later" poems are more comic than my "early." And I'm not speaking of funny poems or light verse, or wit or cuteness or puns as such, though those things may be used. My early poems are not comic in the sense I'm using the word. *I* was comic, but my poems generally weren't. Unless the whole mad act of writing poetry, organizing words rhythmically on the page, and scratching your head with a pencil is itself comic. Chaucer is comic and Burns and early Donne and Byron. And Blake, Nietzsche, Rimbaud, Auden, and Villon. I should probably say comedic. Dante of course called his great work a comedy, but that's something else. I believe what we call comic and what we call tragic have the same roots.

It is possible that what we do now can *only* be comic. Some writers are salted such that every word is comic, every effort. Now we are at last talking about Kafka as comic. When he read *The Metamorphosis* to Max Brod, Brod's wife reported, they both fell off their chairs laughing. Though God, I'm serious when I'm comic. And, truthfully, I don't even smile when I scratch around in my notebooks. And if there is one thing I *hate*, it's when someone, after a reading, tells me I'm a stand-up comedian, but please to look at the God-damned poems. Nor is it only Tourette's, which every clown, comedian, slack-rope walker and baseball player has. Nor is it only fear—or anger. You know what it is? Clarity. Clarity on the highest level. *Klarheit.* Maybe musicians and painters understand it more than poets. "The Preacher," written in 2007, a twenty-seven-page "takeoff" on Ecclesiastes, is a comic (and deadly serious) celebration of the hole in the universe, whatever that is; and "I," only just published online, is a thirty-five-page version and a weeping mockery of Isaiah, or "The Isaiahs," as seen across the street from an abandoned synagogue on 30th Street in New York from inside of a Greek diner.

Jewish comedians I love and hate. Lenny Bruce, of course, but I'm mostly irritated now by Woody Allen. I love Mel Brooks, his heart, his mind. I'm not very fond of the Nouveau Assimilated, but I deeply admire Jon Stewart's intelligence and humanity (though for a stand-up he mostly sits down), and—I'm sorry—I like Lewis Black, his mayhem, his nervous patter, his loud voice, his tough social observation, his craziness. I think it is good news—and healthy—that Jewish humor still persists; we haven't lost our memory altogether. Though I haven't kept up with Jewish comedy in Holland and Switzerland. I *do* like the idea of an Alaskan Jew talking to polar bears. Before he's eaten.

As grace would have it, I turned on the television last night to a Marx Brothers extravaganza—a better word, for them, than "festival." There were four films—I could have watched till three a.m., but I got tired. Everything in the way of irreverence, mockery, bathos, the ridiculing of institutions, wordplay, hijinks, disrespect, craziness, and anti-authoritarianism was there. But it was, to my eyes, gentle. There must be some connection with Talmud and Midrash, the passion for words—for talk—(though Harpo, if noisy, is silent); and there is pride, revenge, and absurdity, shtetl staples; and there is brilliance—much respected—and irony; and victory. It's called "over-the-top" now, isn't it? Is that a term from trench warfare, does trench warfare account for earthiness, one-liners, extravagance, and speed? Certainly earthiness. Speaking of trench warfare, I'll tell a joke from World War I—in English. Two short guys heed Uncle Sam's plea, join up, go through basic, take a train to New York, board a ship (amidst waving handkerchiefs), arrive in France (more hankies), are sent to the front; a whistle blows, they climb up the ladder and start to charge toward the Huns. Bombs are bursting, people are falling, and one of them turns around and runs back. "Where you going, Jake?" "You can get killed here," he says. (Better in Yiddish.)

There is nothing more clear than convoluted reasoning. The Babylonian Jews, who spoke Aramaic, called it *pilpul*. It originally meant to spice or season but came to mean "to dispute violently." The Babylonian comedians actually fought each other on the stage with sticks. Only later did they resort to words, which were more violent and hurt more. Rago's Auction House, here in Lambertville, has some Babylonian items in its catalog, and among them are "comedian's sticks," with a number, a proposed price, and, of course, an image. If the bid is not too high, I'll buy one and put it in my umbrella stand, next to my basket of softballs and my plaster-of-paris pig. I'll beat the first poet who knocks on the door and asks for a blurb.

I got a book in the mail today—for everything comes on time, as Maimonides says, called *Seriously Funny*, an anthology that contains my poem "Grapefruit," written in 1985. It's, as it says, a book of poems that are funny. Yet *serious*. I'm happy to be in the book, and I'm grateful to the editors, but I never thought of "Grapefruit" as a comic poem, though when I read it now—from a stranger's point of view—I see that it truly is, full as it is of mockery, false holiness, bluntness, and weird presence. But I never *presented* it as funny. It's as if the poet (me, in this case) was possessed and didn't care where his metaphor dragged him. Love to both editors. The real secret of comedy is higher and lower co-mingling, co-mocking, confusion; man and God, Yiddish and Hebrew, Alabama and Harlem, light and heavy, exalted and workaday. It's interesting that Samuel Clemens was a lecturer, a stand-up, as well as an exquisite writer. Maybe the poets, some of the poets, have sticky feet on both branches. Maybe it's mostly my own feet I'm writing about, trying to stay upright in the branches. Being close and far away at the same time.

This is what happened on the three hundredth anniversary of J. S. Bach's birthday. I was sitting in my office—at the University of Iowa—when I got a phone call from Steve Berg, one of the editors of *American Poetry Review*. I would be getting a call (he said) in a minute from a retired banker (in charge of culture at the Mellon Bank) asking me to write a poem about Bach and read it—in Philadelphia at an Episcopal church. The price was a thousand, Steve said. When the banker called, I squeezed another thou' out of him—for the reading itself—plus expenses. It was 1985. I labored at the dumb poem for weeks, trying to tone it down, calling Berg endlessly for advice. When I was through, I hated it and, as fury would have it, when I drove down the river from Easton to Philadelphia and stopped in Frenchtown, New Jersey, for breakfast, there, to my horror, was my poem on the front page of the *Philadel-*

phia Inquirer. I helped rename an alley Johann Sebastian Bach Way, Berg and I had lunch with the cultured banker, I read the poem that evening, along with some organ music, and I was interviewed the next day by Terry Gross on *Fresh Air.*

She wanted to talk about Bach, but I moved the conversation to the bombing of the MOVE compound—an African American urban cult in Philadelphia—and Mayor Goode's role: getting a "device" from the FBI and supervising the bombing. Goode was a technocrat and thought the world was mathematical. I called him Mayor Bad, and talked about how information was handled in America and what *our* forms of censorship were (partial, almost hidden). Terry was upset, for poor Bach was being ignored, but I thought it was more important to discuss the official view of a crazy, quasi-religious, school-denying, garbage-flinging cult, everyone with the last name of "Africa," who were called "terrorists" and murdered because they were noisy and disobedient; and because of the horde of weapons they supposedly had—that turned out to be one revolver and one shotgun. Hardly enough for one ten-year-old truck, say, in southern Georgia or northern Pennsylvania. Nor did the *Inquirer* print this information, but a small group the mayor had appointed—priests, social workers, and the like—wrote a report that you had to go to an obscure vault in the main library to obtain. I have a copy of the report; I'm fairly certain the Philadelphia Library hasn't destroyed the other copies. Six children died.

It's bizarre, except for the murders. I called Goode "Nero" and said he fiddled while Philadelphia burned. The compound actually *did* burn as a result of dropping the "device." From an airplane. What I did I did for clarity, for justice. But I'm not altogether happy about it. I don't like balancing in the foliage on my two sticky limbs, singing songs of righteousness. I don't know if the beautiful note, the *vibration*, is not itself too much of a motive or cause. One that Aristotle missed. John Edgar Wideman wrote about the event in his novel *Philadelphia Burning*. In the city of Brotherly Love, there is no remembrance, no remorse anywhere. I doubt if it's talked about in the schools.

When I first started I was an aesthete—I separated poetry from the rest; but I came finally to include every wart and pimple, or at least most of the warts and pimples. That's what poetry should do—as it does other things. Though so doing (warts and pimples) is not itself what poetry is about. And anyhow, who knows? For one thing, you're different when you're older than you were when you weren't older, and anyhow mankind cannot bear very much reality, as Sarah Silverman says, or said.

Which reminds me somehow of the gathering of Jewish poets in Boston a couple of decades ago. We were standing in an anteroom, and the rabbi in charge, after lecturing us, asked us if we had any questions. I said, "When do we get paid?" And he accused me of anti-Semitism. We were all staying at the Worst-Western or a Qualityless Inn, which featured a large mirror against the wall, beside the bed, which more or less doubled the size of the room. At the time I couldn't see too well, though now—after cataract surgery—I have 20-20. I woke up in the half-dark and thought I saw someone in bed with me. I looked at him—it was a him—waved and said, "How ya doin'?" He waved at the very same time and said the very same thing, but it took me a long twenty or thirty seconds to figure out it was the mirror. After that, I must admit, I spent a good half-hour exchanging pleasantries. I must confess I kissed him—or he kissed me. That shadow.

But it's 2010 now, and stand-up has become a plague. Idiots of every stripe performing on "Comedy Stupid." Expressing their deep feelings—about toothpaste; or someone has written a piece for them about mouthwash or erectile function. And, of course, it's disgusting. *De rigueur*. And the audience is laughing and clapping and enlightened beyond measure. It's trivial humor, of no social or any other significance. Flippant, narcissistic, embarrassing, and useless. Cognate, in part, with the other arts, but lacking even their attempts at the New Vulgar, without purpose, connected to nothing. One fool went on for twelve minutes—I timed him—about the weirdness of bathrobes. It could be a good subject, but he knew nothing about those robes and their history and how class was involved, and pretension, and central heating. He ended up making toilet jokes, something about the belt caught in the commode— but it was a one-liner—he couldn't *build* on it. If I were more Zen I would have slapped him, but I didn't want to hurt Anne Marie's TV. I have enough trouble just turning it on.

Richard Pryor is perhaps the best comedian of the twentieth century. With due respect. The key to Pryor's humor is that he speaks to black issues, and as a black man, but it—finally—is a *human* issue he's speaking to, so that white audiences as well as black can be moved by him; and, further, in so doing, the particulars of African American life, the *particulars*, become more and more familiar to the overriding white audience, nor does he have to drive the point home that we're "all one," he doesn't have to lecture, for that point, so to speak, takes care of itself. It turned out not to be so huge and overwhelming a problem as we might have thought it would be. Italian life, Jewish life, have their particulars—language, culture, custom—but it is not appreciated only, or merely, by Italians and Jews. Even WASPs discovered that they had particulars and that they were WASP particulars, not the universal by which everything else is judged. And it was Pryor's own humanity, his life, his understanding, finally his huge heart, that made this possible. He went from short fuse, in the beginning, to a kind of untransformed and raw tenderness at the end. He allowed pain, confusion, and suffering—his and everyone's—to be rendered literally, though filtered, accompanied, by his comic genius. It's as if nobody had thought of it before. He was irreverent and emotional, a true

expressionist. If he was shocking at first—even revolutionary—
he was quickly accepted and, finally, revered. It was black street
humor and satire; it was blasphemy; but it was always *personal* and
absolutely honest. And it was hilarious. Nor was he the first to let
the words just take over. Lenny Bruce—and others—had done it
before, but not so completely. He himself was the character he cre-
ated. There was no distinction. Style and substance integrated. He
was difficult and disturbed, but what comic isn't—more than this
one, less than that one.

What is amazing is that African American humor became
mainstream. "Pride, self-mockery, blunt confrontation of reality,
double-edged irony, satiric wit, assertive defiance, poetic obscen-
ity, and verbal acuity"—Mel Watkin's words. In Pryor's case it
was—in the end—deep sanity, and humanity. The comedian's gift.
He will be remembered for that.

Bert Williams, Charlie Chaplin, Harold Lloyd, Mel Brooks,
W.C. Fields, Lenny Bruce, Groucho Marx, Harpo Marx, Buster
Keaton, Stan Laurel, George Carlin, Lucille Ball, Jack Benny, Fred
Allen, Richard Pryor, Gilda Radner, Chris Rock, Whoopi Gold-
berg, Sarah Silverman.

Roses

There was a rose called Guy de Maupassant,
a carmine pink that smelled like a Granny Smith
and there was another from the seventeenth century
that wept too much and wilted when you looked;
and one that caused tuberculosis, doctors
dug them up, they wore white masks and posted
warnings in the windows. One wet day
it started to hail and pellets the size of snowballs
fell on the roses. It's hard for me to look at
a Duchess of Windsor, it was worn by Franco
and Mussolini, it stabbed Jews; yesterday I bought
six roses from a Haitian on Lower Broadway;

he wrapped them in blue tissue paper, it was
starting to snow and both of us had on the wrong shoes,
though it was wind, he said, not snow that ruined
roses and all you had to do was hold them
against your chest. He had a ring on his pinky
the size of a grape and half his teeth were gone.
So I loved him and spoke to him in false Creole
for which he hugged me and enveloped me
in his camel hair coat with most of the buttons missing,
and we were brothers for life, we swore it in French.

— GERALD STERN

Grapefruit

I'm eating breakfast even if it means standing
in front of the sink and tearing at the grapefruit,
even if I'm leaning over to keep the juices
away from my chest and stomach and even if a spider
is hanging from my ear and a wild flea
is crawling down my leg. My window is wavy
and dirty. There is a wavy tree outside
with pitiful leaves in front of the rusty fence
and there is a patch of useless rhubarb, the leaves
bent over, the stalks too large and bitter for eating,
and there is some lettuce and spinach too old for picking
beside the rhubarb. This is the way the saints
ate, only they dug for thistles, the feel
of thorns in the throat it was a blessing, my pity
it knows no bounds. There is a thin tomato plant
inside a rolled-up piece of wire, the worms
are already there, the birds are bored. In time
I'll stand beside the rolled-up fence with tears
of gratitude in my eyes. I'll hold a puny
pinched tomato in my open hand,
I'll hold it to my lips. Blessed art Thou,
King of tomatoes, King of grapefruit. The thistle
must have juices, there must be a trick. I hate
to say it but I'm thinking if there is a saint
in our time what will he be, and what will he eat?

I hated rhubarb, all that stringy sweetness –
a fake applesauce – I hated spinach,
always with egg and vinegar, I hated
oranges when they were quartered, that was the signal
for castor oil – aside from the peeled navel
I love the Florida cut in two. I bend
my head forward, my chin is in the air,
I hold my right hand off to the side, the pinkie
is waving; I am back again at the sink;
oh loneliness, I stand at the sink, my garden
is dry and blooming, I love my lettuce, I love
my cornflowers, the sun is doing it all,
the sun and a little dirt and a little water.
I lie on the ground out there, there is one yard
between the house and the tree; I am more calm there
looking back at this window, looking up
a little at the sky, a blue passageway
with smears of white – and gray – a bird crossing
from berm to berm, from ditch to ditch, another one,
a wild highway, a wild skyway, a flock
of little ones to make me feel gay, they fly
down the thruway, I move my eyes back and forth
to see them appear and disappear, I stretch
my neck, a kind of exercise. Ah sky,
my breakfast is over, my lunch is over, the wind
has stopped, it is the hour of deepest thought.
Now I brood, I grimace, how quickly the day goes,
how full it is of sunshine, and wind, how many
smells there are, how gorgeous is the distant
sound of dogs, and engines – Blessed art Thou
Lord of the falling leaf, Lord of the rhubarb,
Lord of the roving cat, Lord of the cloud.
Blessed art Thou oh grapefruit King of the universe,
Blessed art Thou my sink, oh Blessed art Thou
Thou milkweed Queen of the sky, burster of seeds,
Who bringeth forth juice from the earth.

– GERALD STERN

21   Sports and Business

This Sunday, April 4, 2010, there was an interview in the Business section, which I read now after Sports and Styles, because it offers a mindless twenty minutes of staring at numbers and looking at photos of middle-age males who are good at deceit and manipulation.

Andrew Cosslett, the CEO of InterContinental Hotels Group, was being interviewed and it was titled "Where Are You When the Going Gets Tough?" What interests me—about the interview—is the metaphor that drives it, the utterly banal, overwhelmingly trite metaphor that compares business to sports, in this case being the captain of a rugby team to running a hotel—or a chain of hotels. Of course, the captain in this case is British—since it's rugby—and I guess the hotels are British too, or the headquarters are. I didn't believe people still talked this way—the fields of Eton, smell of 1910. In response to the question, "Can you elaborate on that?" (The issue, a little vague, is whether becoming a manager is, was, an easy transition for you, him, at first.) Here's his answer: "The whole thing about staying alive on a rugby field is about reliance on the guys around you. You need to get them on a team (*ah!*) but each one responds individually. So it's about dealing with them on their terms, not yours. I'm very sensitive to how people are thinking and feeling at any given moment. That's really helpful in business because you pick things up very fast. It's also about laughing at yourself, and living on your own from the age of sixteen and having contempt for corporate orthodoxy, and being a man of the people, and looking for a gimmick, and talking 'straight' to underlings." Tough-guy stuff. But rugby dominates. Maybe it's an attack on British caste. I certainly think the head of Holiday Inn should arm-wrestle the head of Sheraton, no question there, or they should have a bragging contest about the miserable breakfasts they serve.

When I left Philadelphia to teach at Indiana State College in

the early 1960s—it was later called Indiana University of Pennsyl-
vania—Pat and I had to attend a dinner for new faculty. We sat at
small tables, older seasoned couples and we new ones. I remember
Pat had to wear a hat, so I designed one from a green Egyptian
headpiece, a kind of yarmulke. The food was astonishingly bad and
the seasoned couple with us praised it endlessly. With a movable
blackboard at his side and some chalk in his hand, the chairman of
the board of trustees gave the talk, in which he compared the insti-
tution's success to that of a football team on the thirty or forty yard
line—still a long way to go, but. *determined*, and tough. We were
in a state of shock that we had moved here—there—and seriously
thought about moving back, but we didn't have the money.

Just before we made the move from Pittsburgh to Philadelphia in
1956—to start my college teaching career at Temple University—
I was invited to come there to be interviewed for a job at Friend's
Select, the first Quaker school in the U.S. I would be teaching lit-
erature, history, and French, at an astonishingly low rate of pay. I
was good at interviews and the job was mine—I knew it after five
minutes. The issue remained which sport I would coach, and I
think we settled on junior high soccer. It was late in the afternoon
and it was late August as the headmaster, one of those very tall,
preposterously thin types, leaned back in his chair and started on
sports and character. Eton again—but I was very impolitic then and
pointed out that, at least in Pittsburgh where I came from, the rela-
tionship was an inverse one, and in most sports, we played as dirty
as we could get away with, and we cheated as a matter of course. I
described particularly the brutality of football, the true sport of my
city, and not only how we kneed, elbowed, and choked our oppo-
nents but were taught the priestly secrets by our coaches. In a sec-
ond, the job was gone. He would be in touch. It was nice meeting
me. This after we were already discussing the price of apartments
in the city. I remember that in Scotland, where I taught for a year

in the early 1950s at Victoria Drive Senior Secondary High School, there were no organized sports, and if the students wanted to kick a ball around they did it on their own time, at their own expense. Though that was a while ago. Nor did anyone ask me—of course— to coach anything; and when the faculty played against the students after school one day, we won 2–0, and the students served tea. It was very black and served with cream, in nice cups, with some lovely cakes to boot.

22 Deicide

It was the same Sunday and the same newspaper, though a different section—and Easter Sunday by the way—that the Church was under universal attack for concealing information about its pedophile priests and worrying more about *their* "spiritual" journeys than about the thousands of young boys they had abused. The "Church" in Ireland, Germany, Holland, France, America, Italy, and elsewhere was in turmoil, but the Vatican, a kind of country, called it "gossip" and the pope's preacher, a type of body-builder, compared the "attack" on the pope somehow to the murder of Europe's Jews in the 1930s and '40s, for which he later apologized since it caused such a furor among Jewish and Catholic leaders, especially in Germany. The preacher was a little carried away and, for a moment, unhumble and sunstruck. Imagine, using the Jews for cover. After the two thousand years. Me with my radar, a little concerned when the "aggressive" spokesman for the Vatican began blaming the *Jew York Times* for their problem.

The fact that the "Church" denounced its critics was to be expected. Coca-Cola would naturally denounce those who exaggerate (expose) the amount of sugar in a Coke. But the pope is not *just* the head of a state, or a corporation. He occupies the throne of Peter, he's the bishop of Rome, the Vicar of Jesus Christ on earth, and the Pontiff Supremo of the universal church. And, in morals and faith matters, he's infallible—by his own admission. He can therefore not be subject to scrutiny. If he overlooked a certain memo a decade or so ago, he overlooked it. He was thinking of other things.

God knows that I don't want to join the chorus of the watered and reborn in its dull endless attack on the papacy, but God also knows that I read Garry Wills's *On Papal Sin* and love how his mind works. What interests me most is neither this or that pope's view of masturbation or infallibility, but the Church's view of Jews as deicides, which according to Wills was the central, if you will, "eternal" view, at least, supposedly, until 1965. I take the attack on me, when I was five and on my way to kindergarten, although I could have been six and on my way to first grade since I have come to respect false memory, as a message from a concerned angel that I—since I was a Jew—was a Christ-killer, whatever that meant to a five- or six-year-old. I know there is a new race of Jews in America and elsewhere, and I don't want to embarrass them with my stubbornness, but Pius XI said in an encyclical (when I was twelve and Germany was already showing its true hand), that "Jesus received his human nature from a people who crucified him." Is it strange news that Catholic preachers over the centuries continually made the deicide charge, that seminaries taught it and persecutions were based on it, as Wills emphasizes? And isn't it strange that the Second Vatican Council, which exonerated the Jewish people, said nothing about the Church's past record and expressed no penitence or sorrow, as Wills says? Or maybe it's strange that the German government—as it upped the ante, denying its Jews civil and legal rights, making them wear identifying and humiliating badges, bringing false charges against them, and describing them as less than human (though they won a third of Germany's Nobel prizes from 1910 to 1932)—found an eerie model in Christian Europe—

France, Germany, Spain, Russia, Poland, Ukraine—for its behavior. May I say, even in murdering them? But how did I get here on a peaceful Easter weekend when the trees on my street are just about to blossom? And the newspapers are spread out over my Mexican rug.

And is it a fit thing on such a blossomy day to bring up Luther, the god of thunder, who furiously turned on the Jews when they didn't take his side in the Christian War, and wrote an anti-Semitic pamphlet called "The Jews and Their Lies," which was, in its way, a preparation for the Holocaust (*nicht wahr?*). He said their synagogues should be set on fire, and whatever is left should be buried in the dirt so that no one may ever be able to see a stone or cinder of it. Jewish prayer books should be destroyed and rabbis forbidden to preach. Homes of Jews should be "smashed and destroyed," and they should be put in a stable like gypsies, to teach them they are not masters in "our" land. They should be banned from the roads and markets, their property seized, and then these "poisonous envenomed worms" should be drafted into forced labor and made to earn their bread "by the sweat of their noses" (*ah, le nez!*). In the last resort they should be simply kicked out "for all time." Calling all Jews usurers, he said they should be broken on the wheel and hunted, "cursed and beheaded." A marvelous stylist, Luther. Calvin was a little kinder but still forced the Jews out of Calvinist cities, and Erasmus, whom we all love, wrote to the Cologne Inquisitor, "Who is there among us who does not hate this race of men? If it is Christian to hate the Jews, then we are all Christians in profusion."

Though all this time I am thinking of the beliefs of ordinary people and how my irony and rage is perhaps irrelevant when it comes to their faith and the customs they follow to sustain that faith, various as they are in religious language, culture, ritual, ceremony, and learning; and though it sounds stilted and may be forced, I want to take off my hat—or put it on for those very people—in spite of their priests and high priests, whatever crook is in *their* hands, whatever shrunken head they worship or want the rest of us to, however the jangle of coins ring in their ears, whatever the constraints, how in or out of tune the voices are. I myself come from a religion half-tribal, half-philosophical, indefensible and dear in spite of anything and everything. I am eighty-five and God knows I will be still soon—liberated into a raucous world—and I don't want to just sit on a mantle and I do want to half-hear the Aramaic prayer over my box. And I want the box to be made of cedar.

23 War Work

It was hard getting people to work on a temporary basis for government agencies during the war. They used 4Fs (guys unfit for service) mostly or students who could take a day off. My friend, Nick Tancosic, and I were on their list, and when they (the government) needed someone for a day or two, we were always available. The pay was terrific, twenty-five dollars a day—a good sum then. Nick was from Duquesne, Pennsylvania, outside of Pittsburgh; he later became president of the Serbian Club in Duquesne, but we lost track of each other. I don't remember what he was studying—economics, political science—but we spent hours together, sitting on the Pitt lawn, making up songs. He had been a steelworker, maybe in Braddock, Pennsylvania, a branch of U.S. Steel, but he got fired—and blackballed—for his political activities. He had three fingers missing on his right hand, which was the reason he was 4F; with me it was eyesight. Blindness. But they relaxed the rules later.

In 1943 or '44 there was a campaign, probably by the Department of Agriculture, to urge people to eat more potatoes and less meat, since we were apparently inundated by the lumpy fruit. I saw it on billboards everywhere, and in newspapers and magazines. Nick and I were hired to knock on doors and see how successful the campaign was, so we went to all those isolated ethnic communities, on hills and in valleys, wooden sidewalks or broken cement, to the small soot-ridden houses to find out. Sometimes we went together, sometimes separately. The living rooms were small and dark and there was a picture—generally of either Jesus or FDR—on the wall. Almost everyone we talked to was either suspicious or terrified of the two young men in suits and with badges who knocked on their doors. We represented authority—for all they knew, the police, the FBI—nor had they probably noticed the billboards, and mostly they denied ever eating a potato. Certainly not since the war began, and they were—mostly—anxious for us to leave. Many didn't speak English, so Nick's Slavic tongue came in handy. After a while, because of the meager results, we retired to a bar—it might have been early afternoon and the bar would be empty—to question *each other* about potatoes (and fill out the forms). God knows what we said, in what languages and with what accents, and how we made distinctions between sweets and yams, and how we talked about roasting, boiling, and frying, and God alone knows how the figures in that laboring city were skewed, this way and that. We went everywhere and we did it for a week or more. And we did it mostly in bars over a cold beer or two, sometimes a ham and cheese sandwich. Nick was skinny and tall, with high cheekbones, long straight hair, and glasses, always with a smile on his face. Mischievous and cunning.

Another time, toward the end of the war—maybe afterward— there was a vote to be taken, in the steel mills along the river, about an impending strike, and we were hired by the Department of Labor to help administer the vote—our names were certainly obtained from the "list." My God, was Nick happy! We went from plant to plant, wearing suits and ties like good bureaucrats. Neither management nor labor knew we were *per diem* workers and that we made twenty-five bucks for a day's work. Mainly we had to decide whether ballots that had been challenged by one side or the other should or should not be counted. The bosses took us out for a fine lunch and we let them pay, which certainly made them feel we were on their side. And they were red-faced and furious when we made our calls, always on the side of the union. Two twenty-year-olds making major decisions in the heart of the steel business. I think this is the time Truman seized and nationalized steel, which, I think, was challenged and overruled in court, but I'm against doing research today. Nick and I celebrated when the vote was counted and congratulated each other. I think we took a street car (no. 68) to Kennywood Park and rode on the roller coasters. Maybe it was Serbian Day, or Austro-Hungarian, or Amazon Rain Forest. We didn't care—we were just happy.

Why things happened to me, I don't know. I think a certain angel provides, her eyes red from weeping, and laughing. In 1966, a little over twenty years after the visitations in Pittsburgh, she came to me again when I was teaching at Indiana University of Pennsylvania. I think she lived in Indiana. She arranged for someone from Movie Headquarters in Pittsburgh to phone and ask me if I wanted to pick the movies, classic and foreign, on one of the dead nights—Tuesday, Wednesday—at the main theater in town to attract faculty and students from the college. They might then have fifty or sixty show up instead of ten. In return for this little service, I would get a "Class A Golden Pass" that would allow me entry into any movie house in the area, including drive-ins. (There were no multiplexes yet.) I agreed, had lunch with the owners (Lebanese from Pittsburgh) and the manager. I remember we all ordered steak, salad, and wine, and the manager—maybe he was the assistant manager—ordered a toasted cheese sandwich and a glass of milk. The theater, a 1930s job, was large and elaborate and situated in the heart of town, on Philadelphia Street. The assistant manager, maybe thirty-five or forty years old, came to consult with me in my office at the college. He had never before been in a college or sat in a professor's office and smiled and bowed his way in. He was wearing a cheap suit and a brand-new pearl-gray fedora with a fairly wide brim. He hung it up carefully on a coat rack after brushing it with his forearm, the way you did in the movies. My friend, Lorrie Bright, who was chairman of Freshman Composition, saw the hat and assumed it was mine, since I favored such things. A big guy, Lorrie, and a would-be novelist, who lived in the country with his wife, Jessie, and their three children; one of my closest friends there. He removed the hat from its perch, put it on the floor, and proceeded to jump up and down on it, shouting and laughing. The assistant manager didn't move a muscle, and I waited an extra few minutes before I told Lorrie the hat was not mine, but belonged to my visitor. Lorrie picked the wounded fedora up, re-creased it, brushed it off with his forearm, and re-hung it. Not a word of apology. We finished our business, the assistant manager put his hat back on, and we shook hands goodbye. There was the very slightest of twitching in one of his cheeks and even one loose tear. He brought me my Class A Golden Pass, which I used endlessly, especially at the drive-in, and lent, ferociously, to my friends who knocked on our door on Klondyke Avenue to see if it was available. It was a highly successful venture. I selected the famous Russian, German, English, French, Italian, and Swedish classics, as well as the American, and I took my family to the drive-in dressed in their pajamas, as was the custom. I should have apologized to the assistant manager—maybe I did—and I should have given him Lorrie's huge freshman textbooks, full of the usual advice as regards the Rhetorical Types, or better yet, the first draft of his novel to jump up and down on.

24 Learning Poetry, Living Cheap

I am willing to answer one or two questions after a reading, for I
don't know yet how exhausted I am from the desperate attempt at
trying to communicate, trying to reach them. The question I hate
the most concerns "revision": "how do I revise?" "*do* I revise?"
"how long does it take?" I often say that I don't revise, or I don't
remember, or it's a secret. Of course, what I'm saying, as a way of
not talking about it, is fairly close to the truth. I am amazed at the
question. I am amazed that anyone is interested. I'm indignant that
they invade my privacy, that they want to destroy the freedom and
the mystery. I still believe in "the poem." I don't want to tell them
about the accidents, misreadings, procedures—the process. The
closest I get to it is to admit my sloppiness and haste. The words,
phrases, interruptions—sometimes in pencil, mostly unreadable—
that force me to re-create the poem, take it somewhere else, and
always, especially in my recent work, make it seem that I had writ-
ten it offhand, quickly, as an afterthought, in a few minutes. I go
crazy when I see students of mine with sheet after sheet, num-
bered and organized, sometimes a whole new page for one or two
changes, as if that itself counted, as if the stages in writing Leviticus
were being revealed. (Ah, on page 22 of my revisions, I will not
combine sleeping with goats and sleeping with aunts on my father's
side in the same sentence; I'm so glad I thought of that.)

My favorite questions are sociological and political. "What was
it like in 1948 with you and your friends? What did you do? Who
were you reading?" This gives me an opportunity to talk about
D. H. Lawrence and Robinson Jeffers and Hart Crane and Dylan
Thomas and Yeats and Auden and Pound. And about my attrac-
tion to and resistance to Eliot. And about the thin volume of *Four
Quartets* I had then and how often the books were so much thinner
than they are today and how I physically adored them. And kissed

them. And what a joy it was building a bookcase inside the small closet in the living room of our apartment, and painting it.

The best question is the one someone asked me in Cologne—though it took much coaxing and deep listening to get it out of him. He may have had a Polish accent, or a Turkish, and it would take ten minutes of back and forth and bringing him up front and bending over practically on top of him till I understood—or think I did. He wanted to know whether my poems were written by a little man in the back of my head. I'm sure that's what he asked—or said—after we talked and pushed and pulled; and I'm sorry he was so dumbfounded when I told him, yes, it *was* the little man at the back of my head who wrote my poems, nor did I say "so to speak" or "not literally" or it was a "little woman," leaving him stranded, which I didn't really want to do, nor did I want to humiliate or embarrass him, and he just stood there as there was another ripple of applause marking the final final and some people walked to the doors and some began forming a small line in front of me—for the books and autographs—and I sat down on a cold metal chair and reached inside for a pen and thought of how quickly I might escape and began my scribbling as the line began to grow, but it wasn't true. I mean the little man.

Hotel Webster Hall, where Jack Gilbert, Richard Hazley, and I ate our potato salad and olives, was more or less across the street from Pitt's Cathedral of Learning, with its classes, its library, and its places of congregation, but we never connected it in any way with our activity. We were former students at the university, but there were no other poets there or any interest on the part of the English Department or classes or workshops or clubs. There were young poets at Princeton, Columbia, Harvard, and elsewhere, and they might have—they probably did have—their learning arrangements, but in Pittsburgh we had none. In 1979 or '80, when I was teaching a graduate workshop at Pitt, I told all this to my students, to show them how lucky they were. They only idealized the situation and begged me to tell them again about the dark days, as if they were children at a campfire, their hands clasped about their knees, the fire roaring, cracking and throwing up huge sparks, the woods pitch-black beyond. Ed Ochester, who runs the Pitt Poetry Series, tells me I was the first poet in Pittsburgh, which is of course ridiculous, for certainly there were many who wrote musically about love and death, but he insists I was the first to bear the title, even if shamefacedly. Though Gilbert did publish a collection first. I wrote about this in a book called *In Praise of What Persists*, and I'm probably repeating some of my information. My essay is called "Some Secrets." I don't know the statistics, how many students are taking creative writing courses, undergraduate degrees, MFAs, and PhDs in poetry, the novel, screenwriting, playwriting, or courses online, or in alternative modes or in performance, New Media, Critical Writing, or while sitting on computers. I have—for good or ill— spent much of a lifetime teaching writing and I am, given the style of the time, both comrade and elder or some peculiar combination of reverence and irreverence. There were close to nine thousand writers at this year's AWP convention in Denver. I don't know if there are five thousand, ten thousand, or twenty thousand students at any given time in all the programs. There is a running battle going on about how to make a poet, and I'm sure it's different than making a flood. Both fools and wise men attack workshops, the AWP, and the university as the appropriate surround for poets. I am mostly evasive on the subject even as I tend to side with mystery, hard work, libraries, and solitude, though it's nice to get some support and some quick information. Even some money. If the drag-down, the égalité, and the herd-sense are worth it. Though I do wish I was in Iowa in 1953, with Berryman, or on the Black Sea, with Ovid. The only rule I have is that the founder or teacher must be a writer I know and respect, not a recent graduate student or a hack from the English Department. When I told Iowa in 1981 that I hadn't applied for the opening there because they were too far from New York and I wasn't sure I believed in teaching poetry, they fell in love with me. Though maybe it was my green eyes. I've had four very special students, maybe five. I've had twenty good ones. The waitress at the Siam tonight said she read poems to jazz at college and she had a very fine poet as her teacher. I didn't catch his name. I asked her if she read poetry, and she said she hopes to get back to it. If I had a short fuse I'd say there were too many writers; and too many stand-up comedians. Though I have to say that our best poets *have* got their "education" through the MFA programs—Iowa and elsewhere—and will continue to do so. Was it those born after 1925? 1928?

My problem is I had my feet in two worlds and there was a huge crack. Those who become poets are those who are capable of resistance and finally create *themselves* not because of their world, or not that only, but in spite of their world; although it's a rough and hairy coat that doesn't fit exactly I describe. I am constantly amazed at the wildness and the unexpectedness of its happening. I am shocked and delighted and deeply puzzled. Most of all, surprised. That they burst from an unknown and unforeseen cocoon with sticky legs and wings intact, but with a new, unknown, and unforeseen stripe or fuzz or luminosity somewhere—near the mouth parts or the ear, sometimes the legs. But no one has ever asked me "how do you make a flood?" or, for that matter, a "fissure." And no one expected there to be nine thousand writers one day at two or three giant hotels in Denver when a few elders first conceived the idea of using our universities as facilities for helping younger poets. Removing their fears, giving them some help, giving their teachers some.

It's money though, isn't it? I searched everywhere in the late 1940s for cheap places to live and even contacted embassies when I went to New York. I had a friend named Irving Spector—one of many Irvings I knew—who had some ambition to be a novelist and who was still obsessed with Thomas Wolfe almost a decade after the others, really most others, had changed their minds about him because of his overblown rhetoric—and wrote a comparable poetic prose, including much italicization and mourning; and already had accumulated a few hundred—or thousand—pages and knew in his heart of hearts that some editor in New York would save him, as Perkins did Wolfe. He and I were on our way to Mexico—in 1948—in the green '34 Nash his mother had given him, but first I had to teach him to drive. It was hard shifting gears in those days and Irving wasn't good at coordination, and sometimes the clutch was confused with the brake, so we ended up, me in the death seat, him driving, not so gently tapping a car at a busy intersection— Pittsburgh, of course—after driving to the unknown destination beginners always flounder in. He didn't have a learner's permit and I didn't have a driver's license, so that may be why we left hurriedly, but a streetcar motorman saw us from his perch, caught our license number, and Irving's poor mother had to pay the piper. When he told the story he ended up fleeing the country with a huge trunk on his back, off to Greece or Portugal, to live on fish and fine-tune his book. I saw him a few times before he went to dental school, but eventually we lost touch.

A year or two later, still thinking about money, I was getting ready to board *The Edam* out of Hoboken on my way to Antwerp and thence to a corner of Switzerland near some corners of Italy and France where a few of my creative friends had holed up in a castle, painting, writing, and dreaming about money. There were four or five, and every week one of them would spend a morning trading Swiss francs for lira and lira for French francs, coming back to the castle with enough profit from the negotiations to keep the group going for another week. They had been doing it already for a year or so. Their resources were maybe four or five hundred dollars, everyone included. I don't know the order—they may have gone to France first and then to Italy, since the borders were close, but the actual *work* each of them did was three or four hours every four or five weeks. I don't know if roast chicken and Swiss chard are especially good when they're just about free or whether the idle rich in that castle were capable of real work, since no one suffered, and practically no one had talent, but the day before I went by Greyhound to watery Hoboken I received a telegram—the only one I had ever received—announcing the end of the scheme, since it was all based on the English pound, which was suddenly devalued. Five dollars to two dollars eighty. The telegram said: "we are ruined stop," so I made my way to Paris instead, since I had the G.I. Bill as a backup, and started courses at the Sorbonne, traded my conspicuous fedora in for a beret, and settled into my ancient hotel on the river, writing ten bad lines a day, walking for hours, and going to the American Embassy once a month to collect my seventy-five dollars and live in splendor.

25 Dragonflies and Being

The dragonfly doesn't live in sorrow. Neither does the tiny spider trapped in my porcelain sink, or the murdered squirrel who was torn apart by the red-tail hawk, or the male robin who fights his image in the sun-drenched kitchen window for hours, staring it down, madly lifting himself to do battle, his wings beating, his beak attacking the glass, his eye staring. When he dies, when he died, he was not Tolstoy, nor was there a railroad station. We learned about beasts, their ignorance and joy, in seventh grade and never forgot it. Actually we learned it before we were twelve, wandering through the woods, smelling death, picking violets. We understood it when we were six or seven. But we couldn't yet locate it. My heart goes out to the biblicals who were so wrongheaded about nature. Or outraged by it. But Eden is the last thing I want to write about, where we lived in equality with the other animals. The Greeks too; they were too upright. When you *write* about "Being," the main thing you're writing about is foreknowledge. Death. Dragonflies have "Being" but only humans make statements about it. This could be a sadness or it could be a joy. Where does mercy begin and endless love?

26 Uncle Harry and the Robin

The robin is still fighting his reflection, but he seems weaker and comes less often. He is unkempt and ruffled and takes long rests on the fence or on a lower branch of the dogwood or in the ravaged rose of Sharon. He is only resting, or sighting, but he looks as if he is thinking. He goes to the rose of Sharon to think and periodically smashes into the window. When the sunlight fully appears and the reflection is once again luminous, he will be more active. His desperate and noisy presence at the other side of the glass lasts for five or six seconds now, sometimes much less, and he seems only to knock his head against the window. Just now he flew up against the glass and searched, as it were, through the yucca plant without striking. He was reconnoitering and he seemed then as quick-witted as any member of a search party, his body going up and down, his head going this way and that, even turning slightly sideways as if a thumb were on his chin helping him think, all this time his wings sustaining him.

It's absurd, but I kept thinking of my Uncle Harry all the while this was going on, and since metaphor rules I was trying to find the connection between the two, the robin and Harry. The only thing I could come up with was the word "reconnoiter," for I remember my uncle was, during World War I, sent on missions in the front lines in France. But to reconnoiter is to observe and to do it secretly, to spy, to gather information, and he, because of his small size and his speed and his intelligence, was a messenger, who ran through the trenches, a five-foot-two pigeon with a message attached to his brain, not his purple neck. Whereas the robin does it for competition—love and worms.

Harry was born in Poland, in Bialystock, in 1895 and was my mother's middle brother. There was an older one—Simon—born in 1893. I know the family came to America in 1905; that the two boys left school and went to work when they were fourteen or so; that they lived on Townsend Street in the Hill; that they had an outdoor toilet; that their father—my grandfather—killed chickens and taught Hebrew; that they both had stores "after the war," Simon in Rimersberg, Pennsylvania, Harry in Wheeling, West Virginia; that Simon went broke in the early 1920s and didn't recover till the 1950s when he became a star salesman (with a tape measure around his shoulders) for Robert Hall and a union organizer and labor leader; that Harry ended up owning the largest department store in Wheeling but lost everything in the "crash"; that, like their father, and my mother, they were depressives; that Harry married Aunt Bess and ended up owning small dull stores in northern Pennsylvania, in Clarion and Corry; and that he probably suffered from what we now call post-traumatic stress disorder and spent months at a time in Veterans' hospitals and died of cancer in his early sixties. And the more I go into detail, the less there is a connection with the robin, unless it be in the desperation and the stubborn attachment to pain and, on some level, the hatred of reflection, though human hatred is different from bird hatred.

I used to visit Uncle Harry and Aunt Bess—they had no children—a week or two in the summer in their small towns up north, where they sold furniture in one case and women's clothing in another, both stores empty for hours at a time, and take long walks in the countryside and sit down with them at dinner where—I

remember—there was a bell under the table to summon the maid
and gorgeous porcelain lamps beside each of the upholstered chairs
where we sat and read in the evening and went to bed at ten o'clock.
One morning at ten or eleven when Harry and Bess were both at
the store, I made love—I had sex—with the farm wife who was
doing their ironing. She was probably thirty-five, I was just four-
teen. It was my first time. I have to say she was the seducer. Very
French. In 1919, after the war, Harry made his way to Palestine,
which had just become a British Mandate. He bought property
in what would become part of Tel Aviv—with a deed in Turk-
ish—which he left to me in his will. When I went to Israel sixty
years later, I discovered the property was downtown, a drugstore
by then, but I—wisely—made no attempt to claim it. Bess had a
nephew—her sister's son, who owned a hotel near Central Park
and the horses. Once a year she—and Harry—went there for three
or four days. Harry, who was rich in his thirties and owned a big
house and belonged to a country club, took it in stride, but Bess, a
Jewish country girl from some Pennsylvania shtetl, was in constant
amazement. When she got home, she and my mother talked for an
hour on the phone. Bess said the food was good in New York but
it was better at the Elks Club. In Corry.

The robin looks as huge as a small rooster when he attacks the
window. Anne Marie has put out silver foil to delude him and keep
him away. Delusion of the deluded. He knows nothing of elegant
hotels, he never played golf, and he never heard about shell shock
and the sweats. Nor did he know what Hooverville was or sit in
the rear seat of a 1950 Packard convertible when it was the VFW's
turn to pass by the stands on the Fourth of July, nor did he sit on
a red velvet chair reading *The Grapes of Wrath* and adjust the light
with his left hand. How Uncle Harry would like being compared
to an angry and desperate robin I don't know. He was very fond of
me, and once, when *I* was in the army, he and Bess and my father

and mother stopped to see me in Baltimore, on their way to Florida, and he slipped me thirty dollars, which I will never forget. If he and I ever talk about it we will have to mention the parade after the return home from France and how he was cheered in front of the Fifth Avenue High School. We will have to do it fast since both he and the robin will be lost in a few seconds. Let him pick up a cracked egg or a blue eggshell somewhere south of Toulouse where he is recuperating from the war and sending his mother postcards of the villages in southern France, and let my robin return to cocking his head and listening for prey a few inches under the black earth, particularly after a short rain shower, and let them find each other, as all things do, and—both of them—understand the insane thought that finally brought them together, April 21, 2010, in Lambertville, New Jersey.

27 Lucille's Death

Lucille Clifton's death was a blow to me. Though she was close to it a number of times, I expected her to last, idiot that I was, indefinitely. Even though seeing her, the last time, at the Dodge Poetry Festival in 2008—I knew that wasn't the case.

There are some deaths that you never fully recover from—such it was, for me, with Bob Summers and Larry Levis and Bill Matthews, and so it will probably be with Lucille. She was to receive the Frost Medal from the Poetry Society of America at the annual event on April 1, 2010, and I had the sad honor of being one of the speakers. Her beautiful daughters were there and her half-sister. Michael Glaser and his wife, always there to support her, were in the audience. Cornelius Eady also spoke and Lauren Alleyne.

Those who speak of Clifton's poetry emphasize an abiding strength—faith is a better word—in the face of affliction, misfortune, and adversity, both hers personally and that of the larger world. Her poems, as I see it, though often angry and ironic, are finally, as in a kind of miracle, not only celebratory but even joyous. Her style is called frugal or unadorned, but what I take with me are not poems of austerity or linguistic exclusion—as, say, the opposite of Wallace Stevens—but a language that is specific, personal, and absolutely—always—to the point. In our greatest poets—in our great poets—there is no way to account for them, for their language or their poems. It just happens, certainly after a life of hard work but, it seems, with enviable ease. No critical language can explain Clifton's work. She is the embodiment of the dream: she herself is the poem, her own words are the words of the poem. She is much greater than many of us thought; and she will be remembered.

This is the poem of hers I am reading today.

it was a dream

in which my greater self
rose up before me
accusing me of my life
with her extra finger
whirling in a gyre of rage
at what my days had come to.
what,
i pleaded with her, could i do,
oh what could i have done?
and she twisted her wild hair
and sparked her wild eyes
and screamed as long as
i could hear her
This.   This.   This.

She was born with six fingers (I explained). It was her "greater self" that preceded her—she, her lesser self, was deprived. I remember saying that evening that she was one of our prophets and that she was—variously—thoughtful, angry, shrewd, sensuous, ironic, bitter, compassionate, joyful, funny, and vulnerable. And I talked about her eyes.

I ended by reading three of her poems:

c. c. rider

who is that running away
with my life? who is that
black horse, who is that rider
dressed like my sons, braided
like my daughters? who is that
georgia woman, who is that
virginia man, who is that light-eyed
stranger not looking back?
who is that hollow woman? who am i?
see see rider, see what you have done.

the tale the shepherds tell the sheep

that some will rise
above shorn clouds of fleece
and some will feel their bodies break
but most will pass through this
into sweet clover
where all   all will be sheltered safe
until the holy shearing
don't think about the days to come
sweet meat
think of my arms
trust me

fury

   for mama

remember this.
she is standing by
the furnace.
the coals

glisten like rubies.
her hand is crying.
her hand is clutching
a sheaf of papers.
poems.
she gives them up.
they burn
jewels into jewels.
her eyes are animals.
each hank of her hair
is a serpent's obedient
wife.
she will never recover.
remember. there is nothing
you will not bear
for this woman's sake.

She died on February 13, 2010, at the age of seventy-three.

28   Four Crises

In spite of the foil, the robin keeps attacking the window, though
he doesn't seem as persistent as he was. It could be there are several
robins and one is more desperate than the others. Certainly there
is a nest nearby. There are *three* large windows to bang your head
against, though I notice that when a female cardinal appeared at the
feeder the robins disappeared. One is more desperate, as I say, than
the others, and, as I said, he takes refuge either on a branch of the
dogwood or in the rose of Sharon. This must be a great crisis for
him, a life-and-death matter; and it's not altogether unlike the cri-
ses that human males might go through—or females—though we
tend to prefer guns, razors, knives, fists, hammers, and such instead
of head banging. I don't know what his other crises might be—
being born? dying? facing a cat? Humans, because of their minds,
because of their social organization and their knowledge of their

own futures (and their thumbs and voice boxes), have one crisis after another, health-related, job-related, love-related, age-related. One of the famous ones is the crisis of forty, the *crise de quarante,* and I remember going through it right on schedule—or maybe a year late—and associated, for me, with deep depression (I thought) over how my life as a poet was going; followed, or accompanied, by a new language, or mode; or submission, or awareness, that stood me in good stead for another four decades and more (second telling).

I didn't really have a crisis at eighty or at eighty-four, nor am I having one now—at eighty-five—unless the desire to finish this work before I pass is, itself, a crisis of sorts. I know, by the way, people are dying (if I may say so) to ask me what it's like to be eighty-five. Especially when the Jewish Bible says my allotted time is seventy. "Are you still writing?" they ask. "Are you vertical?" "What diseases beset you?" "Do you still get it up?" "Are you bitter?" "Was it a waste?" "What should you have done instead?" Make a list of the books you didn't read; the musicians you never heard; the forces you didn't confront; the women you didn't love. Shouldn't you have been meaner, more stubborn, less responsible? Who cares now? What are you most regretful of, and most delighted in? Why didn't you become a painter instead? Why didn't you join a theater group and proclaim? Why didn't you study philosophy more? Why didn't you play the cello—or write a novel? Wasn't it something to swim around the Steel Pier when you were fifteen? Would anyone believe the size of those waves? Wasn't it something to be the one spokesman, the one confronter, the one dissenter, time and time again?

Ah, who is having a crisis now at Yale, and whose voice was the loudest and clearest at the Christopher Smart reading? What was the name of the thin beautiful Puerto Rican nurse I met in Baltimore when I was twenty-two and in the army, and where did we go for our picnic? Am I the only one who reads Byron? Heine? How hard it is to read Hölderlin in the English—how hard it is for me, his German. I actually do love my enemies, don't I? All of them? Is it forgiveness, pity, humanity, loving-kindness, understanding? Is it a weakness? I remember how I had to get angry to get beyond a certain point—before I would speak up, and when I reached *that* point, I was unforgiving, deadly, unified, relentless, fully uncompromising. What sort of character was that in fiction? What was the psychology? Wasn't my father once or twice in his life like that? Wherein did theater, satire, irony, extreme detachment, pure justice, enter?

But what I'm *thinking* about is the young pianist and composer (in 1950) who washed dishes in Zak's Restaurant at the corner of 103rd and Broadway, no longer there. The dishwashing was immediately in front of me—at the counter. I was getting a master's in comparative literature at Columbia and living on the G.I. Bill, seventy-five dollars a month. I ate two skimpy meals a day and bought globe grapes, fifteen cents a pound, to ward off hunger. He was my age, maybe younger, a wild, black-eyed Italian, with musical dreams. I listened to him play his compositions, mostly improvisations with classical melody and bravado along with jazz rhythms in the tiny practice room nearby on a scarred upright, the room paid for by a benefactor—a benefactress—who encountered him, singing at his soapy sink. When I came back, after a year in France and Italy, he was the first one I looked up. I had a room then on 103rd Street, up the hill on the right. Across from the synagogue. He was dead, the manager of the restaurant told me, but I never found out whether it was suicide, an accident, or disease. He was from Little Italy, I know, though he never told me much about his family, his stern father, his loving older sister. He wanted to go to Juilliard, still Upper West Side then. I'm sure they would have taken a chance on him, he had such a powerful presence, but I'm not certain if he graduated high school. I don't know if he had time for a crisis; or if his whole life was one. I was still penniless myself, but I had the wild idea of helping him somehow.

There were several other musicians. What I did was sit and listen to them. The flautist on St. Mark's Place—on the stairs—a door between us. The violinist in France, and on the boat going over I used to hear practice every day—for months—John Rablowski, a gentle socialist who ended up writing a book on Pop Art. Marion Berger, who played the harp for me in her living room, still in high school. Whom I wrote a poem for fifty years later. Who died in her sixties from early-onset Alzheimer's. And there were painters whose workplaces I used to haunt so I could smell the turpentine and watch them stretch the canvases, when that was still done. One of them, Robert Ranieri, made fires in a makeshift stove—really an outdoor fireplace, on the stone floor of his loft in Soho—when there were still cheap (illegal) lofts in Soho—and cooked the most amazing pork chops there, which we chewed on while coughing in the smoke. I have several of his paintings, which I treasure.

The musician I was closest to was Ken Gabura, who was head of the experimental music department when I was at Iowa. He lived a city block away from me, and we visited each other's houses regularly. Ken, who was my age, was originally from New Jersey. He played jazz trumpet at first, then had the classic "fifties" education and transformed himself in the late 1960s, as many others of his generation did, to words, random sounds, and the like. He was addicted to literature—especially poetry—like the others, and had a small press on the third floor of his large Victorian. He insisted that my long poem "Bread Without Sugar" was a musical composition and invited me to address his graduate students on the subject. One of his pieces, about the life and writing of Ben Franklin, had the performers sitting in the orchestra seats, or standing, and the audience sitting on stage, a familiar reversal. The speeches, mostly ad hoc, were spoken willfully, randomly, even chaotically, again a familiar pattern, but I must confess that I did like the music. Some of the performers sang, but aside from the voice there were no instruments. Iowa, in a typical budget wipeout, took most of his money away—universities do this particularly with successful programs—and he was planning on starting a new program somewhere in New Mexico, which he talked about and dreamed of. I hadn't seen him for several months when one day, as I was leaving Mercy Hospital in Iowa City after a routine examination, I ran into him and he announced, matter-of-factly, that he had just been told that morning that he had cancer—I think prostate—but he was going to beat it by going to Mexico and getting vitamin injections. The cancer was in an advanced state and he died three or four months later. At the end he had extended visits from his children, whom he hadn't seen for several decades.

I think, when you talk about "crises," there is a period of intense pain, regret, anger, and deep isolation, but it's combined with "hope." There has to be hope, a cessation, if it can be called a "crisis." If there was a crisis in Ken's life, it occurred probably when he moved from the formal mode of the 1950s to the experimentalism of the 1960s and the abandonment of the one for the other; and equally important, when the university dried up his money source, forcing him to halt his musical investments. The "hope" was New Mexico, new funding, new experimentation. His sickness and death was not a crisis as I am describing it. Though it was a cause of much pain, sadness, disbelief, and shock for those of us who loved and admired him. Not to mention of course his own hopelessness.

One night I had a dinner party in my house at 650 South Governor Street, the old original farmhouse set back from the street, redbuds and oaks in front, lilacs and apples in the rear. There were probably eight people, including Ken. I know that Peter Feldstein, the photographer and printer from Oxford, Iowa, was there and his wife, Josephine, a painter. Those were the days when I cooked and I probably had a giant stew, or a pork roast. We had peach pie—I know it was peach—and ice cream for dessert. I was standing up and serving seconds of ice cream; Ken said he would like some and I dug out a huge serving for him and flung it at his plate, only it hit him in the face, the white and black cream running down his white beard. Maybe I tossed the spoon or scoop at him. He had roving eyes, magnified behind his thick lenses, and poor reflexes, so he missed it. He was surprised, confused, and hurt by my action, and I was immediately apologetic, really horrified, at what I had done. Peter says it's because he was flirting with my girlfriend—who was sitting next to him—telling her long stories about his music and his plans. I have never forgotten that and never forgiven myself.

Memoir

   For Marion Berger

I already said we put each other's eyes out
above the garages and we crawled down the catwalks
behind the apartments to look at our parents undressing
and bathing and fucking. We pissed on the weaklings, we stood
in a circle pissing, we fucked the maids, we got
in line to take our turn, we hid in the bushes
waiting, a block away from Schenley Park, we
fought the hunkies with homemade blackjacks, I was
already a general, I made inflammatory speeches,
and once, with three other cripples – it was World
War II and we were cripples – I threw bottles
and bricks and dirt into the windows of
our enemy's little dark stores; and as for schooling
the closest we got to our books was when we covered them
with Kraft paper every September but I had
a girlfriend who played the harp and she was thin
and wise and I was stupid with her; and forty
years later I was hosting a brunch in an elegant
downtown hotel with my wife and my teenage children

and aging mother and aging aunt and aging
friend of my mother's tortured with arthritis and there
was that girlfriend playing the harp again on a small
stage beside the tables and we stared
and exchanged numbers but I was still married and she
was changing her life again after spending thirty
years with an angry urologist; her eyes
were wet and joyous, large and trusting, out of a
drugstore novel, I was stricken, I walked for
years with that, my life was hell, the moon
never forgave me once; I love the harp
above all things, I love the lifelong vibrations,
what the world was doing, how I exploded.

— GERALD STERN

29 Fifty More Pages

The leaves on my redbud are slowly replacing the blossoms, and my
Japanese maple, my dogwood, and my apple are suddenly in full
leaf now, creating the canopy I love so well, for it should be dark
on the ground, and there should be a walkway of red brick run-
ning the length of my yard, from my back porch to the wire fence
facing the towpath, midway between the two wooden side fences,
and it should be two and a half feet wide and set in some sand and
dirt, a little loose, as it were, and it should curve around to the left
going east as I face the back and connect first with the stone, then
with the red brick around the left side of my house (I call left since
I am facing the rear), which, were I on the front porch facing the
street I would call right, and then I'd have the largest holly tree in
the world to consider, its sharp leaves hating everything within
sight and sound.

And I should wait for a few days, certainly less than a week, say
May fourth, or fifth, for my dark irises to appear among the bushes

in the small dirt space in front of my front porch, for then forget the word "spring" altogether for we are in summer, full-bloom, if windy and rainy, though with temperatures some days in the low nineties and some in the low sixties, now that the earth is askew. And I am wearing a T-shirt now and walk to the corner and drive my Honda the six blocks north on Union Street to Rojos, the best café in fifty miles, the doors wide open now and those girls at the machines serving me my rich half-cup named Midwives' Moonshine, for Dave the coffee-grinder's wife, and there, with the wind blowing on me, I can read the *Times* in my deep leather chair and reach over to the table from time to time for a sweet brown mouthful, my eyes never leaving the page.

It is only the beginning and we haven't by a long shot reached the longest day and the shortest night, which by the calendar is called the beginning of summer though we are as yet now six weeks before that time, called grace for us who live by light and begin our mourning early when the long shadows are still on the painted brick wall.

I was in Rome, we were, from January 20 to February 3—three months ago—so I have to figure what portion of my eighty-six pages (May 6, 2010) were written before—and after—and assign a beginning, as I am now beginning to assign an end, to this thing I am doing, this book I'm writing, assuming I'm writing at a systematic pace, so many pages a week, or a month, give and take, and so be able to assign a date, a time, even a month, for the beginning since I never kept track, since I never keep track hardly of anything, and thus name a date—if even a month—and (thus) I can assign myself an ending, since there must be an ending if it's truly going to be a book. And since for the last six, or maybe five, months I have been thinking about "eight months," then I think I'm nearing the ending, the great final stretch, though since I'm writing this in the twenty-first century I can't have a twentieth- or a nine-

teenth-century ending, even if I was born at exactly the first quar-
ter of the twentieth and am given to worship honor respect adore
and tributize (hear, oh twenty-first) the time before me, before
that even, even long before that even. So, if I began on November
10, 2009, I should be done by about July 10, 2010, if I am going to
honor the eight, though I think I started before then, for which
I'll figure something out when I retrieve the whole manuscript,
typed—printed—as it is, somewhere in this house, in a drawer, on
a table, a shelf, a desk, under a book—or over—or lost in a shuffle
or in *the* shuffle.

Not counting sections that may occur, that might come—unex-
pectedly—my way, I now have seven, or six to eight more in mind,
so if things go right, I have, could I say, six to eight weeks to go,
and if each of those sections is, say, seven pages, then I have about
fifty more pages left, which, added to the eighty-five, makes one
hundred thirty-five, but since we are talking about typed pages,
that might be one hundred sixty or so pages, which is a nice-sized
book. Though I am probably wrong. I know I am wrong. I know
this sounds compulsive and driven but so it is with me, alas, and
haven't I already said that I count steps and stories and stairs and
even count aloud, but I'm not as bad as Peter Feldstein. Nor should
you think I'm crazy for I haven't counted the number of blocks
from Anne Marie's house to mine nor the exact time it takes to get
to Philadelphia or New York on which day at which hour.

Nor are there apples on my apple tree, which is against a fence
and therefore an espaliered apple, I was advised didn't need another,
and indeed the first year did produce one apple. Which is nothing
compared to the two, I thought, dead trees in my backyard in Iowa
City, far back near the lilacs, both white and purple, near the alley
and near the dirty mulberry at the far right corner *facing* the alley
as you looked from the kitchen back, or from the Chinese wil-
low. And of course to the property on the other side of the alley,

bushed and treed for hundreds of feet as if we were in the country, the apples, not counting the worms, the sweetest and hardest I ever tasted, the ground full of them, the alleys with deep ruts where the heavy wagons had once rolled.

Though why eight months instead of nine—or seven—since eight is the least sacred number, or why not one year, the most obvious, I can't say—except that any number is arbitrary and I'm anxious to get back as soon as I can to my poems since I seem unable to do the two things at once as I once was able to do five things, or they are too close and drive each other crazy. But I am willing to honor nine or even ten.

Also I'm reading Marie Ponsot's book *Easy* and Charlie Williams's *Wait*, though it's not either competition or envy for I love both books and am at peace with them. Sometimes I get so angry at bad poems that I must "correct" them by my own writing. But not here. In Charlie's book I am moved by the new tenderness, the deep humanity, the bitterness, and, well, the wonder. "Cows" is such a beautiful poem, "some spotted heifers in a field, each with a numbered tag / in her ear . . ." "Those" (he says), "by next year, unless / they're taken to slaughter, / will be middle-aged ladies / with udders, indifferently grazing." I have to write out, to type, one additional poem. I am choosing among "Fish," "Rats," "Ponies," "Butterflies," and "Lucre." Here is "Fish," a kind-of new Charlie:

Fish

On the sidewalk in front
of a hairdressers' supply store
lay the head of a fish,
largish, pointy, perhaps a pike's.

It must recently have been left there;
its scales shone and its visible eye
had enough light left in it
so it looked as they will for a while

astonished and disconsolate
to have been brought to such a pass:
its incision was clean, brutal, precise;
it had to have come in one blow.

In the showcase window behind,
other heads, women's and men's,
bewigged, painstakingly coiffed,
stared out, as though at the fish,

as though stunned, aghast, too –
though they were hardly surprised:
hadn't they known all along
that life, that frenzy, that folly,

that flesh-thing, would come
sooner or later to this? It hurts,
life, just as much as it might,
and it ends, always, like this.

Better stay here, with eyes of glass,
like people in advertisements,
and without bodies or blood,
like people in poems.

And here is Marie Ponsot's poem "Dancing Day II," absolutely
gorgeous; overwhelmingly deadly, stripped of falseness, deep with
feeling. To say she is ironic is not enough; or philosophical; or
strange. Or that her music stops you, or slips by you. She is a viola:
strict, deep, mournful. Athena.

Dancing Day II

Once, one made many.
Now, many make one.
The rest is requiem.

We're running out of time, so
we're hurrying home to
practice to
gether for the general dance.

We're past get-ready, almost at get-set.
Here we come many to
dance as one.

Plenty more lost selves keep arriving, some
we weren't waiting for. We stretch and
lace up practice shoes. We mind our manners –
no staring, just snatching a look
    – strict and summative –
at each other's feet & gait & port.

Every one we ever were shows up
with world-flung poor triumphs
flat in the back-packs we set down to greet
each other. Glad tired gaudy
we are more than we thought
& as ready as we'll ever be.

We've all learned the moves, separately,

from the absolute dancer
    the foregone deep breather
the original choreographer.

Imitation's limitation – but who cares.
We'll be at our best on dancing day.
    On dancing day.
We'll belt out tunes we'll step to
together
till it's time for us to say
there is nothing more to say
nothing to pay   no way
pay no mind   pay no heed
pay as we go.
Many is one; we're out of here,
exeunt omnes

      exit   oh and save
      this last dance for me

on the darkening ground
looking up into
the last hour of left light

in the star-stuck east,
its vanishing flective, bent
breathlessly.

We both save the last dance.

30 Alana Rose

I can buy new asparagus in May—right now, May 12, 2010. I
can also buy small strawberries in June and corn and tomatoes in
August. Though, whatever I eat, I keep the first taste separate, for
everything must be savored of itself, as it says in Numbers.

And it says, "You should love life and not starve yourself." And
you should love anyone whose name is Alana Rose for that is the
name of my new granddaughter. And it says that Alana Rose must
always remember Heraldo. And whatever name you give the ghost
it doesn't matter, for she is a voice.

And when you say "God" you should never leave out letters—
and put in dashes—whatever your rabbi told you, for G–d is not
"The Name." And all the mystics are alike. And all floods are.

And it also says you should not get angry if someone asks you
if you're still writing. And since everything is there in Revelation,
you might as well know that the testimony of the three CEOs of
British Petroleum before a Congressional committee was predicted
two thousand years ago, and in their trial before the Lamb they lied
through their teeth as they blamed each other, like three chimpan-
zees who tore open a piggy bank. And the song, "Yes, we have no
bananas," was written for the three chimpanzees, and their punish-
ment for ruining an ocean and destroying a river will be for them to
tread water in the middle of the slick with weights on their feet and
white shirts and neckties on their miserable bodies. And one of the
punishments (just one) for BP should be that they must pay for the

next three years the salaries of the three hundred thousand teachers who were fired in our recent depression, whatever the modes and methods. Justice as in the final scene of a Shakespeare play where all is set right by a wise prince who is not encumbered by legal bullshit but metes out his decisions sometimes in an unexpected but always a good way, so life can go on.

31 26 Vandam

The thing about 26 Vandam was how it sat in the air, so to speak, like a tree house, isolated, distant, and self-contained. It was on the top floor—the fifth, one of four apartments surrounding a small hall and two side-by-side toilets just the other end of the staircase, with more steps leading up to the roof, which nobody except me and my friends ever used, and accessible for years until one day it was padlocked, either for safety or from meanness. I was in 5FW, number five, front west, and I didn't have to use the hall toilets because I had a small, a very small, bathroom inside the apartment consisting of a commode and nothing else, with a large mural on the wall facing you, when you were standing up and pissing, of a half-naked woman with a sexy come-hither look reminiscent of some displaced Lily Marlene or Marlene Dietrich in all her 1940s glory, which I never painted over in the twenty-some years I had the apartment, nor did Pat Stern who occupied it the years she was an art therapist in a hospital in Brooklyn, even when our son, David, redid the apartment for his mother's comfort, replacing the ancient tub in the kitchen with a shower, putting in a new sink—and cabinets—knocking down walls and such.

It may have been the early 1970s that I first took over the apartment. I remember that it was Deedee Massena who handed me the keys, that she had lived there for several years with her teenage daughter and that she formally introduced me to the landlady, who lived on the second floor, and how she and I both bowed as we looked each other over, the landlady and I. She was Chinese and didn't, so far as I know, speak one word of English. She recognized me immediately as an "artist," and whenever we encountered each other on my slow climb up the stairs she would grin and make the motions of playing a violin, acknowledging my "work," with respect and humor, even if she was a bit wide of the mark. There was no lease, but I paid her on the first of the month or as close as I could come to it. She wouldn't accept a check so I had to give her cash, which she immediately hid in the pocket of one of the many skirts she wore. I think the rent was ninety dollars a month, maybe a hundred, all the years she and her son, a chemistry professor at Queen's College, owned the building. There was no record. Though a few years later her son and I did negotiate in the front seat of his VW station wagon; he got a few more dollars, and I got my first lease.

The front room, the living room, was square, of decent size, a dead fireplace, a mantel, some plaster carving and two large windows facing the street down there, one of them giving off to a fire escape that once or twice was used when something fell awry, say me throwing the keys down to the sidewalk and not making it over the iron steps. The primitive kitchen was at the other end of the apartment, and in between was a small dark sleeping room and a "dining" room. The entrance gave more or less onto the bedroom—the kitchen to my left and the living room to my right. There were two windows in the kitchen–dining room area and an airshaft in the "bedroom." I think 350 square feet in all.

There were twenty apartments, five floors, small variations in each one. All the tenants were Chinese except an older Italian couple on the third floor and a young "Caucasian" woman opposite me who kept her bicycle against the rail in the hall. Gradually, over the years, most of the Chinese disappeared, the Italian couple died, one at a time, and the building came to be occupied mostly by actors, dancers, singers, and even a stray poet, trying their luck in New York. Vandam was a block long, maybe it was two blocks, Sixth Avenue on one side, Varick on the other, the Holland Tunnel traffic maneuvering late in the day from lane to lane, horns blowing. The building was quite old, originally a hotel for sailors. The land to the west beyond Varick (or Washington), and this side of Hudson, was landfill, and no. 26 preceded the additional acreage on the lordly Hudson, or so I was told. It was the only domicile on the one side; the other buildings were storage, office, and manufacturing; but across the street were a series of two-and-a-half-story brick row houses, built by Aaron Burr as part of a real estate speculation, beautiful colonial buildings, similar to the ones in Philadelphia, built at the same time, for stately residences. I don't know what they were in the 1920s and '30s but when I lived at no. 26 they were quite upscale, and Leontyne Price and Paul Taylor lived there. There is, I understand, a common backyard for the whole block of houses, a kind of park instead of a series of narrow yards.

One of the things that I dearly loved about my apartment was the view from my living room windows. I had a direct shot at the Empire State Building on 34th Street—"the red and blue beacon of Empire"—as well as the roofs of the low-lying buildings this side of 14th. It was one thing to stare out at the Delaware River in Pennsylvania, especially from the second floor of my house on old 611; it was equally moving to look out on lower Manhattan or to open the window a foot or so and listen to the hum. I spent days on end there—it was my personal Yaddo. Most of the time I didn't have a phone and, except for the nine months I gave the apartment to my son who was spending his junior year in New York at the Institute of Urban Studies on 40th Street, I could have been on a mountaintop or in a cave, so little did I have contact with others in the city, in that building or beyond, especially in the years before my former wife "modernized" it, for I was much given to red tubs in the kitchen and the wind driving through the airshaft. I did easily half my work there—before I left for Iowa in the early 1980s—and when I came east, it was a (sacred) place to come back to.

I count steps—I said that before—and I'm sure that at one time I knew how many steps there were to the fifth floor, and I'm sure that I deliberately miscounted them or pretended there were fewer—or more—and reconciled differences and held my breath and leaned and bent and sang, sometimes in several languages, as I continued climbing. I have written before somewhere, or I have said it in conversation, or at a reading, how there finally was no way to fool the body for you might go slow, or you might run, or you might close your eyes or do a circle on the landings, but eventually you were at the third floor—and breathing—then the fourth with your mouth open, and finally the fifth, with your legs turned to stone. There maybe were thirteen steps to each landing, or twelve or nine, but there were eighty to a hundred steps in all, which was a little difficult at fifty-five years but much harder at seventy. And it may be, more than anything else, more than the legal threats from the landlords or Marlene Dietrich's life-size image in the loo, the reason that I finally gave the apartment up.

It was the happiness of being in New York, and it was the excitement, and awe, of being at the center, even if the true centers were as often as not not there but ninety miles away or nine thousand. Aside from which I always loved New York as a city, as a place to live, to *be*, and, although, like all the other "older" denizens I preferred what it *was,* what it used to be, and regretted what it had become, it was still home, even if a home away from home. Each of us has his or her own narrative. I like to go back to Lewis Mumford and *his* memories, even to Whitman and his. Certainly I miss the Jewish dairy restaurants, Ratner's and Rappaport's; and I miss the bookstores on Fourth; and the distinctly ethnic neighborhoods, full of their delightful hate; and, well, the time before I was born, or barely, the great Yiddish theaters on Second, the coffeehouses, the Jewish newspapers, and, above all, the crowded synagogues, though as a cosmopolitan anarchist and hater of superstition I would have none of it. Not to mention the music uptown, and Soho in its illegitimate splendor of secret studios; and the speeches in Union Square; and the cafeterias, and just sitting there—or the nickel—then dime—subways and the sixty-cent dinners; and Klein's Department Store. And I inveigh against the poverty of only six pairs of shoes in a window in Soho and tourists walking around like zombies looking for nothing. I loved to walk down my five flights in the morning and have a coffee and roll on a bench in a tiny park on Sixth and talk to a purple bird before I climbed back up for my less serious work. Or I loved a morning walk as far east as Tompkins Square Park before or after its "temporary" closing so I could watch the Chinese exercise or the homeless lay down their burdens or mothers taking their children to school or a Greek priest or a Jewish mystic, both bearded and with books, as they frowned their way across, each (also) with a burden.

I am not a true New Yorker, I am from Pittsburgh, as everyone within my reach knows, but it's been partly my city since I was thirteen—even younger—and traveled there with my father on his buying trips and stayed in the hotels on 7th and 8th, the Governor Clinton, the New Yorker, the Edison, the Pennsylvania; and spent the day going up and down in the elevators or walking for hours, or riding the cheap subways everywhere, getting out for a while, going back an hour later. The Greyhound to New York was eight or nine dollars and I was constantly on it when I was sixteen, seventeen, eighteen. And later. My walks took me everywhere and simple hunger drove me into cheap restaurants—German, Italian, Jewish, Greek—where I talked to the ancients and learned a little from the waitresses. I loved the Village like everyone else, but I also loved the Upper West Side, which was seedier then, and the Lower East among the Poles, Ukrainians, Jews, and Puerto Ricans, but mostly Midtown, before Disney changed it. I knew every movie house on 42nd and what I did not learn from the profound images on the screen I picked up from the random activity in the orchestras and the balconies.

I didn't have many visitors at no. 26—I didn't want any—certainly no students and no one wanting anything—that was not allowed, but there were a few poets who came to see me, Ed Hirsch, Phil Levine, William Merwin. Merwin had a similar apartment and he had it for years—in the neighborhood of St. Vincent's, which I hear they are closing, only he was on the sixth floor and, as I recall, the steps were in a circle, built around a central pole, and from hall window to hall window, as you climbed, there was an endlessly tall tree of heaven close by that was determined, it seemed, to go where you went, or, if needs be, even higher and higher, out of sight—but not mind.

One night John Gardner and his wife, Liz Rosenberg, stopped by to pick me up and drive me back to Pennsylvania on their way to Binghamton, New York, where they were both teaching at the State University. John was, like Joe Louis, a slave to the IRS, which garnished his wages and left him with little for living. Only two nights ago, at a small gathering in Princeton, Joyce Carol Oates and I remembered Gardner's first wife hiring a plane to drop leaflets on the campus of the Bread Loaf Writer's Conference declaiming his infidelity, which, by the way, made him into a kind of hero, whereas a later (ill-informed) accusation of plagiarism (not dropped from airplanes) turned him into a villain—almost as bad as a student—from the point of view of the English teachers, gathered for their annual feast of death. It was winter, John had an ancient tiny car, but when we were inside and settled, the engine wouldn't start, though we tried for at least an hour. It was about 9 p.m. so John, Liz, and John's sister, who was also there, spent the night in my small apartment. The sofa opened up so there were two beds. John slept beside his wife and I got into bed, in the other room, with John's sister. She looked remarkably like John, so when I woke up from time to time and looked at my bed partner I almost thought it was him I was sleeping with. John, for his part, paced the floor from kitchen to living room practically the whole night, troubled as he was by poverty, cancer, a rusty car, and lost dreams. The interesting thing was that he had been trying to raise the money, and a great deal of it, to bring me to Binghamton as a poet-in-residence, a do-what-you-want-to job. And two days after I arrived in Iowa and began teaching, and a day before he died in a dumb motorcycle mishap, I got a telegram from him that *he had the money*. It wasn't until seven or so years later that I *was* proffered a position at Binghamton, and though I was already looking for houses in the Catskills I knew deep down I wouldn't go—for six reasons, one of which was the heavy load and one of which was the weather.

Varick Street at night is very quiet after all the cars have entered the tunnel. One night—oh, 1990—my subway line broke partially down and we had to go south to Canal, cross over, and go back north to Houston and get off there. It was after twelve and there were four or five of us waiting. I proposed a cab but everyone was suspicious so after waiting a half-hour we got into a noisy "repair" car. A young woman got off the subway with me, or ahead of me, and we both made our way south, me trying not to "follow" her, she frozen with fear. While still walking I told her my name was Gerald Stern, I was a writer, I lived on the next street and I meant her no harm. To which, she replied, "My God, I'm just home from Greece, the Aegean School in Paros. I was supposed to look you up." I don't know why she was heading down Varick but she came to my apartment. I offered her some food, we talked for two hours, and I gave her my bed while I slept in the living room. She lived uptown, in Inwood. She came by to see me once more. I think she ended up in some kind of commercial art—clothes, I think.

I have put the angel with the huge eyes and fat cheeks that's in the front of no. 26 on the cover of *Paradise Poems*. Before it was covered over with a stupid thick plaster that practically effaced the image. It's "*26* Vandam" even though the title of my poem (of the same name) I mistakenly published in both magazine (*New Yorker*) and book (*Lucky Life*) as "*96* Vandam." The disease of confusing, conflating, and combining numbers has a name I'm sure, but I'd probably get it wrong. I gave the apartment up in 2002, gave my furniture and dishes away, and celebrated by buying everybody breakfast at a nearby Greekery. I was paying $240 a month at the end, which, I'm sure, another zero was immediately added to for the next tenant. I got a few hundred dollars; spent half of it on that breakfast.

The Roar

That was the last time I would walk up those five
flights with a woman in tow, standing
in the hall patiently trying my keys,
listening to my heart pounding from the climb.

And the last time I would sit in front of the
refrigerator, drinking white wine and asking
questions, and lecturing – like a spider –
and rubbing my hand through my hair – like a priest.

Look at me touch the burning candle
with my bare palm and press a rusty knife
against my left eyelid while she undresses.

Look at me rise through the cool airshaft
and snore at the foot of the bed with one hand
on her knee and one hand touching the white floor,

the red and blue beacon of Empire
just beyond those little houses
as familiar now as my crippled birch

and the endless roar out there
as sweet as my own roar
in my other dream, on the cold and empty river.

— GERALD STERN

96 Vandam

I am going to carry my bed into New York City tonight
complete with dangling sheets and ripped blankets;
I am going to push it across three dark highways
or coast along under 600,000 faint stars.
I want to have it with me so I don't have to beg
for too much shelter from my weak and exhausted friends.
I want to be as close as possible to my pillow
in case a dream or a fantasy should pass by.
I want to fall asleep on my own fire escape
and wake up dazed and hungry
to the sound of garbage grinding in the street below
and the smell of coffee cooking in the window above.

— GERALD STERN

32 Signs over Gates

When the Jews dragged themselves through the gates of Babylon, they could see inscribed in the wood and scratched on the metal the following:

Nebuchadnezzar King of the Jews,
Spell that in four letters and I'll give you my shoes.

There are four cities with a motto written over them. This is a shame and should be rectified. The great sign under Trenton's railroad bridge was probably thrilling—full of oxygen—when Trenton was a living city. "Trenton makes: the world takes," it said. The sign is still there but reading it only produces laughter. There was a sign in a city called Hell that urged the walkers to "abandon hope, ye," and though Europe as a whole had few if any signs over or in front of their cities, they did have some at the entrance to the camps. Europe is good at museums, parks, and the like. The Romanians and the Slovaks are terrific. They can actually remember where the murders took place, even the names of the murderers. The French are a little forgetful. In Auschwitz, where a train went in and another went out, is a memorable sign. The trains apparently were bomb proof.

33   Dragonflies

Dragonflies flourished millions of years before the dinosaurs; they are one of the oldest of the insects and were probably not much different in their primitive forms than they are now. Though even those had ancestors, maybe without wings or without fully developed ones or maybe extra ones, say in front, that could have provided stability at low speeds as the flaps of an airplane do—as I, in my ignorance, understand it. We are talking 300,000,000 years. Think of this and think that we may have only five—or ten—years before our dear planet is modified, certainly for the worst, by the humans that "own" it, or pretend they do. Not by the ants, who do own it, or by the dragonflies who eat from it and fuck on it. There were giant dragonfly-like creatures then, in Kansas. With wingspans of twenty-two inches. And there are deposits everywhere— France, Brazil—preserved in one amazing way or other of extinct species, dead-ended, Buddhistic. There were suborders, for example, that were abundant in the Mesozoic and probably perished with the dinosaurs, though living representatives of the groups may still exist—in the Himalayas or Japan. There probably is confusion among the scientists as they wander in the fossil beds or study the DNAs, just as there is confusion among the literary critics as they wander on lost floors of their hotels in the critical cities, concerning beauty maybe and its vain and complicated wings.

The myths—and legends—about dragonflies are universal. In the south, when a "snake doctor" landed on a fishing pole they would soon get a bite; you could predict rain—heavy, light—by how high the dragonfly was flying; "devil's darning needles" were poisonous, they sting; the devil takes the form of the dragonfly; they perch on snakes' heads; they sew together the fingers or toes of scolding women, saucy children, profane men; they enter your ear and penetrate your brain; they were, along with ants, various beetles, bats, and locusts, one of the original twelve "people" (Navajo); they guarantee water's purity; they are represented by a vertical and horizontal line, the first crosses (among Hopi); they weighed people's souls (in Sweden); they were called "draculiu" in Romania; another (European) name is based on their scientific term: *Libellula*. Maybe from *libel* (the wings spread as in the pages of an open book [libel]); or *libella* (balancing scales) [when the dragonfly is hovering over the water]. *Libellule* (France), *libelle* (Germany), *libelula* (Spain) *libelinha* (Portugal); balance fly (English).

And since they are water animals, they have watery names: water nymph, water peacock, water spirit, keeper of the fish, guard of the tubs—in German, Dutch, French, and Italian. And they are horses: devil's horses, devil's riding horse, witch's horse, devil's little horse, hunting horses, our dear little horse, little golden horse, God's horse, little horse, and horse and wagon. And snakes, evil beings, sharp instruments, harmful agents, other animals, people, God knows what: snake with a head, bull snake, small snake, devil's needles, devil's grandmothers, king of death, Judas (of course), sorcerers, greenish pointed thing, needles, pins, knives, arrows, finger cutters, eye stickers, finger gnawers, nostril cutters, horse killers, bull stingers, little gentlemen, little nuns, priests, queens, tailors, chaplains, shoemakers, sky goats, salamanders, crickets, peacocks, green streaks, glasers, autumn insects, pearls, pissers, pounders, salt fish, flat bellies, skinny pricks, and long pricks.

One of the old names for Japan is Island of the Dragonfly. The dragonfly was a favorable symbol of strength among Japanese warriors and was called the invincible insect. They were used for decoration on warriors' helmets and they are signs of good luck. The poets have written about them for centuries, especially Basho. During the Buddhist holiday of the Spirits of the Ancestors, the dead return to their homes, and dragonflies serve as mounts for the spirits. In China, a dragonfly thrust describes the motion of a boxer as he darts in close, delivers a quick blow, and darts back. Tu Fu and Liu Yu-hsi wrote gorgeous short poems about the dragonfly.

34 My Big Mouth

My big mouth gets me into endless trouble. I blurt things out, I intrude, I intervene, I break boundaries—and I am not proud of it. I attribute it to Tourette's syndrome, another word for big mouth; and I half forgive myself. My poem "Stern Country" details such an intrusion, even the biting of a (beautiful) woman's shoulder, which is an *extreme* intrusion. It happened in Prague, and Ed Hirsch and Phil Levine were witness to it. A group of us were sitting at a restaurant table, and my neighbor on the right asked me about my Tourette's, and I explained how I invaded and took over, and ended up biting her shoulder. It was Mary Morris. When Anne Marie returned to the table after a visit to the loo, Eddie, in his broken voice, said: "Anne Marie, Jerry just bit Mary's arm." To the joy of everyone there.

A year or so later, I was part of a group reading at the Poets House in New York, a crowded audience in front of us, including Bill Murray, a patron of poetry and a frequent visitor to the Poets House, and when it was my turn to read, I read "Stern Country" and told the story of the bite. But I couldn't leave well enough alone and had to up the ante by attacking Bill and *Groundhog Day* and insisting I knew Punxsutawney—and the groundhog—better than he did (which I do) and when I was done reading my two or three poems, he rushed up and bit *me*—on the left shoulder (as I had done Mary) for he probably has Tourette's too. The only complaint was from several young ladies who were critical of him for biting that old guy when he could have bitten them, or critical of me for offering my shoulder.

Ann, the young lady living next door to me (on the south) gave birth last week (early June) to a baby girl (Karis—as in charismatic), and her parents were up from Nashville to visit for a week. Her father and mother are involved in church work. He was a United Methodist, then a Unitarian minister, and he is now—in his sixties—"contemplating," as he describes it. I'm not sure exactly what it is she does, but they both have degrees in divinity from Boston University, where they met. Richard (the father) and I had coffee and talked in the morning, and I gave him a book of my poems and lent him Willis Barnstone's *Restored New Testament*, an extraordinary version of the Christian scriptures, for the two of them to look at. I went over for a minute to see the baby and was touched by the love in the house, especially on the part of Richard and his daughter, Ann.

Early evening, 7 p.m., I was about to get in my car to drive to Anne Marie's when I saw a little gathering on the sidewalk, in front of Ann's house, the five of them, father, mother, grandfather, grandmother, baby in a carriage, people next door, one or two others. "You look like a bunch of subversives," I shouted, in my insane mode. "Are you on strike? I know, the baby's on strike, she won't drink any milk!" It was beyond a gaffe, it was a horror. I was immediately mortified—I wanted to run over and embrace everyone; I wanted to pick up Karis and kiss her fifty times. (Still crazy: other side.) I was in a medieval nightmare. I had cursed the mother's milk. I was possessed by an evil spirit. In my world,

straight out of Poland, you didn't even praise a baby lest evil fall
on her; you chewed thread, when your grandmother was sewing
a button on you, to divert the devil; you said your prayers in exact
order, twice a day; you watched for signs. But they (next door) were
"modern," thanks God, even the Methodists, and didn't seem to
realize the extent of my madness; maybe they didn't even hear me.
Maybe I had the gaffe all to myself. Maybe my blunder was of the
sort where you're all alone and bang your knee out of clumsiness or
absentmindedness or it's dark and you wander around your house
in excruciating pain from one room to another, cursing yourself or
holding your breath or counting till the pain goes away; or worse
yet, you trip, or slip, on a broken sidewalk and have to pick your-
self up all alone and see where the pants are torn or the blood is and
the scab will be.

But that wasn't all, that memorable day. Anne Marie and I went
to dinner at a close friend's house a half-hour away, in the beautiful
New Jersey countryside. I had a large scotch with my cheese and
crackers before we sat down at the table and my big mouth wouldn't
stop. When you combined my wild talking with my self-pity and
quick resentment you had to end up hopeless before my onslaught. I
told story after story; I resented any interference. How we got there
I don't know, but I was telling the three others about an old girl-
friend of mine reuniting with a daughter she had given up at birth,
and since at our friend's table I couldn't stop, I went on about birth
mothers and such, realizing but not realizing, as if I were watching
myself from up there, say on the ceiling, that the friend I was lec-
turing had herself reunited with her first child, a daughter born in
Italy when she, the mother, was young and alone, I don't know the
details. My friends kept looking at each other, and Anne Marie was
staring in disbelief but I went on. And I couldn't sleep that night,
partly from the alcohol and partly from the gaffe—worse than gaffe,
which is merely a blunder, a faux pas—regret, remorse instead—

and called the next day to apologize but was generously forgiven, my behavior attributed to my love of narration, for a story is a story, which almost convinced me, but I will wait for seven years or so till I apologize to Karis, may she forgive me for my big mouth, and her parents too, and her grandparents.

35 Trip to New York with Poet–Potter

I have come to respect confusion and imperfect memory, nor do I insist too much anymore on *my* version of the facts, nor am I embarrassed, nor do I weep when evidence of one kind or another contradicts my version. I am even somewhat at peace—somewhat—with forgetting an important name, or when it was that an event took place, or what the car was I was driving at the time.

Last night, at 2:30 a.m., I got halfway up in my bed trying to remember the name of the potter, the huge bearded 1960s artiste who came to my house in Indiana, Pennsylvania, in the spring of 1966 or 1967, whom I drove to New York with for a three-day jaunt. I don't remember exactly how we met. I think he was a friend of the poet Bob Mezey, who was giving a reading at my college, Indiana University of Pennsylvania, and the potter may have come along. Mezey became a kind of prisoner of Will Stubbs— alas, dead—a colleague of mine at the time in charge of readings. Stubbs wanted to keep Mezey to himself and wouldn't tell him I had phoned him, several times, but we finally did meet after midnight, Bob Mezey and I, and played pool in the student union for a few hours, two lost poets.

Angela Hazely remembers the year as 1965, the potter's name, she said, was Joseph, and he was—he had been—a visiting teacher in the art department of Slippery Rock State College for a semester. Slippery Rock was two hours away from Indiana (PA), northwest. Bob had possibly visited Joseph there on his way to Indiana, or stopped to give a reading. I don't remember if Joseph stayed at my house or if he came back a few days later or if he had a car or came by bus, but we left for New York, in my '62 Rambler if it was 1966, or my '50 Buick (Roadmaster) if it was 1965.

It turned our that he had never been to New York City or, for that matter, anywhere east of Slippery Rock, fifty miles north of Pittsburgh. And hardly that, for he was only visiting western Pennsylvania; he had never really been east of Chicago for any length of time.

We drove east on Route 22 to avoid paying a toll on the Pennsylvania Turnpike and—also—to see the old cities and not be bored by the tunnels. I did all the driving, as I usually did. He was going to spend a long weekend—four days, probably—in New York as the guest of an old friend who ran a bar on 14th Street, near Klein's Department Store, and lived upstairs. When we drove through the ancient spaces in eastern Pennsylvania east of Lancaster, he looked at the old houses and asked me when they were built. When I told him the Germans came there, and the English, as early as the middle of the seventeenth century and most of the houses were built in the 1720s and '30s, he couldn't, physically, comprehend it. "You mean they're over a century old?" he asked. He tried to figure it out on his fingers.

I of course gave him the quick overview of New York so when we arrived at his friend's bar late at night and he took his things out of the back seat and hugged his friend hello, I thought this was the beginning of a grand adventure. We hugged goodbye and I arranged that I'd pick him up Sunday, or was it Monday, for our ride back. We may have started early, or in the afternoon, but I was there on time for the seven- or eight-hour ride back to western Pennsylvania. I was staying at Guy Daniels's house on 120th and the river, west side, Guy who came from Iowa and was a Russian and

French translator and lived in quasi-poverty and fought constantly with his wife and drank raw eggs in the morning and argued with publishers and waited for checks and danced freestyle in the morning for exercise and was born maybe six years before me and adored Gil Orlovitz's poetry.

Joseph and I began the return quietly—it must have been morning, and chilly, for I recall his coat collar was up, his eyes were closed, and he had a slight smile on his lips. We drove through the Holland Tunnel and over the Pulaski Skyway with almost no traffic, a blessed, unusual day. I asked him if he had a good time and he nodded yes and looked at me with pure happiness. "Did you walk around Union Square?" I asked. He shook his head no. "Did you see all the bookstores on Fourth?" No. "Well, did you see Washington Square, Fifth Avenue, the Empire State Building, the Brooklyn Bridge, the Lordly Hudson, the Village?" No. "How about Times Square, the dirty movies, Central Park, the horses, Seventh Avenue, the flower district, Bloomingdales, the galleries?" No. "The library on 40th, the Metropolitan Museum, the Modern, the Guggenheim?" Again, no. He had spent four days inside the building on 14th Street, either downstairs at the bar or upstairs in the apartment. There was plenty to eat and drink and smoke, he had a comfortable bed, and there were visitors and good talk all the time he was there. He was totally pleased with himself. The visit was a huge success. Not only that, but he talked the whole way back about how great New York was, and how he wanted to come back there to live—when he left his wife and provided for his kids. We hugged goodbye, probably at a bus station in Indiana, and he was off, back to Slippery Rock or Chicago or all the way to LA, thinking, I'm sure, of the joys of New York as the bus climbed west and the bags downstairs in their allotted compartments shifted ever so slightly as the bus tipped sideways in its ascent into the Alleghenies.

36 James Schuyler

I don't know what this book is, a way of remembering, a disgrace.
I try desperately now to reach out to those I want or who want me
before it's too late. Once I knocked on a door and they told me, "He
died yesterday; I thought you knew it." I love clarity, above all else,
but for some reason I combined—in an earlier version—the narra-
tive of Joseph the potter with a short meditation on James Schuyler.
I know it doesn't make sense. I think, in my mind, the connection
is with Joseph's stay in New York—not leaving his friend's apart-
ment on 14th Street, calling *that* the magic visit, glorying in it—
and Schuyler's habitation, his room and a bit, at the Chelsea Hotel
on 23rd Street. Not that Schuyler never left *his* room; only that I
thought he would adore Joseph's visit to NYC and understand it
like no one else.

I have been to the Chelsea a number of times—I have even
stayed there once, lulled to sleep by the sweet scent of potpourri
descending a hallway, but I have never been on the fifth floor, and
I have never knocked on room 526. I have studied Schuyler's poems
for years, and I know and admire what he does. And I know a lit-
tle about his life, the more public part and the more private. I love
to discover, in every poet I read, his—or her—mystery, the thing
without which he is not he, or she is not she, and the thing with
which he, she, is. Though it's disgraceful (now that I'm using that
word) to call it a "thing." I'm like the others, I am amazed at how
he holds it together, especially in the long poems, as I'm amazed
at his knowledge—what I'll *call* knowledge—and by his aesthetic
stubbornness. I don't know what critical observer used the phrase
"seeing as a form of feeling"—maybe it was Barbara Guest—but,
of all the statements, it is the most accurate. I love an essay I read on
"Schuyler's Poetics of Indolence"—Mark Silverberg wrote it—and
I love how poets of different beauty seizures respond to Schuyler. I

love how he looks at things, and what happens to the poem through the looking, and how it's not devouring. I know how he (apparently) doesn't want to "change anything," doesn't want to tamper, even if that runs counter to so much I myself believe in. And I love his tenderness, and his willingness to include "the horror," and his secrecy, and his courtesy (in the poem), and *his* kind of ecstasy. What I would call his "Dutchness."

I would have loved to have sat with him in the lobby, or next door at the Cuban restaurant, or (best) upstairs. For maybe an hour. I certainly wouldn't "interview" him, but maybe, among other things, we could talk about Auden and Ginsberg and Dylan Thomas and Hart Crane and Emily and Walt. What formalism was, and why he didn't like bard-ism; or I could get his view on Warhol and Pearlstein. Or maybe we would just talk Carmen and Ischia, the boat from Naples and Valéry's grave, what it was like walking across Italy in 1950, or his first reading of Dante, and where, and the text; or Villon; or Rabelais. Or something simple: the ice cream we loved best, or the cigarettes, say Picayuni.

I get too soft when I talk to the dead for I forgive them everything. Though who am I to do that? I did want to ask him about the poem "Sometimes." There he is remembering a synagogue in Amsterdam—and I can't tell if it's the Portuguese or the Ashkenazi, or some other smaller. The brass chandeliers make me think it's the Portuguese. I know there's a painting by the Dutch painter Emanuel de Witte, done in 1675, of the interior of that synagogue. I have the feeling that either looking at it in an art book, or seeing it on a wall—in New York or elsewhere—generated a memory of the *exterior* and "what time and weather abraded." But that's only a theory. For one thing, the painting contains many people, calmly standing there, different from the poem. The poem is divided into two parts; lines 1–9, ending with the phrase I have mentioned, are devoted to the exterior, and lines 10–16 to the interior. It's a poem given to absence and to stillness, though given the occasion, the silence ("terrible") and the emptiness are heartbreaking. It is empty because the vibrant Dutch Jewish community, there for hundreds of years, was viciously destroyed by the Germans during the war.

Sometimes

I remember the synagogue at Amsterdam
        a tenderly overcast day
                ripe leaves
fell and floated
              cobbles and
      toned nuances of pink brick
               aglow
tenderly, tenderly
          what time and weather abraded
epochs of refinement
       reflected in mute lights
cross cast by shined brass chandeliers
        a kind of Quaker hush
so quiet
       and wonder how such terrible silence
came into the world

— JAMES SCHUYLER

It's a Schuyler poem, unheroic, deeply observant, tender, and detailed. No one else was like him.

37 Dog Eat Dog

I called the dragonflies water animals. They live and die by streams, ponds, and lakes. Some actually reproduce in watering troughs, birdbaths, washtubs, and buckets. One commentator said the name comes from the fierce jaws they use for ripping apart their prey. But I didn't know dragons had such jaws.

They hatch their eggs in two weeks and live for a month. They can see from twenty feet away. They have three pairs of legs but can't really walk. They use their legs to rest on twigs and leaves or to scoop up their prey in flight. They chew their prey while flying. Males are very territorial and often stay attached to the female while she lays eggs. They can stay submerged in water, breathing oxygen from the liquid that enters the gills along the thorax. They do not need to surface as they shoot the water out of these gills. They can also shoot water out of their anus to propel themselves away from enemies.

The abdomen of the dragonfly has ten segments. The primary sex organs (of both sexes) are on the ninth segment. For mating to occur the male must move the tip of his abdomen forward to transfer the sperm packet from the organs located in the ninth segment of his abdomen to the secondary set of sex organs in the second segment. This frees the abdomen and the appendage on the tenth segment to capture a female. Females have structures on their heads and the first sections of their thoraxes that accept the males' terminal appendages. These appendages, called claspers, project backward from the last segment of the abdomen, and are species specific. Female dragonflies do not always have a choice of mate—the male will usually attempt to grab any female that passes by. The female "accepts" the sperm pouch by moving her abdomen up to the secondary organs of the male. She can lay her eggs while flying over water and leave them to wash away to their individual fates; or she can flip her eggs away from her as she dips her abdomen into the water; or she may have egg-laying organs—ovipositors—that dig into plant stems or even dead wood, or on plant material floating in the water; or in soil or mud.

Dragonflies rarely fly at night. They are purely carnivorous and predatory—they eat any flying insects smaller than them, even other dragonflies. They themselves fall prey to a number of other predators—birds, spiders, robber flies, and other dragonflies. Their larvae are a favorite food of fish and, in some places, people. It takes fourteen days for a male dragonfly to reach sexual maturity, and they can live eleven days after that—twenty-five days. The larval stages last longer than the adult stages. Some migrate, but we don't know where they go and how long they take. Their swarms are endless—sometimes as much as forty miles long. It takes generations. Males fight each other in the air and maneuver like World War I airplanes. Many carry old battles scars, torn wings and the like. They eat and fuck. And fight. Males, that is. Adult males.

Would a glass of water do? Or a bowl, or a *shissel*, or a thimble? Do they not murder, even if they destroy mosquitoes? When Darwin said "dog eat dog," who or what was he referring to? What Lion and what Lamb? What are vegetables? Give me a vegetable and I'll give you the world! I have, in this briefcase, the names of six card-carrying vegetables in the state department! I have, in this briefcase, the bodies of six bread-eating damselflies. I have the name of one dragonfly who has eaten all of them. I have the name of six Isaiahs! I have the husks of six ears, I have the skeletons of six nymphs. I have six nymphs in this card-carrying fish-case. I have six fishes in the bellies of each nymph. I have one tadpole. I have the discarded tails of four thousand dead and transformed proto-frogs. I have one frog for each finger. I have the mouth parts of the most efficient insect on earth. I have his six legs, his two thousand eyes. I have his brain, which is spread out over his body. I have his think! Give me a handshake and I'll give you my hand. What is quicker, a buzz saw or a dragon saw?

We should be called *walks* since flies (who fly) are called flies. We should be called *runs*. Jesse Owens outran a horse. Then he ate it. See eating habits of frogs. Keep your mouth open at long last. Speak softly and carry ten segments. Speak softly and carry a big one. Speak softly and carry your cane. Speak softly in front of your grandchildren. Speak softly if speak you must. Lie down together and eat carrots.

38 Academy of Arts Medal

Yesterday, May 19, 2010, at the annual meeting of the Academy of Arts and Letters on 155th Street (NYC), I received the "Award of Merit" medal for poetry, given every six years to a poet chosen by the academy, or as these things go, chosen by a committee of academy members. It was an all-day affair, consisting of wine, gossip, kisses, a formal luncheon, a photo session, and a very long two hours of speeches, presentations, applause, induction of new members, and, finally, more wine, hors d'oeuvres, kisses, and farewells.

I sat on the large stage (of the auditorium) along with members of the academy and other honorees. Wives, husbands, friends, and the interested public filled the seats in the theater. We had numbered places on stage, and it was well organized. Bill Moyers received an award for distinguished service to the arts, Garrison Keillor, wearing red socks and red shoes, introduced Hal Holbrook, and two foreign honorary members were inducted. James Levine and Meryl Streep were inducted as honorary members; several dozen awards were given in architecture, art, literature, and music; and there were special awards in the arts, given by various families and foundations.

I could be cutting, as Holbrook's Mark Twain was, but except for the heat and my tight collar, I was mostly happy, even touched, by my award, even though my other machine was at work, the ironic one, and I found myself more and more accessing it, especially when the speeches were boring or unnecessary or the introductions excessive. But, for God's sake, they weren't wearing powdered wigs and red robes, and I'm sure almost everyone carried within him, or her, his or her own bullshit detector and wasn't mistaking either awards or membership as some kind of barometer for artistic excellence (I hope); and the door to the street was open and once a dog poked his head in; and we didn't die from it; and Tony Kushner was there, and Chuck Close and Stephen Sondheim and Marilynne Robinson and Edward Albee, and I actually liked the ritual—the theater—and I must admit I adore medals. And squeezing into his seat just in front of me (no. 39) was Philip Pearlstein, who was my locker-mate in Allderdice High School in Pittsburgh, and we reminisced like two dislocated beavers studying each other for signs of age and still visible signs of youth. He actually didn't recognize me—so much for a painter's eye—but I knew him immediately, and I reminded him of his high school graduation party—on Lilac Street—and the bottle of Schenley we downed, and asked about Dorothy, his wife, whose family owned a wholesale fish business; and we talked fish, art, and houses, but it was brief and we didn't get into children, health, and dreams, nor did I remind him, nor did he ask about, Pat Miller, his classmate at Carnegie-Tech, whom he came to the Carnegie Biennial with in 1949 and whom he introduced me to and whom I married and had two children with and stayed with for twenty-seven years, nor did we talk about Andy who also was with him that night. My memory is that he was sort of courting Pat and warned her against me since I was rough at both the edges and the center, which probably made me attractive to her. But I'm sure his memory is different since Robert Browning reigns supreme, *The Ring and the Book*.

I walked down the steps to get my award after sitting there for almost two hours; hanging on to the chairs, supporting myself on the shoulders of one loving artist after another, musicians, architects, writers, painters. Phil Levine presented me with the award and read the citation. He also kept me away from the microphone with his right arm. I kissed him in front of the three hundred or

more people there, maybe four hundred. I love him, that crazy
Detroiter, and I love his poetry.

There actually was a medal, and as far as I know, it was made
of gold—and not gold plate over something inferior. One side had
a wreath in the center surrounded by the words (on top) "The
American Academy of Arts and Letters" and "Award of Merit" (on
the bottom), in a perfect circle; and on the other side was a figure
of Apollo—with a loose garment hanging uselessly and artistically
over an arm and a shoulder, almost three-dimensional, his right
arm outthrust, holding the hyssop in his hand, his left arm clasp-
ing a small lyre, a wreath in his hair, his left leg forward, his right
leg supported by his (left) toes, standing on a kind of platform,
the sun and the sun's rays rising up beneath him. He is young and
muscular with a small cock hanging down, unobtrusively, and the
words "Opportunity, Inspiration, Achievement" circle the disc. I
don't know if the words come out of an Apollonian tradition or if
they were chosen by the artist, academician Herbert Adams, or if
a committee made the choice. I am happy enough with that Greek
god for I like foreigners, but I don't know if the medal would be
exactly appropriate for a woman, the cock exposed like that. But
why not? Anyhow I don't know when a woman was last chosen
for this honor.

Did I say that Paul Muldoon was sitting on my left (no. 40) and
that he introduced Dan Rhodes (no. 44), an English novelist who
was getting the E. M. Forster Award, and that my friend Peter Cole
(42), who was getting a literature award, was on my right. And, on
Peter's right was Francine du Plessix Gray (no. 43), whom I had
supper with one night many years ago in Rome, and Bruce Smith
(no. 45), dear Peter Everwine (no. 46), and Charles Simic (no. 47). I
blew Meryl Streep (no. 2) a kiss when I was at the podium, which
is as far as I would allow the Tourette's to take me.

There was a certain tedium as the hours wore on, especially

when academicians were giving awards—and speeches—to other academicians, and after a while I began to sneeze from the powdered wigs and the heavy red robes, which hadn't been dry-cleaned for maybe six hundred years; and the other machine was starting to rev up, though quietly since it was well-oiled. This was only the second time I had been at the shindig; the first was in 1980 (I think it was) when Kenneth Burke, another Pittsburgher, got a medal or a kiss or a nod and came on stage wearing a homespun gray suit and house slippers. Let's remember Kenneth Burke, who founded Theory, learned Greek in high school, never went to college, divorced his wife, married her sister, and had wild parties in western New Jersey with the likes of William Carlos Williams and Malcolm Cowley. He was a terrible poet, but his philosophical tracts are priceless. I don't know if he should be forgiven or not for sleeping with Djuna Barnes, but he was a great soul and a true original.

39 Meister Eckhart

I find myself attracted to the teachings of Meister Eckhart, but I realize the impossibility of dealing "quickly" with such a subtle, complex, strange theologian and mystic, speaking and writing in another language from me, in an oddly different century and in an absolutely different culture and religion. And way of thinking and explaining and understanding. Moreover, in this case, as seen through the eyes of an interpreter, Matthew Fox, who has his own ideas on Christianity and whose most famous book is called *Original Blessing* (as opposed, obviously, to "Original Sin"), and whose book (on Eckhart) I blithely reached my left hand out for as if to catch a few truths, which I describe in section 3, whatever page it's on.

Fox describes Eckhart as a theologian whose "this-worldly spirituality went underground (after he was condemned posthumously by a papal decree, the year he died), where it fed many of the most significant movements of Western cultural and intellectual history." He (Fox), in his dedication, calls Eckhart a "creation-centered brother," "exiled for six hundred fifty years." As he praises Eckhart, I don't know if the concepts he describes more properly belong to Fox or to Eckhart, but I tend (from what I've read) to trust Fox, though he is accused of both popularism and new-ageism, and I think I might not like his taste in art.

Essentially, Eckhart (according to Fox) rejects a dualistic Platonism for a nature-based dialectical Aristotelianism, with the inevitable paradoxes of that approach. I think one would have to be a German shoemaker living in Thuringia in 1310 and speaking the local dialect to fully understand Eckhart, or partially, as the case may be. He is full of rich and shocking statements that are poemlike in their simultaneous simplicity and elusiveness.

Eckhart talks of "letting go and letting be." And he says that laughter might be the agency—or basis—of that. He says we should begin eternity now. He is a lover of life, of nature, of animals, of the body, of art, of this life—even of death. He says: "I pray God to rid me of God." He is obsessed with justice, but the way to it is both mystical and social. He is a joyful optimist, yet without illusion. God is in all things; for all we know, God *is* all things. Being is God. If you go into the desert, take a child with you. If you write a big book, have a dog at your side. All creatures are equal. God is a pregnant woman. God is fire. Empty yourself so as to give birth to God. We contain the spark. If we can face the darkness within, we can face the darkness that is God. God is a nameless nothingness. Those things that belong to the intellect are, as such, nonbeing. All deeds that are authentic call up the original deed of creation. We have to learn to be empty if we are to be filled. All things are created from nothing. Outside of God "there is nothing but nothing." If I ask for nothing, then I am asking rightly. We should stand empty and should will nothing. The letting go of all things is the act by which we enter into nothingness. The person who has learned to let go is one without objects in his or her life; even life itself is no longer an object. A good synonym for letting go might be reverence. The detached person is one who is at home in the world of things, who has a new relationship to creatures, who understands them for what they are, who lets them be. Evil is nothing but a defect or shortcoming. No one can take your joy away from you. Deep within us we are not separate—my life is not my life. When I offend another person I offend humanity. Opening up and entering in are but a single moment. If a tree has a thousand leaves, all of them turn their right side to the lightning bolt. All things become nothing but God. The soul loves the body. You can never be better off than when you are completely in darkness and ignorance. From knowledge we must come to a state of ignorance. Darkness can be a means of seeing the light more fully.

We are to become as God is. All things have been drawn from nothingness; that is why their true origin is nothingness. To be silent is to have let go of all images. God was born in nothingness. Birth itself is taking place all the time. Love is between equals! Love is the end of separation. To be in God is to be God. It is in this life that a person is born as a child of God and to eternal life. A word is something that flows out but stays within. As true as it is that God becomes a human, so true is it that humans become God. The spirit is never satisfied. The desert is God. Ecstasy does not allow divisions. The spirit, like water, displaces emptiness. Fire recognizes fire. Where God is, we are. The seventh age is eternal rest. It is a great crime from the livelihood of the poor to increase the luxuries of the powerful. Compassion is the best name for God. Justice is God. True work is ecstasy. There is joy in equality. It is an evil thing that I see under the sun—that a fool is placed in a high position.

I am picking cherries, as I did when I was seven, on the roof of our garage from our neighbor's tree, quickly, in buckets, what was easiest to reach. There are branches that I hate and will not touch. They irritate me and bore me.

You might say I am picking my own grapes, or I am picking *my* grapes. Ones hard to reach, ones I don't want, I don't pick. Strawberries, too, and out of ignorance! Though I am too tired to bend. Too stiff. So is Fox. Is it Fox or is it Eckhart? If it's Fox, then it's Meister Fox. I am pretty much content with that for I was illuminated then. So:

> Come, get together
> Let the dance floor feel your leather,
> Dance as lightly as a feather
> Let yourself go.
>
> Let yourself go, relax
> Let yourself go, relax
>
> You got yourself tied up in a knot,
> The night is cold, but the music's hot
>
> So, come, get together
> Let the dance floor feel your leather,
> Dance as lightly as a feather
> Let yourself go.
>
> – SONG FROM THE '40S

40 Larry Levis, Caravaggio

In "Caravaggio: Swirl and Vortex," Larry Levis, our dead poet, so occupies, so *enacts*, the great Roman painter that he all but becomes him, even as he portrays and reenacts the early 1970s, the inhuman new suburbs of central California and the hideous war in Asia; as well as the early days of the Vietnam Memorial in Washington and the heartbreaking mementos: notes, rings, ribbons, and joints left there. Here is the poem; it's long, but it's beautiful:

Caravaggio: Swirl & Vortex

In the Borghese, Caravaggio, painter of boy whores, street
   punk, exile & murderer,
Left behind his own face in the decapitated, swollen, leaden-
   eyed head of Goliath,
And left the eyelids slightly open, & left on the face of David a
   look of pity

Mingling with disgust. A peach face; a death mask. If you look
   closely you can see
It is the same face, & the boy, murdering the man, is murdering
   his own boyhood,
His robe open & exposing a bare left shoulder. In 1603, it meant
   he was available,

For sale on the street where Ranuccio Tomassoni is falling, &
   Caravaggio,

Puzzled that a man would die so easily, turns & runs.

Wasn't it like this, after all? And this self-portrait, David holding
   him by a lock
Of hair? Couldn't it destroy time if he offered himself up like
   this, empurpled,
Bloated, the crime paid for in advance? To die before one dies,
   & keep painting?

This town, & that town, & exile? I stood there looking at it a
   long time.

A man whose only politics was rage. By 1970, tinted orchards &
   mass graves.

■

The song that closed the Fillmore was "Johnny B. Goode," as
   Garcia played it,
Without regret, the doors closing forever & the whole Haight
   evacuated, as if
Waiting for the touch of the renovator, for the new boutiques
   that would open –

The patina of sunset glinting in the high, dark windows.

Once, I marched & linked arms with other exiles who wished
    to end a war, & . . .
Sometimes, walking in that crowd, I became the crowd, &, for
    that moment, it felt
Like entering the wide swirl & vortex of history. In the end,

Of course, you could either stay & get arrested, or else go home.

In the end, of course, the war finished without us in an empty
    row of horse stalls

Littered with clothing that had been confiscated.

                           ▪

I had a friend in high school who looked like Caravaggio, or
    like Goliath –
Especially when he woke at dawn on someone's couch. (In early
    summer,
In California, half the senior class would skinny-dip & drink
    after midnight

In the unfinished suburb bordering the town, because, in the
    demonstration models,
They finished the pools before the houses sold. . . . Above us,
    the lush stars thickened.)
Two years later, thinking he heard someone call his name, he
    strolled three yards

Off a path & stepped on a land mine.

                           ▪

Time's sovereign. It rides the backs of names cut into marble.
    And to get
Back, one must descend, as if into a mass grave. All along the
    memorial, small
Offerings, letters, a bottle of bourbon, photographs, a joint of
    marijuana slipped

Into a wedding ring. You see, you must descend; it is one of the
   styles
Of Hell. And it takes a while to find the name you might be
   looking for; it is
Meant to take a while. You can touch the names, if you want to.
   You can kiss them,

You can try to tease out some final meaning with your lips.

The boy who was standing next to me said simply: "You can
   cry. . . . It's O.K., here."

                           ■

"Whistlers," is what they called them. A doctor told me who'd
   worked the decks
Of a hospital ship anchored off Seoul. You could tell the ones
   who wouldn't last
By the sound, sometimes high-pitched as a coach's whistle, the
   wind made going

Through them. I didn't believe him at first, & so then he went
   into greater
Detail. . . . Some evenings, after there had been heavy casualties
   & a brisk wind,
He'd stare off a moment & think of a farm in Nebraska, of the
   way wheat

Bent in the wind below a slight rise, & no one around for miles.
   All he wanted,
He told me, after working in such close quarters for twelve
   hours, for sixteen
Hours, was that sudden sensation of spaciousness – wind, & no
   one there.

My friend, Zamora, used to chug warm vodka from the bottle,
   then execute a perfect
Reverse one-&-a-half gainer from the high board into the water.
   Sometimes,
When I think of him, I get confused. Someone is calling to him,
   & then

I'm actually thinking of Caravaggio . . . in his painting. I want to
    go up to it

And close both the eyelids. They are still half open & it seems a
    little obscene

To leave them like that.

The painting is called *David with the Head of Goliath*. The paint-
ings I referred to earlier, in Santa Maria del Popolo (see section
6), were not as gruesome or as personal. The head of Goliath *is*
Caravaggio's head, still frowning, mustachioed, cheeks empurpled
and eyes leaden (as Levis says), while David, holding the head by a
lock of the hair in his left hand, his robe open and his left shoulder
exposed—as it also was in *The Musicians*—telegraphing, according
to Larry, that he was available.

The painting is in the Borghese, as Larry announces at the
beginning. David has a face of sorrow, even pity, as he stares with
half-closed eyes at the severed head. It's our favorite subject of com-
bat, the smaller newcomer unexpectedly defeating the invincible
professional. Jimmy Braddock destroying Max Baer, Billy Conn
almost beating Louis, the (upstart) Americans beating the Russians
in ice hockey at the 1980 Olympics. Not much is said about Goli-
ath. He was either six-foot-seven or nine-foot-six, depending on
the Hebrew letters (numbers). How old he was, how many wives
he had, whether he was past his prime, slow, and living only by
reputation, we don't know. Was David as terrified as Cassius Clay
in his first fight with the murderous Sonny Liston? And what was
it that made Caravaggio identify with the giant?

Larry's poem is about the 1970s and the Vietnam War and the
Vietnam Memorial and the heartbreaking days of high school in
northern California in the early 1960s. The connection with Goli-
ath is the memory of a high school friend who looked like him—

like Caravaggio—when he "woke at dawn on someone's couch" after a night of skinny dipping and drinking. My own connection with Larry—here—is seeing the Caravaggios in the Cerasi Chapel and suddenly remembering Larry's poem and his love of horses, which, in the poem, he refers to only by mentioning the abandoned stables. It's why I so identified Larry with *The Conversion of St. Paul*, where the horse is so prominent, the horse, according to Caravaggio, that Paul was riding when the fit seized him. It is the horse that's most illuminated in the painting, that illumination which Caravaggio used as a technical tour de force but which can also— here and elsewhere—be seen as an example of the divine light that invests itself in material objects and descends upon them lovingly; in this case, as I say, mostly upon the horse. And it's Caravaggio here and elsewhere who is merciless, theatrical, realistic, vulgar, histri- onic, insouciant, emotional, and wildly original. St. Paul lies on his back. He has just been thrown by the horse or else he's fallen during his seizure. His hands are up in the air in a futile attempt to protect himself. Somehow, a servant, or attendant, is calmly restraining the horse by holding the reins in his two hands. The horse is a Pinto, his muscles everywhere, his mane long, one shod foot, the right fore- leg, in the air—as if about to step on Paul. I like it that the horse is Larry, or that Larry is the horse. I certainly wouldn't want him to be the retainer, nor would I want him to be the prone Paul, con- fused among the legs, his shirt rolled up above the elbows, a kind of orange or pumpkin-colored leather vest over the shirt, his eyes almost closed, or appearing to be from the beholder's viewpoint, still overcome by his strange, confusing, unexpected visitation. As is often the case in medieval and Renaissance painting, the horse, albeit agile and powerful, is too small—or the men too large—as if to accommodate its body to the canvas and to emphasize the mad drama. Luckily Larry will be there for many more years, centuries probably, waiting—in the dark—for some tourist from Korea or

New Zealand or Oklahoma to put a coin in the slot in order to add our pathetic electric beam onto the already brilliantly illuminated figures, there forever in their wild struggle.

In Larry's poem, I almost thought the beginning of the last line of the first stanza, "A man whose only politics was rage," might refer to Caravaggio, he who killed Ranuccio Tomassoni in a street brawl and ran. Though it's truly Larry himself, even grammatically, and it lets us move into the main text of the poem, the tinted orchards of California, with their memories and associations, and the mass graves of 1970 and beyond.

The flower children are leaving the Haight, "the song that closed the Fillmore was 'Johnny B. Goode'" ("as Garcia played it, / Without regret,") and the neighborhood is being gentrified, American style, into a hideous, peaceful shopper's paradise. Like an imprint, the memory is there of the war protestors but it was only something to wonder at, to gawk at, for the damage was being done, mercilessly, as we said in our own hysterical poems, and, in a personal note—*his* imprint—Larry tells us that "the war finished without us in an empty row of horse stalls (the divine light gone) // Littered with clothing that had been confiscated." The weapons, the lopped limbs, the ruined minds and broken hearts, we left behind. While that Goliath—his friend Zamora—who "woke at dawn on someone's couch"—a thousand years ago—walked off a path and triggered a land mine when he heard or thought he heard someone calling his name. Caravaggio certainly.

What's left is the Memorial, the one we sighed over and wept at and gave our offerings to—even hopefully—as if we were in a Mexican church. The one Reagan added conventional heroes to, soldiers with bayonets, for to him it was always Iwo Jima.

The last stanza of the poem moves it in an unexpected direction. A doctor is telling Larry about the shells—the whistlers—during the Korean War, where he (the doctor) "worked the decks of a hospital ship anchored off Seoul." "You could tell the ones that wouldn't last / By the sound, sometimes high-pitched, as a coach's whistle, the wind made going / Through them." The doctor too had a memory—a farm in Nebraska, no one around for miles. And the poem ends with his friend Zamora—he is diving from a high board but someone is calling to him and he's Caravaggio—in the painting—and Larry wants to go up to it and close both eyelids for they are "still half open and it seems a little obscene / To leave them like that." Though it's Larry, and he's the horse stepping on St. Saul and he would be sixty-four or five at this writing, June 2010, and I think of him always.

Eggshell

The color of life is an almost pale white robin's green
that once was bluer when it was in the nest,
before the jay deranged the straw and warm flesh
was in the shell. I found it while doing my forty-five
minute walk between two doors beside some
bushes and flowers. I put it in one of my pockets
keeping some space around it to protect
the pale green, an idiot carrying a dead
child inside him, something that may have broken out
anyway, a blue afterbirth, shoved out of the
nest. I lay my dead like eggs on the table,
twelve tombstones to a box. I buried
dread that way, my telephone calls and letters,
and on the way I walked into a side yard
and straightened a brick – for it was May – and chased
a garter snake into his rainspout; and since it was morning
and it was hot already I put the eggshell
under a leather chair and thought of our trip
to New Orleans and used the end of a broom
to prop up a rosebush, the way we do, sweet Larry.

— GERALD STERN

41 Angela Hazley's Death

June 1, 2010, I got a call from Pamela Hazley, Angela Hazley's daughter, that her mother had died the night before, in a hospital in Pittsburgh, from complications following a heart attack just on the day they were going to release her and send her home. Pamela, who is fifty-eight, thought she was calling my ex-wife, Pat Stern. She must have gotten my number from Angela's address book and confused one—hurriedly written—number with another. Angela, I loved so much. Pamela and I talked for twenty minutes, mostly about arteries, valves, procedures, and very little, I now realize, about Angela's last hours, where her mind was, what she expected, what she said, or what was said to her. It would be impossible for me to get to her funeral, yet I wanted to go there, to be with her children whom I knew so well, and her grandchildren. She was the center of a large family who came to her every Saturday night for dinner, as did many of them during the week. She lived in the oldest stone house in Indiana County, Pennsylvania, near an absurd town called Homer City, which I found for her—and Dick—in the mid-1960s when they moved from Slippery Rock, PA, where Dick was teaching at the state college, to Indiana (I.U.P.) to join me where I was teaching after I left Temple University in Philadelphia—in 1962, I think—not quite voluntarily.

Dick, who was a part-time hypnotist as well as an English professor and the head of the state teachers' union, died, or was found dead (in 1995) in a hospital parking lot in one of the small towns in central Pennsylvania where he was putting Bell Telephone employees to sleep or making Westinghouse secretaries howl like wolves or dance the tarantella. He was my closest friend in the late 1940s and early '50s—we were in New York together and Paris and southern France—and his early poems were excellent. Hart Crane and Dylan Thomas were the poets he was closest to. When Pat and I went to

Europe in the early 1950s, I wrote asking him to come over—with
Angela and Pamela—for an extended stay and even offered to lend
him—or give him—the money for it, maybe rent a big house, since
prices were insanely low then in Europe. (We paid seven dollars a
month for a small apartment in Vienna, about fifty cents a night for
a huge room in Florence, near the Duomo, and could eat a decent
meal, cheap wine included, for about twenty cents, also in Flor-
ence.) But he had already bought a sixty-acre dairy farm, near But-
ler, Pennsylvania, and was raising cattle and baling his own grass
as well as working as a foreman at the National Biscuit Company
on Penn Ave in Pittsburgh and selling eggs to the women on the
line. He wrote his poems in an old dairy house, which he had fixed
up as a study, and was planting trees, repairing roofs, and spread-
ing manure in his fields as an alternative to roaming through the
Pitti Palace or staring at Ghiberti's doors; or walking up a steep hill
to smell the apples instead of doing the *passeggiata* at sunset on the
Arno. We wrote each other dozens of letters, and when Pat and I
came back—after three years—with about twenty dollars in our
pocket and I sold handkerchiefs and socks in my father's store in
Detroit as a way of debriefing, we lived with them on the farm till
we accumulated some cash through dumbbell work. Two months
maybe, before we moved into a furnished apartment in Pittsburgh.
While we were on the farm, I'd get up every morning at 5:30 or
6 a.m., shave, put on a suit and tie, and get in the front seat of Dick's
Ford coupe, which smelled of rotten eggs, to make our hour-long
trip into Pittsburgh—where he went to work at Nabisco—then
take a streetcar (no. 73) downtown and sit, and sleep, in the lobby
of the Hotel Henry until it was time to visit the employment agen-
cies or have interviews, week after week. Then go back home with
Dick. We talked poetry, surrounded by eggs and soggy cartons. It
was 1956, and in six months Pat and I would take a train, or bus,
down to Philadelphia for my first college teaching job, at Temple

University. Ginsberg had published *Howl*, the rimesters were leaving the stage, Williams was coming into his own. I was reading Roethke, Lowell, Williams, and Stevens. And the French poets. Trying to ground myself. It was more than ten years after Frost had stayed away from Williams's lecture at Bread Loaf, and advised the fresh meat to do the same since Williams was "no real poet"; and a couple of years later that Williams, in a letter to a student in the Navy V-12 Unit at Middlebury College, would distinguish American, as opposed to English, verse and would acknowledge Pound, his old friend, as an ass and Eliot as a slimy liar. Everyone was hanging onto rocks as the dirt was sliding all around them, just as they're doing now.

Angela cooked meals for us and, after she put Pamela to bed, came downstairs to talk till late at night. She was the glue that held us all together, from the very beginning a caretaker. I thought she was the most beautiful woman I'd ever met. Thin, with thick black hair, and close-set eyes. At college, she had acted and danced. She was graceful, intelligent, and kind—and I think of her that way all through her life. I talked to her every few months and we always negotiated our getting together. Luckily we never lost contact.

We left Indiana in 1967 when I was forty-two years old, the same age as Angela, and after that I only saw her from time to time, when I visited the area or when she and Dick made one, maybe two, trips to see us in Raubsville, Pennsylvania. I remember her house, room by room, as being filled with antique furniture, sofas, beds, corner cupboards, dining room tables, lamps, chairs, rugs, almost all of it collected at sales and local antique stores, the amazing buys we were still able to make in the 1950s and '60s. As I said, it was the oldest house in Indiana County, and there were—discovered by the previous owners—letters from the original settlers describing the Native Americans—I don't know which nation and what the particulars of the history were—burning the crops and cutting down the fruit trees. There was a certain chaos that crept into the house, especially late at night, when inert bodies could be found on daybeds and chairs and sofas. Dick was gone a lot, especially in the spring and early summer, doing his "shows" at fraternity houses and for small companies having their annual celebrations in the bleak half-empty dining rooms of empty hotels in western Pennsylvania, Ohio, and West Virginia, he who would merely shake hands and put people under, a whole stageful reciting, weeping, dancing, hopping for the best—and cruelest—hypnotist in the tri-state area.

Later in life, Angela got involved in flower arrangement, in competitions I think, the sort of activity that in our more cynical moments we males of the liberated sort might make fun of. And, of all things, she opened a bridal shop, a salon, for the virgins of Indiana County and their June transformations. What kept her sane, though, was a certain quiet irony, even a bawdiness, and a merciless tongue. Something that caused confusion in her listeners, especially the unexpected objects of her disdain. But those she loved, and those she cared for, were showered with tenderness and concern. Two things I'll never forget are the pet deer in the kitchen and the circumstances surrounding the 1958 Oldsmobile 88 I gave her son Jonathan. I bought a 1963 Nash Rambler from a friend in 1967 and, rather than junk it, I gave the enormous Oldsmobile (a gift in 1963 from my father) to Jonathan. He was born in 1954, so he was thirteen years old at the time and his brother, Marshall, eleven. The eight-cylinder motor was perfect but the transmission was gone, as well as the shocks, brakes, and electricity. For starters. Jonathan and Marshall built a huge track in a field down from the house and raced the car—at terrifying speeds—by the hour. Angela was furious. And rightly so. The deer (a fawn) was confined, as I recall, to the large kitchen. There were barriers on one side into the dining room and the other into the hall. He—she—walked and slid around on sharp hooves over the stone floor and rested by the huge fireplace. It must have been boring for the poor animal. I once petted and kissed her for a half-hour. Her name was either "My Dear," or "My Deer." I don't know if they took her out on a leash or if she ate and defecated on the spot. The day she escaped she was killed in minutes by a large Mercury nearby on Thompson Road. Which I recounted in a poem. Dick continued to grow flowers and plant trees on the twelve acres, an abandoned railway line running through it on one side—a master of the natural.

It's always surprising how effortlessly (and unexpectedly) death comes, and how indifferent it is to what it leaves in its wake. My own greatest worry is that my passing will cause too much pain to those who love me. I want to, oh, sing for them, so they can weep only at my song; or tell a crazy joke so we can all scream with joy and outrage. For me, the pain and confusion will come from what I'll miss, from losing what I love, for it going on without me. The least the Malachamovitz can do is give me an outline of the rest of this century, though what does he know except for suffocation and flies laying eggs and dogs eating corpses. I suspect that a few great Frenchmen and Germans wondered—with great self-pity and deep concern—how the world would get along without them, but I have great respect for the world and its forgetfulness.

I think the last time I saw Angela was at Pat Stern's eightieth birthday celebration at the Sette Luna, a magnificent Italian restaurant in Easton. She drove down with Pamela and they stayed at the hideous Holiday Inn across the street from the dirty, cholesterol-ridden Golden Arches. There were no shootings the two nights they were there nor did they trip over any diseased and bloody needles. I was planning on visiting her in September (2010) when I was due to read in Pittsburgh. The truth is I'm brokenhearted. Though I'll have someone drive me to Homer City so I can visit the children. I understand she was cremated and her ashes are in an urn on one of the mantles. I hope they'll be scattered soon, but

I don't think so. Dick is out in the fields, maybe underneath one of the walnuts he planted years ago, surrounded by daffodils, under a heavy stone. I'll take a look when I get there.

My Dear

This I learned from Angela, a fawn's
ass has to be clean or he won't shit,
and if there is no mother to lick him, you have
to use toilet paper, lovingly, this way
you become his mother, you get to name him
and get to find him on Johnson Road, a '74
Mercury heating up beside him, the owner
in tears, and you, the mother, consoling *him*
as you both drag the body into the woods
which keeps you calm although your hands are shaking
and you are breathing hard from pushing the one
remaining leg into the ground without
disturbing the bloated stomach or the nose
that wants to stick out of the leaves nor do you
lower the shovel and flatten the ground
for you have babied the universe and you walk
with fear – or care – you walk with care – and wipe
your face with dirt and kiss the murderer.

– GERALD STERN

42 Playing Jacks

It's interesting how excited we were for a while about the disaster in Haiti and how uninterested we are now. It's like an election that totally absorbed us. It was all we could think of, but after a while we couldn't remember the names, not even of the loser but the winner as well. Which year, or decade. Maybe the oil spill in the Gulf takes precedence. Unlike wars, we can only do one disaster at a time. In Haiti maybe, by now, certain things have been set into place. Maybe there's something of a hum in the air or maybe the ex–American presidents are gearing up for something else, protecting the Outer Banks, playing jacks. Certainly every ex-president should be debriefed by renewing his interest in jacks. Imagine the glory of sweeping up those little metal, or plastic, star-shaped objects. What is the game about? Did soldiers play jacks in between slaughtering each other? Were the jacks spelled "jacques"? Were they once made of stone, or dung, or eyeballs? If I went to a toy store, would the jacques be the same, if they actually had jacques? Would they be purple? Would there be illuminated tips? Should I go to Wikipedia? Did the Mongolians do it; or the Japanese?

I'm going to choose "Haitians-at-Fault" as the radical and ultimate Matrix, the Cause. It is more subtle, though, than most race-baiting. It's not that, or not just that, Haitians are ridiculed as "lazy" or "sex-driven," it's their "culture," a safer, and vaguer, word. Even if one pointed out—again—the invasion by Napoleon and the endless debt and the fact that the United States didn't recognize Haiti till 1862, after the southern states had seceded, and before then had interfered in a dozen ways, not to mention after that. The central nightmare is how did a country that was so blessed by forests and by sugar, coffee, and cotton plantations which were the richest in the Americas, and France's richest colony, become so barren and poverty-ridden? Could it just be French management? (Read European, read white.) What if there were Polish, or Hungarian, or Chinese managers, anything but black? Are blacks, at least Haitians, hopelessly self-destructive, shortsighted, ungifted, and corrupt? Ah, we need good theorists to subtly explain all that. Let's not leave it just to the fools and ignoramuses, the Pat Robertsons. If it has to do with defining power—and wisdom—by skin color, then let's call it what it is—white racism. (God, are we in the second grade or the fifth?)

There was a dream, for a moment, that Haiti would remake itself, with the help of Europe and the U.S., perhaps even Canada or Mexico or Brazil. It would decentralize, federalize, replant, be forgiven its debt, be the prime target of aid, the subject of the well-paid economists and social scientists, the special concern of Washington and Paris, given the history. But this is a *forsook* dream from a greed-ridden society that has 20 to 30 percent unemployment among the poor, that can't manage gangs in its cities, that is drug-ridden—in *all* its classes—that fights stupid wars maybe to just get rid of the excess military crap it spends billions to pay for, at the cost of everything productive, useful, and human. That has the permanent disease of hating its own government as well at hating the mind and living in weird myths accompanied by bad food. Maybe Haitians should help *us*.

The *New York Times*, at the end of March 2010, suggested transparency, accountability, and effectiveness at a "donors' conference," where billions were discussed; and a strange thing called Haitian involvement, and self-sufficiency, and tapping the diaspora—doctors, lawyers, teachers—in Brooklyn, Miami, Boston, and Canada; and (the usual) decentralization. It was full of optimism, in spite of Haiti's "tragic history." Of course, the tragic history continues as Haitians are treated differently (still) from Cubans and as they are "detained" (for months) even when they were flown here by American planes.

Naomi Klein suggests that Haiti is not a debtor nation but a creditor one. It should not only get full "forgiveness" of its foreign debts, it should receive reparations and restitution for the devastating consequences of debt. "In this telling," she says, "the whole idea that Haiti is a debtor needs to be abandoned. Haiti is a creditor and it is we in the West who are deeply in arrears." There is first of all the slavery debt, she says. France had three centuries of free—and forced—labor. As late as 2003, President Aristide, while facing a crippling economic embargo, announced that Haiti would sue the French government over its debt. France was concerned and tried to keep the case out of court, but the lawsuit disappeared when Aristide was removed. In addition, the IMF and the World Court were trying to collect money that the Duvaliers had stolen and put in Swiss bank accounts, over $500,000,000, a U.S. District Court in Miami found. Klein says that "even if Haiti does see full debt cancellation, that does not extinguish its right to be compensated for illegal debts already collected."

Maybe Haiti went to Hell under the burden of its debts; maybe the ex-slaves still had a slave's mentality; maybe they just couldn't resist the world's opinion that they were worthless and their work—their lives—were shit. It's called "internalization" (fifth grade), and Klein feels the rich white nations owe them for that. Not to mention the requirements the World Bank and the IMF made on Haiti—to deregulate its economy and slash its public sector still further, presumably to pay the debt. For which failure to comply was met with a punishing embargo from 2001 to 2004, "the death knell," she says, "to Haiti's public sphere." She wants a re-reckoning.

Noam Chomsky feels the West should stop being "benevolent" (read destructive) as they were under U.S. Marine occupation from 1915 (vicious Woodrow) to 1934 (Roosevelt), and they should stop "restoring democracy" (Clinton), which Haiti never had in the first place, and who (the West) shook with terror and whose cold blood turned colder when a president finally was—in 1990—popularly elected (Aristide); and who did what they had to do to undermine him since they were appalled by the election of a populist candidate with a grass-roots constituency just as they had been appalled by the prospect of the hemisphere's first unslaved country on its doorstep two centuries earlier. Under Bush I, Chomsky says, America shifted aid from the legitimate government to "democratic forces," "the wealthy elites and the business sectors," who, "along with the murderers and torturers of the military and paramilitaries had been lauded . . . in Washington for their progress in 'democratic development,' justifying lavish new aid." "The praise came," Chomsky said, "in response to ratification by the Haitian people of a law granting Washington's client killer and torturer, Baby Doc, the authority to suspend the rights of any political party without reasons." The referendum passed by a majority of 99.98 percent and called to mind a 1918 law granting U.S. corporations the right to turn the country into a U.S. plantation after the Haitian parliament was disbanded at gunpoint by Wilson's marines when it refused to accept this "progressive measure." Passed by 99 percent.

It goes on and on. A military junta overthrew the Aristide government after seven months. It accused Aristide of violence. The CIA is involved. Emmanuel Constant, who founded FRAPH, a paramilitary force, lives in Queens. Clinton and Bush II dismissed extradition requests. Clinton undermined the embargo against the junta by authorizing the secret shipment of oil. Clinton sent in the marines—again—to "restore democracy." The news of this was *buried*, American style, in the business section of the *Times*. Aristide had to meet conditions that Clinton imposed in order to return, which he did, in 1994; and which he will do again.

It could take pages. The business class, the corporations, and the "white" elite were favored over the peasants and the urban poor. The rice farmers were forced to turn to agro-export even though Haiti cannot feed itself. Cheap chicken parts from U.S. corporations were dumped, at low prices, onto the market.

Bush II (he was good at jacks) was even worse. He cut off aid and pressured international institutions to do the same. He—they—despised the Aristide government, and every fool was taught (kindergarten) to talk about *his* crimes.

There is no way of knowing what is what. Aristide was (generally) accused of betraying his mission, urging his "bands" to violence, greedily pocketing aid money, manipulating elections, and engaging in drug trafficking and money laundering. He apparently invented it all. Investigators from the new government couldn't prove any allegations, and a court case brought against Aristide was quietly shelved. It's impossible to keep track, either of timeline, interventions, charges, or countercharges. Aristide claims he did not go into exile voluntarily, but was kidnapped by U.S. forces and sent off to Africa. I mean back to Africa. A neat ending.

Do you remember when the Haitians were accused of starting the AIDS epidemic? Boy, do they do it! Anything that walks, especially grasshoppers. Just like the Jews in the Roman slums (Cicero) and the African Americans in the South (and North). If I rant too much, do you want some real ranting? Check out Amos and Hosea, two bad northerners, one of them married to a whore. Of the two, Hosea was better at jacks for he could switch positions more quickly. He probably had Tourette's.

The most famous game of jacks was in 1948 between Harry Truman and Thomas Dewey. I was in a movie house in New York when Truman won and famously held up the newspaper that announced, in huge type, that Dewey had. (It would have been nice with that little moustache and those size 6½ shoes.) Truman was superb in picking up jacks, with either hand, but Dewey didn't seem to have the same quickness, or nimbleness. I liked when Dewey barked out "onesies" and "twosies." There are many variations to jacks, in Korea, Australia, Ireland, and elsewhere. Stones were used in the early days, or knuckle bones from a lamb shank. Sometimes it was played without a ball. The Alabama state legislators passed a law outlawing the use of red balls. They were considering outlawing the game itself since it was discovered that the North Koreans had a version that didn't even have a rubber ball, and in Eritrea they sang a dangerous song while playing it. Something like "Five pieces, ten pieces, two uncles, eight nieces." Un-Christian, if widespread.

The thing I can't understand is that Aristide was a Roman Catholic priest, yet he boarded the plane for Africa with his wife. He must have left the church; or he preferred women to choirboys. I also can't understand why the poor of the world have such a deep connection to chickens.

43 New Zealand Broadsides

A few months ago I met a New Zealand poet and printer named Jim Wilson who lives across the street from Anne Marie—in Lambertville. He prints broadsides in his shop back home and has them sent over. I understand, from a bookseller in town, that he makes his money by printing announcements, programs, and such for musical groups performing in New Zealand. I don't know the particulars, but he seems "enterprising." We meet in the street or getting into our cars or at the local restaurant or coffee shop. He calls me "Mate."

He persuaded me to give him a short poem—for a broadside—and I gave him "Roses" (see section 20). I understood he was going to paste it to the window of the bookstore, and I and a few others might give a low-key reading there, among the books. The reading hasn't taken place yet (June 10), but he's nailed the poem to dozens of telephone poles throughout Lambertville so that wherever I walk I see my poem, and a small photo and bio at the bottom, beautifully printed, on good paper, perfectly hung.

I was embarrassed to be the only one thus displayed, but in the last few days, he's added a few others since there are many telephone poles in my old city, including a posthumous Robert Creeley poem that Creeley's wife gave him. I studied the Creeley poem for a good ten minutes this morning, on the way to the City Market for my coffee, and I was touched, as I was in his last book, how he returned to—or reached—pure simplicity, pure statement, verging on the literal, the prosaic, even the banal, yet making a last-minute leap into the lyric, albeit that last minute was there even from the very beginning. All the time I was waiting for it to happen.

I don't know how Creeley would feel about his poem—and his puss—on every third telephone pole in Lambertville, but I felt embarrassed. I didn't know Jim was going to do that. It was crazy. And it was crazy explaining to the waitresses, the druggist, the librarian, and the gardener that I had nothing to do with it, that it wasn't my idea, that it was just advertisement gone wild, broadsides breeding, reproducing, pinning themselves to telephone poles.

Think of Yeats or Frost—say Heine, say anyone—confronting himself, his labor, his craft, his narrative, his *feelings*, pasted to a pole like that. Think of Jim Wilson thinking of it. And think of his devotion, his love of poetry and his generosity, however merciless the broadsides were.

> *Old Song*
>
> I'm feeling ok still in some small way.
> I've come too far to just go away.
> I wish I could stay here some way.
>
> So now that what comes wouldn't only be more
> of what's to be lost. What's left would still leave more
> to come if one didn't rush to get there.
>
> What's still to say? Your eyes, your hair, your smile,
> your body sweet as fresh air, your voice in the clear morning
> after another night, *another night*, we lay together, sleeping?
>
> If that has to go, it was never here.
> If I know still you're here, then I'm here too
> And love you, *and love you.*
>
> — ROBERT CREELEY

44 Demystification

I believe firmly in demystification. With true demystification it is not even necessary to have anarchy. Furthermore, true demystification does away with hierarchy. Demystification also leads to natural aristocracy. In fact, in demystification no one takes his hat off to anyone, unless it be in true appreciation of a poem or a song or a speech, or a field of flowers or a plate of spaghetti. It's not that spaghetti or a painting of Caravaggio's are the same or that there is the same mystery or *creation* in the two—it's just that one is not holier than the other, a colonel is not holier than a private, a pope is not holier than a parish priest, for we are all vicars. The shammes (the sexton) is one of the community of ten (the minyan), a nobody—like the rest—for the rest are also nobodies. (Dentist to lawyer, pointing to shammes: look who's being a "nobody.") And it's beautiful that women can now be nobodies.

> Oh, I'd rather be a private
> than a colonel in the army.
> A private has more fun
> when his day's work is done.
> On all his hikes,
> every town he strikes,
> girls discover him
> and just smother him
> with things he likes –
>
> (*slow*) But when the colonel passes by,
> the girlies act so shy,
> he holds his head so high
> with dignity,
> soooo
>
> Would you rather be a colonel with an eagle on your shoulder
> or a private with a chicken on your knee?
>
> — WORLD WAR I SONG

It's hard to explain it in prose and make it convincing or even understandable. I want to say that all great art is antihierarchical but I'm not sure. Certainly the more realistic the details and the more painful the suffering, the more the myth was, is, believable.

One almost believes Adam and Eve were exiled when you walk into the church of Santa Maria del Carmine and see the Masaccio. These are two humans, more earthy than ever before, mourning inconsolably the life they lost and the unknown empty one that lies ahead. Critics refer to the *technique* of the artist, his craft, and where it might have come from and how it developed; but what about the painter's heart—and mind? Did one cause the other or the other the one, or are they one and the same? We don't care about the Jewish Book of Origin, called Genesis, and we stop for a minute the argument between the priests and the anthropologists and archaeologists, who are standing themselves in wonder staring at the painting, tears coming down their own stricken faces, their hands covering their genitals, all mystification gone. One thinks of the cave art that Anne Marie is writing about, the animals—those horses and deer—so perfectly reimagined, so amazingly crafted, that anyone's breath is caught short. They are locked in mystery but are, at the same time, demystified. They are what they are and the wonder of it is endless, but the animals, and the artists, neither inflict, cajole, nor attribute. We can't paint like that, Picasso is said to have said; that is, we can't imagine—perhaps we can't experience—life like that, life as they did; the eagerness, the liveliness, the *holiness*, caught by those amazing hands, and minds. We have probably lost it forever.

I'm going crazy now over the Gilgamesh epic. I'm reading and rereading. There are huge tablets on my walls. My backyard is covered in indecipherable stones. I have a finger and I have a wand. I am chanting in Sumerian. I stroke Humbaba's poor head. He is weeping over his lost neck. I say the names of the gods. I suddenly realize why Yahweh doesn't want his secret name pronounced. It is too foreign, too long, too unpronounceable. Rappers call him "Yo." I call him God because I speak English now. But not God with the middle letter cast out. That's for the rabbis in Princeton and West Oak Lane. They like mystification. Certainly there is obscurantism and confusion in the Gilgamesh narrative. It could be because pieces are missing or that the minds then were different than now, though I doubt it; and there's plenty of talking to one or another of the gods, and concealment and magic and secret power, not to mention oppression, privilege, and violence; but the core feeling, the heart of the epic, is grief, as it was in "The Expulsion" and as it will be in the epics to come, *The Iliad, The Odyssey, The Aeneid,* Job, *Finnegans Wake.* It is—in *Gilgamesh*—that grief, grief over the loss of a beloved companion and grief over the inevitability of death and grief at human loss from stupidity and forgetfulness that comes to dominate, a grief that is unbearable, as it will be in *Lear* and, as in *Lear,* tied to an otherwise sensational, or flimsy, narrative. We are left with basic human loneliness—nakedness— and nothing in the way of sophistry, obscurity, or concealment works in the face of that. The president in his oval office, G–d on his mountain, a movie star or millionaire dying—how could they compare? There's nothing left but heresy and ungodliness. In our literatures, Kafka—and Beckett. I think it's in *Malone Dies* that Beckett's creature is in a kind of prison or hospital. As I recall, he is visited twice a day, slop brought in and slop taken out. He has a stub of a pencil, a bit of paper. And he asks questions, ten, seven, I don't remember. "Why am I here?" "What day is it?" The last one, no. 10 maybe, says "Number your answers." That is not just desperation and clinging to something called "reason"—by his fingertips—that is humanity, shit-smeared, hopeless, and mad humanity—in the face of all denial. Our work is about that. My work.

Baruch Spinoza was surrounded by "friends" who were shocked that he didn't believe in Jesus's resurrection or Lazarus's awakening. His tongue was sharp and what he hated most were "the shackled minds of zealots." When they talked to him about miracles, this is what he said: "This I believe is the reason why Christians are

distinguished from other people not by faith, nor charity, nor the
other fruits of the Holy Spirit, but solely by an opinion they hold,
namely because, as they all do, they rest their case simply on mir-
acles, that is, on ignorance, which is the source of all wickedness."
Spinoza also rejected claims to Jesus's supernaturalism. "As to the
additional teaching of certain doctrines, that God took upon him-
self human nature [in Christ], I have expressly indicated that I do
not understand what they say. Indeed, to tell the truth, they seem
to me to speak no less absurdly than one who might tell me that a
circle has taken on the nature of a square." Unquestionably he was
thinking of his own excommunication in Amsterdam in 1656, "for
not believing in angels, the immortality of the soul, and the divine
inspiration of the Torah; and other not-named abominable her-
esies practiced and taught by him; and for committing monstrous
acts." There was anathema and cursing and someone played with
the lights—for mystification's sake. As to his resort to "reason" and
his "intellectual love of God," he was, in his demystifying mode,
letting a thousand dogs loose, not housing them. I love using my
college textbook *History of Philosophy*—after sixty-five years—by
Frank Thilly. I guess Spinoza believed that God is everything and
everything is God, only he used the word *God* for convenience's
sake since there's no other word for it. Certainly he didn't believe
God was a person or there was a person called God who, for exam-
ple, punished or rewarded you according to your behavior or for
behaving in a certain way, say leaning more to the left or to the
right. God had—God has—no consciousness, as humans under-
stand that word. Prayer may be useful psychologically—it is—but
it is probably useless otherwise. It is surely useless, he might say,
geometrically. In his letters, Spinoza rejects the identification of
God with nature, whatever he meant by nature, but he did say that
God and the universe are one; and the *Cambridge Dictionary of Phi-
losophy* emphasizes nature as being the same as "God" when it dis-

cusses Spinoza's metaphysics and his theology. I could see how one could argue that Spinoza replaces one mystification with another, given his unusual radical nouveau system, but he is not interested in using it or having it be used to force, or persuade, anyone to do or not do anything. One may see a certain coldness or heartlessness in his approach or even a naïveté in his trust of the intellect and his presumed expectation of its fairly widespread use, but that's an optimistic sin, or a sin of optimism, and anyhow it's "determined" or, as the Presbyters say, predetermined, or as the modern philos say, necessitarian. I am touched by his mode of living, an enviable "attribute" of simplicity and dignity that almost looks like wisdom. He ate only porridge, with a few dried grapes, twice a day, and probably would have slept on the floor if it didn't cause too much attention. What excites me about him is not his devotion to reason (seventeenth century) or even his love of the spirit (nineteenth century), but his vision of interconnectedness, infinity, and unity, which shows an anticipation of twentieth-century thought—in physics and elsewhere—as well as an echo of the medieval mystics, Jewish, Christian, and Muslim, a connection with Kabbalah, a reflection of the thinking of Maimonides as well as Averroes, and an amazing connection to—a parallel thinking with—the Vedas. He who would have fixed my watch with his enlarged eye so perfectly attuned to his crystal mind, my watch that fell who knows when, dislodging the perfect innard and jarring the circular outer, so that it wouldn't stay and I had to bring it back to my jeweler who restored it for me and charged thirty-two dollars.

I believe human beings should pay very close attention to each other. They should reach out beyond the family and help the oppressed, the trapped, and the sick. They should insist on security for and from the larger society. They should pay attention to the past, live with grief, make charity personal, teach without end, share food, listen patiently to the young and honor their music, turn their backs on corporations, advertising, and public lying, hate liars, undermine bullies, love June 21, and, on that day, kiss every plant and tree they see. They should love two-lane highways, old cars and old songs. They should eat with relish, and study insects. They should never stop raising children. They should fight for schoolteachers, *pay them*, give them tenure, let *them* make the rules. As Coca-Cola does. They should insist that no one be paid more than ten times anyone else, no matter what or where. They should make fun of war, flags, uniforms, weapons, pulpits, oval offices, square ones, oblong ones, circular ones; and robes, and titles, especially the titles of "Dr." given to education degree holders in state colleges who address each other as "Doctor." They should respect all dogs, love one breed intensely, eat fruit, eat root vegetables, read *Lear* endlessly, and be suspicious of Gertrude Stein—with the exception of her war plays. They should love New York, know two foreign languages, practice both regret and remorse, love their own cities, forgive but not forget, live in at least three countries, work in a gas station, lift boxes, eat pears, learn a trade, respect pitch pines, believe in the soul. They should stop throwing rubbish out the window, they should sit on park benches, marry young, marry late, love seals, love cows, talk to apes, weep for tigers, cheer on the carp, encourage the salmon and the shad, and read twenty books a year. They should talk to their neighbors and eat herring and boiled potatoes.

— NIGHT OF DECEMBER 17, 2009, I A.M.

45 Remorse, Gilgamesh

Hank Evans, one of my college presidents, had a photograph in the hallway of his house in Bernardsville, New Jersey, of himself in a World War II pursuit ship, a P-38, with his two thumbs, as I recall, on the machine gun buttons that, with the slightest pressure, some maneuvering, and some luck, would destroy a German—or a Japanese—bomber, or fighter, in a second or two and, as he ascended into the sun, (he) could see—through his thick, curved goggles—the fiery enemy plane descend, with increasing crescendo into some ocean or forest below in a great crash.

I knew him twenty-five years after the goggles when he presided over a community college in New Jersey, and I was fighting him and his deans and the board as head of the English Department, head of the union, wrecker-in-general and chief enlightener for students, faculty, community, and, as it turned out, the state of New Jersey for a period of four to five years when community colleges were being established—and defined—in the late 1960s and early '70s.

I was the enemy supreme and those were the glory days, what with the cities recently on fire and the whole country in a heightened state because of civil rights and Vietnam and the new radicalism (from the left) and the sickly righteousness (from the right). I made speeches at the public board meetings that were printed verbatim in the newspapers, angry people pounded tables, wept, screamed, and, on one occasion, students pelted the board, seated at a long table in front, with marshmallows as an act of local theater—which of course had the desired effect, left and right thumb on the guns, and crazed laughing students crashing into the water.

I make it sound like a war and it was a little war, though the stakes were ridiculously small and local, if madly symbolic. There were three of us who basically ran the school, or at least decided what and where the battles would be. The other two, the registrar and a computer science teacher, were forced out, but when it was my turn the student body, small at the time, held the school hostage for a while till the board relented, someone shouting uncle somewhere. I was writing all the time since I essentially had two heads, but after a while I got bored with the political one and let the other take over. More than a couple of administrators went, including Hank Evans, but this narrative is not about the joy of vengeance at all, but about pathos, sorrow and regret, and of knowledge over violence.

By my calculations, Hank was born in the period 1915 to 1918, so he was in his middle or late fifties when he became president of what was originally called Somerset County College but is now Raritan, and close to sixty when he ended his brief career as a college president and found a job teaching English in a small private school in North Carolina. The stakes are so low, they're ridiculous. Hank was, I believe, an assistant registrar at Rutgers University when he was hired at Somerset. He may have looked the part or had some pull, but there he suddenly was. Not that all college presidents, ivy or weed, are not foolish in their big offices and with their self-importance—and high salaries. Maybe you need such a small place for clarity. Groucho understood this; Berkeley and Harvard are not much different than Dubois State or the University of Southwest Alabama. The same probably applies to kingdoms and republics. See Groucho again.

I was on a hugely reduced load by the mid-1970s and taking time off to teach writing at Sarah Lawrence and Columbia. In a few years I would give up, go to Iowa to live with the pigs and the bright young writers and stay there, one foot always elsewhere, for the next fifteen or so years. Hank, as I say, was teaching in a private school somewhere in North Carolina. I think of him working his way through *Silas Marner* and *Julius Caesar*, or marking blue books. For all I know he had dorm duties and had to sit at the head of a small table, and bow his head before eating the bad food. It was in the late 1970s when his letters started to arrive, handwritten, hard to read, almost scribbled—page after numbered page, stuffed clumsily into a small bulky envelope. They were an attempt to explain his former situation, to apologize, and to try to reach some kind of understanding with me. As much as anything else, they were a kind of confession—to himself, to God maybe, to the world, as it were, through me, as if I were some kind of confessor and had the power to forgive and bless; but also, since I was, as he saw me, apparently the only person he could "confess" to, and who, as he saw it, the only one who might listen—and understand. It was a strange reaching out, he a right-wing, pro-war Republican and privileged Wasp; me, an anti-war, half-nihilist, card-carrying Jewish activist. And poet. Yet he saw me—and rightly so, I think—as sympathetic and forgiving, across class lines even. I actually liked him, and saw his human side. He was better than his dumb beliefs. And I realized how much he depended on me and on my response to his letters. I was also touched that he appreciated—where he was then—my position and even the metaphoric activity I and my friends engaged in. There may have been three or four exchanges. I had my difficulties with the language and even with the grammar (in his letters), English teacher that I was, but I was surprised by his understanding, his openness, and his gracefulness, almost a kind of modesty or humility. For my part I tried to arrive at a place where we could honestly communicate, and I tried not to lecture or be patronizing. It was very hard work for both of us, and I think we both benefited. I also think we arrived somewhere, or partially arrived, at a place that was beyond the crises and the politics of the times, though there were many sore moments. Looking at it now, I realize we were writing from *different* places, even with different "agendas." But the truth was we were *both* asking forgiveness, in our clumsy ways. I remember once eating dinner at his house where it was agreed we would not discuss politics. I remember the three-martini lunches, as I remember his stiff white shirts, his cuff links, and his red face. And I remember his dream of freedom: two weeks in a Maine farmhouse, a creaky bed, a bare bulb in the ceiling, sticky fly paper loaded with stinking dead flies, swollen windows, miles of new growth. The Wasps called it "camping out." Different from *kuch allein*, in the Catskills, or the Imperial Hotel in old Atlantic City on a run-down street, the halls smelling of sulfur. He was certainly sentimental, and my radical friends, then and now, would be merciless with me, sentimentality the least of it.

For a reason that wasn't altogether clear to me I was suffering from regret—or remorse. I sometimes go in that direction from merely drowning an insect in my sink, but this was a man, one of my species, red face or not, stubborn thumbs or no, trying to account. Spinoza says it's absolutely futile and a waste of time. Gilgamesh, who wants to live forever, seeks help from Utnapishtim, the wisest man on earth, who at the urging of his wife tells Gilgamesh of the plant of rejuvenation. Gilgamesh retrieves it from "the watery depth," but a snake eats the plant while Gilgamesh is bathing in a pond. Gilgamesh's remorse is pure, and absolute.

Hank died of a heart attack at sixty-four or sixty-five, in the early 1980s. I don't know where he was buried and who came to the funeral, but it's refreshing to think of that burdened soul and to think, at the same time, of Gilgamesh and *his* downfall—his agony over the lost plant; his vain labor; his mistakes; he who flung away his tools, who abandoned his boat to bathe in the cool water—in some way or other. Ridiculous, I know.

> Thereupon Gilgamesh sat down weeping,
> His tears flowed down his face,
> He said to Ur-Shanabi the boat man:
>
>> For whom Ur-Shanabi have my hands been toiling?
>> For whom has my heart's blood been poured out?
>> For myself I have obtained no benefit,
>> I have done a good deed for a reptile!
>
> — THE EPIC OF GILGAMESH, TABLET XI,
>   TRANS. BENJAMIN R. FOSTER

46 Etheridge Knight

At our low-residency MFA program at Drew University, Aracelis Girmay, a young and gifted poet, prefaced the reading of her own poems with a short poem by Etheridge Knight called "Genesis." The poem was italicized and presumably served as a kind of introduction in *his* book, *The Essential Etheridge Knight,* to the ninety-two poems that followed.

This provoked some discussion here and there among our community of poets and pushed me to remember Etheridge and the times we were together. I think Jim Wright, Galway Kinnell, and Dave Ignatow were the poets who most connected with him when he was in prison. Bly too—and I met him a year or two later, probably in Philadelphia or at a reading or gathering nearby. There is a brief biographic summing up in the book jacket of his Houghton Mifflin book, published in 1980 and called *Born of a Woman.* "Etheridge Knight," it says, "began writing poetry as an inmate in the Indiana State Prison during the early 1960s. His frank and powerful poems," it says, "depict the fractured lives of black men and women in a divided society, beset by drug addiction—as he was—by violence among themselves, and by conflict with a hostile system." A little patronizing and distant. He was born in Mississippi in 1931 and lived, when the book came out, in Memphis, where he was conducting a Free People's Poetry Workshop. He died in 1991 of cancer in Indianapolis. As I understand it, he got the habit—morphine, then heroine—as he was being treated for injuries—wounds—suffered during the Korean War. He was a medical technician and may have had access at first that way. As he tells it, he robbed a gas station, later, to get some money. I never knew all the details. I knew he was locked up for six years, but what his trial was like, how he was caught, when he started to write, and if he wrote before he went to prison, I don't know. What it was like in high school, say, who his first teacher was. I suspect I didn't want to intrude, or I was more interested in the poems themselves, or was satisfied by that. I know Gwendolyn Brooks was an early supporter and wrote the preface to his *Poems from Prison*. I spent many hours with him but never asked him about that friendship. I remember now that he often stayed with Eleanor Wilner and her husband, Bob Weinberg, on 6th Street in Center City, Philadelphia, and I now think I met him at her house. At the time, Eleanor was an editor of *American Poetry Review* and was a strong supporter of my poetry—as she was of Etheridge's. All he says about it is "I died in Korea from a shrapnel wound and narcotics resurrected me. I died in 1960 from a prison sentence and poetry brought me back to life." In the acknowledgment page of *Born of a Woman*, he invoked the names of the men and women who helped him. The ones I recognize are Robert Weinberg, Eleanor Wilner, Audre Lorde, Sonia Sanchez (his first wife), Judy Ray, Dennis Brutus, Gwendolyn Brooks, Haki Madhubuti, Mary McNally (his second wife), Donald Hall, Alice Walker, Galway Kinnell, Judith Minty, Dudley Randall, and Charlene Blackburn (his third wife).

Maxine Kumin was visiting Drew Thursday and Friday, June 25–26, 2010. She read her angry anti-war, anti-torture, and anti-lying poems at her reading and mentioned that Dick Wilbur admonished her for writing "polemical" poems. It's boring when poets tell others to write like them, and inappropriate. Etheridge never wrote one word that was not grounded in a political situation or that was not grounded in his state of being a black man from Mississippi, a convict, a prisoner, and, from a Caucasian point of view, a stranger. I think of his poem "A Conversation with Myself," in which he is sitting on the abutment of a small bridge in Missouri, hitchhiking north of the "hi / ways // where farmers // fondle their guns"—white farmers certainly and a white cop cruising by and slowing down to look in his rearview mirror and Etheridge wondering what the hell he's doing there and dreaming of Harlem. Too personal, too political, too plain, of course, though we all know what could have happened. I loved—and love—his work because of the overwhelming passion, the variety of form, and the exact appropriateness of the language. I almost didn't realize the nervousness, the "calm hysteria" of the poems, their unity of voice, and their overwhelming political stance. It's almost as if the poet—and his poems—were so grounded, so authentic, that I took that stance for granted. Thus spoke Etheridge; thus *was* Etheridge. I almost took for granted the magnificent art.

A Conversation with Myself

What am I
           doing here
in these missouri hills
hitch / hiking these hi / ways
                     where farmers
fondle their guns
and eye my back
the cars zoom by
                zoom zoom zoom
and disappear around the bend
I sit
on the abutment of a small bridge
and wait
          reading mari evans' book
below me a brook gurgles along
a field of corn, green, waving in the wind
five cows stand swishing their tails
                          in the shade
                          of three cedars
a hi / way cop passes
                 and
                      slows down

peering in his rear / view mirror
I clutch
    I am a Black Woman
                like
a security blanket
I turn and show my teeth
             and
                 the book
the cop gasses the engine
             and disappears
             I scramble
                   down
under the bridge
             and pee in the water
what am I
        doing here
in these missouri hills
wish
I was / up / in harlem
where
I could talk *bad.*

Even his love poems were political, though I realize it was "anti-war" Wilbur was talking about. But what he said was "polemical," as Maxine reported. Here is Etheridge's famous poem, "Feeling Fucked Up":

Lord she's gone done left me done packed / up and split
and I with no way to make her
come back and everywhere the world is bare
bright bone white   crystal sand glistens
dope death dead dying and jiving drove
her away made her take her laughter and her smiles
and her softness and her midnight sighs —

Fuck Coltrane and music and clouds drifting in the sky
fuck the sea and trees and the sky and birds
and alligators and all the animals that roam the earth

fuck marx and mao fuck fidel and nkrumah and
democracy and communism fuck smack and pot
and red ripe tomatoes fuck joseph fuck mary fuck
god jesus and all the disciples fuck fanon nixon
and malcolm fuck the revolution fuck freedom fuck
the whole muthafucking thing
all i want now is my woman back
so my soul can sing

It is the wildness, the heresy, and extreme madness of the sec-
ond stanza that transforms the poem from what would have been
a simple, and good, poem of confession and regret into a supreme
curse, where everything he holds, or once held, dear, is dumped
into the river of loss, dross, waste, and nothingness as an extended
metaphor for the loss of his beloved.

He is given much to self-examination and self-blame.

Welcome back, Mr. K: Love of My Life
How's your pocket / book problem? – your / being
broke problem? you still owe and borrowing mo'
25 dollar problems from other / po / poets?
Welcome back, Mr. K: Love of My Life.
How's your ex-convict problem? – your John Birch
Problem? – your preacher problem? – your fat
Priests sitting in your / chair, saying
How racist and sexist they / will / forever / be
Problem? – How's your Daniel Moynihan
Problem? – your crime in the streets, runaway
Daddy, Black men with dark shades
And bulging crotches problem?
How's your nixon-agnew – j. edgar hoover
Problem? – you still paranoid? still schizoid? –
Still scared shitless?
How's your bullet-thru-the-brain problem? – or
A needle-in-your-arm problem?

– FROM "WELCOME BACK, MR. KNIGHT: LOVE OF MY LIFE"

what now
what now dumb nigger damn near dead
what now
now that you won't dance
behind the pale white doors of death
what now   is   to be
to be what you wanna be
or what white / america wants you to be
a lame crawling from nickel bag to nickel bag

– FROM "ANOTHER POEM FOR ME"

Though essentially he was a prison poet, a man locked up behind
stone and iron. Like Hikmet. Poem after poem after poem. I could
name them now, from memory, "For Freckle-Faced Gerald," "He
Sees Through Stone," "Cell Song," "Hard Rock." Nor did any
other prison poet love more the large and beautiful world he came
into after he was freed. Nor did any other poet of plain speech
appreciate as much the gifts of nature and friendship he received.
Nor was anyone more grateful.

What strikes me now, as I reread him after more than a few
years, is that he was not an anti-war poet, as such, given the fact that
that's where we got started. There is a passing reference or two to
Vietnam and a cunning understanding of power and inhumanity,
but he doesn't write either of Korea or Vietnam directly, the mur-
der, the stupidity, the madness, the waste, the cruelty. This is not
to criticize him—but I should have talked with him about it when
we had the chance. One thing leads to another and what started off
as a short introductory poem at a reading by Aracelis Girmay and a
criticism of Maxine Kumin's anti-torture poems led to a recollec-
tion of dear Etheridge. I wonder what Wilbur thought of Etheridge
and I wonder if he read him. I am sure he did. I want to say that I
didn't always agree with Etheridge's political take. The poem on
Idi Amin, for example—no friend of mine, that hippopotamus,

that cannibal. I heard he ran a bowling alley in Saudi Arabia some-where after he "took refuge." But I love "Poem for the Liberation of Southern Africa" and "On Watching Politicians Perform at Martin Luther King's Funeral," and the Lightnin' Hopkins poem and the poem for Malcolm.

I used to have an idea about Etheridge's language. Though when you talk about language you talk about signals and states of the mind, and of the heart. I thought he was closest to the Provençal poets, that in spite of the bitterness, the anger, and the sadness, he was a poet of spring and exquisite exact and tender language. I can find no American source for him—or English. Should I say Burns? The truth is that it was not a narrative of self but a self allowed to exist in its mythical face, or that it was two things at once. Can you bear the tenderness of "A Poem to Galway Kinnell"?

> Saturday, April 26, 1973
> Jefferson, Missouri 65101
> (500 yards, as the crow flies,
> from where I am writing you
> this letter, lies the Missouri
> State Prison – it lies, the prison,
> like an overfed bear alongside
> the raging missouri river –
> the pale prison, out of which,
> sonny liston, with clenched fist,
> fought his way, out of which,
> james earl ray ripped his way
> into the hearts of us all . . .)

dear galway,
        it is flooding here, in missouri,
the lowlands are all under water and at night
the lights dance on the dark water,
our president, of late of watergate,
is spozed to fly above the flooded areas
and estimate how much damage has been done
to THE PEOPLES . . .

dear galway,
        it is lonely here, and sometimes,
THE PEOPLES can be a bitch

dear galway,
        i hear poems in my head
as the wind blows in your hair
and the young brown girl
with the toothpaste smile
who flows freely because she has heard OUR SOUNDS . . .

dear galway,
        OUR SONGS OF LOVE are still
murmurs among these melodies of madness . . .
dear galway, and what the fuck are the irish doing /
and when the IRA sends JUST ONE, just one soldier
to fight with say the American Indians, then i'll believe
them . . .

dear galway,
        the river is rising here, and i am
scared and lonely . . .

Mary and the children send their love
to you and yours

        always

        Etheridge Knight

Ah, if Oppen had not separated his two lives. If the oppression had only been his subject. Is that presumptuous?

May I tell two stories, though I know fifteen or more? The first is about Etheridge, at least in part. I was on a two-day visit to Allentown College—in eastern Pennsylvania—that included a reading of my poems on Friday night and the organization and oversight of a Saturday convocation of over a hundred high school students. I had to meet the students on Saturday morning, inspire them and assign them to small groups, then meet them after lunch to say goodbye. I spoke to them—in the morning—about the legitimacy

and authenticity of their own language and experience as the basis
of poetry and opened up an anthology to—randomly—read them
a poem. I read one by Heather McHugh about her mother washing
her mouth out with soap for saying the "c" word and while I was at
it, I read, in the same collection, "Feeling Fucked Up." Half-way
through I realized I was going to be cursing Mary, Joseph, and Jesus
(in a Catholic College), but out of loyalty to poetry I couldn't stop.
When I finished the students, at least the boys, leaped up onto the
tables, threw their fists into the air and shouted, "right on." When
we reconvened the mothers and teachers weren't there. They were
in another room talking to the president of the college about me—
but he defended me. He said, "Mr. Stern is a very religious man."
And I got my check.

I either shared the stage or gave the stage to Etheridge a dozen
times. In Easton, Pittsburgh, Philadelphia, New Brunswick, New
York, and Iowa. When word got to us that his lung cancer had
metastasized and that he was dying of brain cancer, I emptied our
small treasury and invited him to come to Iowa City. He was deeply
distressed but otherwise altogether himself. He ate at my house
instead of at a restaurant, and his memory, as always, was keen—
extraordinary. He asked after my children by name and recalled the
meals that Pat had made down to the smallest detail. I had always
been amazed by his deep intelligence, his power of recall, his gift
of connecting things—his metaphorical mind. At this point we
could talk like two ghosts remembering and forgiving each other,
but not quite the world. We were ghosts with muddy shoes and
stained shirts.

I love his poems, but I think I didn't quite realize then how great
a poet he was. And the shame and waste and confusion he experi-
enced maybe prevented him from realizing it himself. I am honored
to have known him. My respect and appreciation grows only more
and more. That king of the hill, in overalls.

To Make a Poem in Prison

It is hard
To make a poem in prison.
The air lends itself not
to the singer.
The seasons creep by unseen
And spark no fresh fires.

Soft words are rare, and drunk drunk
Against the clang of keys;
Wide eyes stare fat zeroes
And plead only for pity.

But pity is not for the poet;
Yet poems must be primed.
Here is not even sadness for singing,
Not even a beautiful rage rage,
No birds are winging. The air
Is empty of laughter. And love?
Why, love has flown,
Love has gone to glitten.

47 Pruning Hooks

The truth is, I hate being a scoffer, a skeptic, and an agnostic. What the hell do I know about Lambs, or anything else? Let someone lean against a wall and howl, if it's her religion. Let biographers twist facts (whatever those are) or let people talk in tongues, their own or someone else's. Let fat men live a little. Let dogs, when they are old, shake, shiver, whine, and bleed when they shit. Let priests wash my feet; let me wash yours. Let me piss on theirs.

Let me consider this life, now that I've lived eight decades. Let me consider whether or not it's an illusion. Let me sit down and read the thirty-two journals that are scattered in three of my seven rooms. Six, to be more exact. Let me bless the one room where the journals are missing. Let me say the names and scorn the third lines, for it's the third line that is most culpable, that, ah, gives it away, that rips the veil and haunts the soul. If I had the time I'd read you the third line of one hundred poems. Next project: an anthology of the third line of one hundred famous poems. If I had the time, I'd tell you about my talk, brief as it was, with Chris Hedges today. I called him at 11 a.m. and he answered at 8 a.m. He was in Oakland, California. He was, he told me, at a convention of the Socialist Party. The decaffeinated Tea Party.

Anne Marie's son, Jeremy, was a freshman at Hampshire College for no more than three weeks when she tried to phone him, but he couldn't talk because he was in New York at a meeting of the World Socialists at Columbia University. Dear Jeremy and ah, Columbia, that drives out old people and poor people from its "properties," and who destroys neighborhoods as it expands into higher regions. With all my heart I love lower regions and smaller ones and quirky ones and bastard ones and throwback and useless ones, stumbling block that I am. I'll join the Socialist Party (if they'll have me) when they address themselves to the subject. After all, if I'm anything I'm a socialist. The Republicans are lower than dog shit, not to mention that in all things save lying, they are utterly stupid. By stupid I mean stupid. Think sea level. Democrats are better by far but every one of them carries either a blunt dagger or a small vial of poison to self-destruct when the time is ripe. Though my congressman, Rush Holt, is a concerned, brilliant, deeply honest man. I actually gave money, I actually read poetry, at social gatherings in private houses. I actually went down to Washington to read for him at one of his reelections. A busload of people came to cheer him on. I met Nancy Pelosi there, and John Lewis. I felt like Walt tipping my hat to the president. Except that president was playing jacks.

Even if it's beating a dead dragonfly, I have to remind us (you and me) how much of the gross we spend on the tools for mass murder and that it doesn't matter a splinter's ass which party. But there's a reason for this. It's to prevent the teachers from taking over. For if we had more gross we'd probably pay them more, and before you could say Charles Lindbergh or wrong-way Corrigan, they would not only be buying the biggest cars but actually swimming in their own pools. Isaiah the pacifist is an enemy of America. Anyone who's read my poem "I" knows that Isaiah spent his time playing his own chess game with the salt and pepper shakers and that he drank blood from his own arm (believe it, oh Jews!), that he spilled his coffee (at the Cosmos Diner), that he was berserk; that he walked on his hands, that he was a little like Cervantes and thought of his fork as a sword and screamed like a woman in labor (see King James). Also that he made a sound like a walrus hungry for halibut and that he made his famous walrus sound at the cash register. But he did love pruning hooks.

As it turned out, no one listened to me when I said McChrystal should be demoted to corporal. He was allowed to keep all four stars, which makes him a hot number on the Potomac. In a little while, he can work for some "defense" contractor, hauling in huge bucks. They used to have barkers on Orchard Street with hooks in their hands to pull in customers. In Tel Aviv they sing their wares in the market. In Amsterdam, they sit in the windows, all berouged and undressed. Of course, the McChrystal was crushed. He was humiliated, "At some point he will make peace with himself," and "move on," some bedecked ostrich in D.C. said. A real psychologist. If he had been made to retire with only three stars it would have sent a signal that he wasn't in favor and wouldn't get a hook. The poor man, who is fifty-five, will receive 85 percent of the base pay of a four-star general, which, with thirty-four years of active service, comes to $181,416. Had he retired as a three-star hooker, it would have only been $160,068. Keep in mind that, in Iraq, he oversaw secret commando operations and aggressively pushed his troops (short hookers) to kill "insurgents." No question that he will be a well-paid consultant, with a giant hook, either in the Pentagon or some government intelligence agency. "Stan will land on both feet, make no mistake about that," one of the bedecked said. He might end up on a stamp—instead of Joe Louis. We could show our appreciation by licking him, over and over. He loves to be licked.

We are either embarrassed or dumbfounded, particularly those of us who wrote down crazy words only five years after the extermination camps were discovered. Where did *I* get it? Was I paying for that huge Bible I carried with me to France; that a girlfriend had bound for me so perfectly, along with seven or eight other books that were borrowed or stolen along the way? Auden was kind to me. Or he realized he couldn't show me the light (the darkness) in one afternoon. I don't know if poets, if critics, would be more offended by leopards munching on grass or by rifles turning into pruning hooks; and if someone said "the lion shall eat straw like the ox," the chorus of course would roar; so dumb was Isaiah; and if someone else said "Thou should love mercy, do justice, and walk humbly before your God," the chorus (of oxen and lions) would bellow. It really never stopped. Micah himself did pruning hooks and fig trees, as well as Zechariah, and the writers of the Sibylline oracles, hundreds of years after, who said there would no longer be war on earth or famine and there will be a common law throughout the whole earth; nor would there be walls or fences, and that lives will be in common and wealth will have no division—no rich, no slave; and that all will be on a par together.

Luckily the Christians transferred it elsewhere or we would all go around hanging our heads. Even if it said "dying will be done" (on earth) . . . why struggle? If you must, you could just detach, say (oh, retina), or eat lunch with monkeys, and if 1 percent of the population owns 90 percent of the wealth, who cares—except me and *Nation* magazine. Anyhow, whom should I bore? Just this afternoon a woman I know told me that her grandfather carried

Eugene Debs's soapbox in the lower East Side. She writes poetry, does healing, and is quite proud of him. She is, by the way, under five feet, so she also stands on a box just like Debs. I stood on a box only once, in Union Square, with a tiny flag stuck in one of the corners. That was the rule. I was protesting some ancient war— or making fun of a president. For which I apologize. Afterward I went to book row on Fourth and bought the collected poems of Tennyson—which I sold later for a dollar fifty. If anyone hasn't read "The Imaginary Jew" by Berryman, you should know it's one of the greatest short stories of the last century; it takes place in Union Square and involves a soapbox. I used to buy my neckties at Klein's, next to the square, but it's all been gentrified. I used to meet people by the statue of Mahatma Gandhi on the western side. I guess it's still there. I had a long talk one day with a cop hard by the statue who was confused that Gandhi had so few clothes on. He almost arrested the statue, but I protested. No one makes speeches in the square anymore. I don't know if it's even lawful. Maybe I'll give it one more try. Or not.

Chris Hedges and his son Tommy visited me this afternoon. I made tea and we talked about McChrystal and *Rolling Stone*. We're going next week to visit Daniel Berrigan. I remember Etheridge was suspicious of Dan and had a short—negative—poem about him. I asked Chris what Israel could have done instead of dropping commandoes down on the blockade-breaking boat. He suggested tear gas and taser. I liked loud Yiddish music. Maybe they could have had a violinist perform in the sky, or are those days over? Would you believe that Netanyahu went to Cheltenham High School outside of Philadelphia and that he was known as Benny the Bully? This fat guy is going to decide how many calories a Palestinian boy—or girl—is going to eat? Ah, Zechariah, walk down Broad Street!

What makes it worse is that the ultra-Orthodox have a lot of little followers, the tzitzits of the males fluttering in the wind. I respect redeeming the dead of Europe, but I must admit my prejudices, whether it's they or the Arab fundamentalists or the Christian, all looking backward to the same river. It's contrary to the whole tradition of Jewish justice, what's happening—for decades now—to the Palestinians. I have to say it plain, once and for all. And I don't give a rat's ass that Arab states are not democracies or that they mistreat, if they do, their own minorities, including Palestinian ones, or that they mistreated, in a hundred ways, their Jewish guests, or that Israeli Palestinians (ah, generosity) can vote and go to emergency rooms, or that there are communities where Jews and Palestinians are friends, or that Jews "bought" their land, fair and square, in the Turkish and British days. None of that justifies. And Israel is a nation, and to be a nation is to compromise, conceal, lie, and misbehave, but some nations are greedier than others, and anyhow Abba Eban said Israel would be a light "to the nations." Nor is it the job of Palestinians to be saints or more gracious, decent, and generous than their oppressors. They can be as bastardly as they want. If some of them are Jew haters or "anti-Semites," then they are idiots and assholes like all Jew-haters, and if the Grand Kishki of Jerusalem loved Hitler, may he rot in some Muslim hell forever, but it's no reason to tear down a house on some fake legal pretext, or burn an olive grove. Nor do the Palestinians have to bow and say "thank you." Nor do they have to love Jews or have European manners. There will be no Greater Israel because the world will not allow it, and, as dozens have said, it will only lead to Israel's destruction, democratically and demographically. All through human history, families, tribes, and nations have treated other families, tribes, and nations unfairly cruelly perversely insanely destructively even suicidally. They have outlawed languages (and still do), they have destroyed cultures and religions on absurd and lying pretexts (and still do). Germany did it, and England and the U.S. and Spain and

Portugal and France and Italy and Serbia and Austria and Belgium
and Russia, and China and Japan and Sweden and Turkey and the
old Arab states, and the Aztecs and Comanches—for starters. Israel
has been more considerate than many of the others. Than most.
But—well—since Israel is a light to the nations, then let her be
a light to the nations. Obviously, she's in the spotlight. If for no
other reason than the three mad religions interpenetrate in that
one place. Nor can Jewish eschatology and vision dominate or
command nor Christian nor Muslim, as it was borrowed and then
diverted. Goyim don't say, "Next year in Jerusalem," but so what?

If American soldiers are "assassins in uniform," as Twain said,
and if King Leopold and King Adolph and King Joseph and King
Mao were unbearable monsters and Bastards Supreme, it doesn't
mean Benny the Bully and his ridiculous mean-spirited racist
underlings should also be. There's the Nixon-gone-to-China bit,
but it's quite a stretch. And dear Europe has changed its mind about
colonial oppression, or so it says, and has turned righteous, like a dog
putting on airs at a hotel or a dog show. Israelis are *not* Nazis, as
left-wing apologists, in league with Arab Jew-haters, insist, in their
stupid reenactments and their willful ugly ignorance of history,
unless China is, and practically every European country, and the
United States itself with its French torch in the sky and its Jewish
verse. Even to think so is barbarous and unforgivable. But they *are*
oppressive, bureaucratic, and deceitful when it comes to the Pales-
tinians. And anyone who makes connections with biblical matters
or confuses myth with history, particularly the idiotic Christian
literalists, should be sent back to the first grade and forced to sit at
those tiny desks. The only eschatological events that will occur will
not be directed by a crazy God but will be man-made or, as we used
to say, made in the USA.

As far as the effect in Israel itself of its expansionist—and oppres-
sive—policies, the longer it goes on, the more helpless—and iso-

lated—Israel will become, in spite of its economic successes, and the more it will develop a siege mentality and hide behind its own walls, physical and psychological. And the more paranoid obsessive and conservative it will be. The consequence will be a less democratic, more authoritarian and rightist state. The discriminations against Arab citizens will increase, and, since a significant percentage of the ultra-Orthodox support such a state, women will be increasingly oppressed and disadvantaged in school, at home, in the workplace, and on the streets. Of course, police presence will increase and civil and human rights will be lessened. I find it personally obnoxious and outrageous that Orthodox rabbis tell us how to live, that *they* define who a Jew is, and that, through their arrogance, egotism, and medievalism, extend their black sway. I am a secular Jew, a proud lover of our radical past and a fierce defender of Israel. It belongs to me. Moreover, as Israel has gone its own unchecked way internationally, it has also done so domestically, and since the "socialist" safety net that once existed has more or less disappeared, the gap between rich and poor has grown wider than in most European countries. I read somewhere recently that one out of three Israeli children now live below the poverty line. This of course includes Bedouin and Ethiopian children since, alas, we must count them. This is the nation that claims Amos and Isaiah and that produced Jesus. Milk and honey always was a weird dish.

I read Peter Beinart's recent article, in the *New York Review of Books,* on the failure of the American-Jewish Establishment (AIPAC and the President's Council) with gratitude—and concern—maybe "fear" rather than concern. It points out, in excruciating detail, the absolute, total defense—by these organizations—of anything that any Israeli government does or says, whatever the truth is, and whatever moderate or concerned Israelis say; and it points out how AIPAC and the President's Council denounce any criticism of Israel whatsoever, ignoring particularly the changes

that are taking place, for different reasons and in different circum-
stances, among both American Jews and Israelis. It is a difficult
article to paraphrase, or summarize, but I am struck by the under-
lying conclusions: that Israel itself is turning dangerously to the
right and is in acute danger of losing its democratic basis—and
beliefs; and that American Jews are divided, mostly by religious
affiliations; and the young—in America—feel much less attached to
Israel than their elders and, irony of ironies, having imbibed some
of the defining values of American Jewish culture, have a strong
commitment to human rights (Palestinian included) and a "skepti-
cism about military force." I wish this courageous article could be
the basis of every Friday night sermon, but I doubt that it will. The
American government will continue to be compromised and para-
lyzed, and the Israeli government will continue to be evasive and
ambiguous as a way of stupidly gaining time and avoiding reality.
A horrible—and false—marriage. A suicidal and divorce-driven
one. Beinart is, of course, a "Jewish anti-Semite," though he is an
Orthodox Jew, like Isaiah.

　　If I sit on a bench nearby the No. 1 subway stop on 110th Street,
or in the park near the cannon-with-balls in Lambertville, New
Jersey, I remember how closely, and with such fear, I followed
the Jewish wars in the first four decades, and how angry I was by
the righteousness self-congratulation complacency selfishness and
ignorance of the generations before mine and how at times I was
confused but mostly not, and how useless my liberal ideas are today.
My cud is white and blue and I'll swallow it alone. I'm enlightening
mine own intestines for the brightness in my mouth was only a light
to the nations. Today I read in the *Times* that some American sena-
tors are scratching their heads over the Gulf of Tonkin Resolution,
that the Republican candidate for governor of Alabama believes in
a literal interpretation of the Bible, and that the Netanyahu gov-
ernment wants control of the land *east* of the proposed but not yet

proposed Palestinian State, hard by the Jordan, to prevent rocks, tomatoes, and bombs from being tossed.

Now say you had a peach pie and you were playing Territory (with plastic knives). Wouldn't that be fun? I wrote on the back of my ticket for the 7 p.m. cruise around New York with my grand-daughter Rebecca that the Palestinians are the nagging conscience of Israel. Is that too banal? I think I'll save that ticket, put it in the drawer with my copper dipper, my Turkish coffeepot, my key to the city of Carthage, Texas, and my Orvis watch guarantee.

48 Charlie I

There's a thin, somewhat bent-over man, maybe in his late eight-ies, who passes Anne Marie's house and the little city park as he walks his dog every morning. He usually wears heavier clothing than the weather calls for, but this morning, July 5, with the tem-perature due to go up past 100 degrees Fahrenheit, he had on a thin white T-shirt and long pants. I was walking back to Anne Marie's house when we passed each other and I stopped to ask his dog's name and pet him, though it was a "her" and her name was Elvira. What struck me was how easily we pass by older people and ignore them, as if they weren't there. And the fake attention paid them—paid us—does not constitute an exception, and the utterly stupid and insulting epithet "young man" is pure degradation. I challenge anyone who addresses me as "young man," whether he's stupidly innocent or unknowingly—or knowingly—contemptuous. Older women, I understand, are likewise addressed as "young lady"; the men are emasculated, the women—crones, witches—are buried.

I have seen Charlie several times, but this was the first time I talked to him. It turned out he had been an editor for various com-panies, including Merrill Lynch, and tried to correct stock brokers and engineers in their use of the language as they wrote for in-house publications. He is a gentle, intelligent man who lives two city blocks away. He has been in Lambertville since the early 1970s, and remembers when you could buy cheese—and fish—here, not just antiques. He was, he told me, raised in some community "on the water" in Brooklyn. He read my poem "Roses" on one telephone pole or other. He has a sense of humor, a clear voice, and speaks French well. Elvira is thirteen and turning gray. She has bad hips and is incontinent but was anxious to get home for her breakfast. His first name is Charlie. I want to get to know him better.

49 Israel

My heart beats like the stone I made soup with tonight, and I put down my cruel book, for another bomb has just exploded. And I'm doing this, alas, at the very same time that my redbud is blooming so that my large window is engulfed in blossom while the wind, what there is of it, gently makes the rich limbs move this way and that, as if dancing for me, a hundred arms gesturing. And were they not lucky, those Jews, during those hundreds of years when they didn't yet have a country and were limited to treating issues of justice and compassion in a small room—in many small rooms—by swaying, pointing with a stick, and closing their eyes instead of in a large room—in many large rooms—of decorated, perfumed, and shiny-booted double-dealers, anxious servants with their tongues out and their perfectly kempt fingers scratching each other's backs, eons away from issues of justice and compassion, though their fingers might not even have been crossed and there may even have been an image of suffering—or a thought—say, a woman with a hand on her mouth, say an orchard uprooted, say a stinking cattle car, say false humming.

And wasn't it lucky they didn't have to appoint judges, raise an army, levy taxes, receive ambassadors, deal with a national debt, have a flag, appoint a secretary of education, or interior, have elections, print money, and keep felt horseshoes available for carrying off and burying a dead king or president? Except for the Judenrate, who administered for the Nazis, our great shame and disgrace. Particularly, they didn't have to go to war, or make peace. Well, they *did* have a secret flag and they *were* allowed a certain amount of self-rule here and there—taxes, judges—but that was only here and there. And they were mostly poor, especially the easterners. And their power was ridiculously local. So the corruption was crazily minimal. Lord Acton said of them that absolute lack of power hardly corrupts at all.

They were called small-timers and their only problems were, aside from disease and pogroms, the fact that their wives sometimes didn't show respect and didn't have much interest in the exalted matters they were obsessed by. It's as if they were all unpublished poets and would—at dinner—try their beautiful lines out on their miserable families. Did they expect a standing ovation? Though I must quietly attest, as myself a poet who still tortures families, that their emotions, their tears even, and the occasional breakthrough decisions and discoveries, buried as they were in the thick books, some of which led to carrying the either thin or pot-bellied argufier on their shoulders, like a hero come home from the war, or like A. E. Housman's dead athlete in his poem "To an Athlete Dying Young"—which moves me into the maudlin—doesn't it—whose color is violet. For their part, the Spanish agreed to pay a few billion for destroying Judaism in Spain and the Portuguese followed suit. The French and the English, too, and Russia, Poland, Romania, Morocco, and Egypt. But they didn't know who to make the checks out to, for Israel *does not* speak for the Jews beyond the Jews in Israel. Or otherwise the Jews of, say, Argentina, Texas, and Canada would have to pay the Palestinians, when they did not, as such, abuse them. I suppose Israel knows who to pay its check to.

All of which leads me to remember de Gaulle, when he decided—after the French left Algeria—to take up the Arab cause, thus reversing everything, so that Israel, which had been the ally, dear friend, and chief customer of French weapons, was suddenly its enemy. Ben-Gurion, who stood on his head, was no longer "one of the greatest leaders of the West," and the Jews were suddenly an "elite people, sure of itself and dominating." This from that arrogant six-foot-five pile of *merde*. He said "Jews," he didn't say "Israelis" or "the Israeli government." It must have relieved a great many Frenchmen, particularly in their nightclubs.

But all this has nothing to do with whether the strings on which the peas climb have to be taut or not; and it has nothing to do with the tiny wrapped candy bars at my cleaners; and the ink on my white shirt; and Sid Caesar's neckties; and kissing the dog goodnight; and remembering—with joy—a terrible job I once had; and trying to remember a name; and reciting lines to myself; and overcoming a foolish loss. I discovered a new restaurant today and I can't wait to taste their potato pancakes; and I adore some of my paintings; and, if you don't know it, Paul Matthews is a great painter; and I'm beginning to appreciate the uneven bricks at the south side of my house; and I wish I had been old enough to work for the WPA; and I remember—with pleasure—the thick white coat with large buttons that fit me perfectly I found in a trunk in one of Edith Stein's cottages in San Cristobal. Because I'm behind enemy lines.

50 Nut Death

There are certain nuts that when you open them there is nothing but intricate patterns of wooden roads and tired, suffering caves where milk could have lain, or oil, but no kernel. These were called walnuts and were, like dragonflies, the top of the feeding machine that no one in his right mind could have created. Though when I carefully opened one such nut I discovered a fat worm, still alive, moving slightly through those caves, but there was nothing of rottenness, not one speck, in the whole nut. The question was how did the worm get in, how did it penetrate—if that's what it did—the powerful and intractable shell? I thought, well, it did so when the nut was still soft (if it was) and it survived all this time by consuming the meat inside the shell. On the side of the roads and in the caves. For worms are meat eaters (some of them) and tend to go for the soft before the hard, which, if they were human and eating their favorite meal, they would consume the mashed potatoes before the meat loaf and probably the loaf itself before the string beans, though here I am only paying attention to *softness* whereas one must take into consideration taste, for even worms have taste— even if it's bad taste. In such circumstances, when the worms consume me—if I go that way—they will certainly consume my heart first since—at least I'm told—I'm softhearted, though I don't know if that's altogether a good thing for it's not exclusively a question, say, of kindness, mercy, and love—those things—but also cowardice, avoidance, sentimentality, and the like. And for all I know, tears soften everything and those who are quick to tear are quick to be eaten. So what?

The worm forgives the robin and I forgive the worm—and that is one good reason to fight the fire, for you can love the segments, but there's no sense loving the match. Diamond or no diamond. I have a couple of medals and many photographs on display on walls, on mantles, and on top of dressers and tables, but I would feel absolutely silly displaying my ashes—in a bowl or a basket or a pot or still on a little silver shovel in this or that porcelain or metal container. Though what am I thinking, it won't be me doing the displaying—that would be revolting, let alone impossible. Nor, since I'm not Moses—or Jesus—I don't want the wind to scatter me from some high hill or other, neither in Cook's Forest nor at the shore nor even in Paris, the city of your dreams, nor Pittsburgh, the city of my nightmares.

Though sometime or other you must deal with facts, even in poems, and if we consign ourselves to the worms, if "worms" will threaten (through their eating habits) that "long-preserved virginity," as beautiful as it sounds and moving—and final as it is—we know, depending on the type of burial, it is probably not worms and certainly not earthworms that I suggest we envision when we hear the word, for they are vegetarian for the most part, but rather maggots, the larvae of flies, who consume the putrid flesh, even if the word is much less poetic, and no poet worth his salt would ever talk—or sing—about maggots trying that long-preserved virginity. Though that was, intentionally or not, the underbelly of Dickinson's poem "I heard a Fly buzz – when i died."

Even through a small study of decomposition you learn—what you always knew—that the change sets in immediately after death, and depending on temperature, exposure, protection, and the like, you become what you were not through the agency of bacteria, insects, and scavengers as well as by internal chemical processes. And there are describable stages. But I'm keeping my distance from putrefaction, out of courtesy, and because I'm fascinated only a little by the details. It's not what happens to a cadaver I'm interested in, though I do have to show some respect and, as far as I'm concerned, I have to make a decision soon. I'm pouring all this out for Anne Marie and my children and grandchildren and for the friends I have and for the women I have loved and for the children and grandchildren of my seventy-three first cousins and for Pat and for the neighbors and their animals and for my nailed-up poem and for the abandoned stone jail in our small public park and for the huge white pine that soars over it and the Chinese dogwood and the crab apples that surround it.

My book—part of it—is a return to earlier last wills and testaments, which, rather than talk only about money and property, address themselves to ideas, to beliefs, and advice, albeit, in those cases, somewhat pompous and elder-driven of the male sort. If anything, mine is more in the way of images and of indirection and, though still elder-driven, is so by different impulses. My grandfather—my mother's father—I somehow discovered, after my mother's death in 1993, had written a long work, in what seemed both Hebrew and Yiddish, maybe a language he had created himself, which is a puzzle to me and also to the few authorities on such things, professors of Hebrew or Yiddish language and literature I consulted at the University of Pennsylvania and elsewhere, which might be a book of this type. It's amazing to me that I can't find the original text, for what I have is a copy, or that I don't know that she even *had* the text—the journal, the notebook—in which it was written. She—my mother—was not given to keeping such things nor did she ever talk to me about it the long decades we spent together. She didn't hold onto the expensive porcelain lamp her brother Harry had given her in 1921 as a wedding gift, nor did she keep the gorgeous samovar her mother—my dear Libby—brought over from Poland—Polish Russia—and she lost the painting I entrusted to her that Andy Warhol gave me, which I have written about elsewhere. She hated anything old and her favorite term was "brand new," which she used over and over again in criticizing my furniture, yet she kept the manuscript, whatever it was. I would love to see how good the writing is, what his mind was made of, what interested him. Yesterday I took the loose pages with me to Rojos, the local coffee house, and consulted with David Waldman, the owner, whose father had been a Yiddish scholar in Philadelphia. Dave is a man of all skills. He is not only the best roaster of beans in this part of the universe but a lawyer, a musician, and a former manager of musical groups—in Memphis and elsewhere. His wife is a midwife and one of his best coffees is called "Midwives Moonshine." The beans come from Costa Rica. He makes periodic trips to Central and South America, and to Africa, to inspect farms and buy coffee. He could make out some of my grandfather's writing and found the names of translators in Philadelphia, New York, and elsewhere online.

My grandfather's document, his book, is actually a "one year diary," and the year is 1911. There is a calendar in front, a biographical fact sheet and every date, important or not, has a single sheet, January 1 to December 31, and every sheet is full of his careful script. Along with footnotes, private symbols, and continuations. The writing is not altogether unified. Sometimes it's scribbled, sometimes careful, even with a flourish. His name (Beryl Barach) and his address (20 Townsend Street, Pittsburg [*sic*]) is in English on the cover page, and since two pages fit fairly neatly on an 8½ x 11 sheet, the size of the diary pages are approximately 4 x 6. As I say, I have lost the original, but I am constantly (in the last few days) searching for it. Some entries seem to be poemlike, some are lists, and some are continuous narratives, or single observations. If one were to judge by looks alone, I would say (crazily) that there appears to be a great deal of intelligence and variety. I may find a translator before I finish *this* book or I may not. But it's suddenly grown very important to me. Beryl himself I remember only vaguely. I was four, I think, when he died. I used to mistake him—as he sat on the sofa—for the man on the box of Bering Cigars, also with a beard. He lived his last years—maybe his last ten years (along with his wife, Libby)—in his son Harry's house in Wheeling, West Virginia. Harry, by that time, owned the largest department store in Wheeling, known later as "Horne's" after a one-time partner. Harry himself lost everything in the crash. Through stupid investments. But all that's another story. Beryl sat in his son's house, as I remember, grateful to be there, a little like a rebbe. I don't remember him ever touching me, let alone hugging and holding me. When my mother was close to ninety, and we were finally "talking," she said to me "he never kissed me even once." But you remember what you choose to remember; that's why I want to read what he says.

It is Villon's *Testament* that comes to mind when we think of bequests, last wills, and such. It is a tender, biting, memory-ridden poem, straightforward and ironic at the same time, and the nominal subject is what he leaves, presumably after he's gone, though I think he was in his early thirties when he wrote it. He leaves creaking doors, broken windows, backaches, and nightmares. It's satire and the bequests are comic but pointed and devastating as Dante's rewards and punishments were. A reader in the 1450s and '60s would have gasped and roared a little more than we do, but there's enough clarity, art, and reality for us as well, though we may read it a little differently. I find Villon to be heartbreakingly obsessed with the past, even including the immediate past, so that his themes are the basic ones of time and death. Either he was *inclined* that way or he lived in an age of great or sudden change where the past was overwhelmingly haunting. Nothing could be better than a last will and testament for such a writer, such a person.

Today, July 10, 2010, I learned of the verdict in the case of the transit cop who shot and killed a prisoner in the back while he was lying face down on the cement floor of a BART Station in Oakland, California. It was buried, American-style, deep inside the *Times*. He was making noise or howling, or singing or protesting when the cop shot him. Maybe he called the pig a pig—I don't care to get all the details right. The cop's defense was he thought he was using his taser and murdered him by mistake. The victim's name was Oliver Grant; he was twenty-two. He was fighting on the subway or watching a fight or leapt the turnstile or some such. Nothing so serious as pissing in a plastic cup. The trial was moved to Los Angeles because it was agreed that that poor policeman couldn't get justice in the murdered boy's city. They would probably have moved it to Alabama if they could. The jury—none of whom were black, as Grant was—bought the cop's story and convicted him of involuntary manslaughter—the very least they could do besides acquittal—two to four years. The cop was white, sort of an off-white, a little yellow mixed in. Ross Gay tells me a friend of his who is an ER doctor told him his hospital in Oakland was preparing for a riot if the verdict went the wrong way. There were several days of rioting after the shooting itself in January 2009.

I don't know what did happen or what's going to happen, but, as far as Oliver Grant is concerned, putrefaction has long since set in. The worms appear to be ruthless, but they are only doing God's work, or nature's. There is nothing perverse or evil in their behavior. Villon would probably have them somehow, obliquely and cunningly, reject the transit cop's flesh when the time came. But faithful as they are, they will—like jurors—swallow anything.

51 Anti-Semitic Cartoons

I lose heart when I see reproductions of Arab anti-Semitic cartoons. I don't know if I'm chagrined, bitter, or sad. They are brutal and stupid. Nor are they the product only of extreme enemies of Israel but also of "moderate" states, Jordan, for instance, or Qatar. It is one thing to depict Ariel Sharon as "bloodthirsty," standing in a cup of blood (*Al-Hayat Al-Jadeeda*, a Palestinian newspaper), for example. It is something else to picture, right out of the Nazi playbook, the Jew with a hooked nose, a hunched back, a tail, and wearing a yarmulke as he thrusts a sword—with a Jewish star at the tip—through the body of an Arab, a swastika on his tail (*Al-Watan*, Oman); or to repeat the vicious medieval blood libel (official website of the Palestinian Authority State Information Center); or as rats wearing Stars of David and skull caps as they run (scurry) through holes in a building called "Palestine House," implying, as the Germans did, that Jews are vermin and should be eradicated by mass extermination (*Arab News*, an English-language daily in Saudi Arabia). I am one of those rats, and I resent the depiction. It makes me feel less like giving my name to any Arab cause. Nor do I want to hear from my radical friends that Arabs are also demonized and that the cartoons will stop if Israel changes its policies toward the Palestinians. These cartoons, in effect, do more than demonize Jews—they forgive Germans, reassign blame, and minimize the Holocaust. I am sick to my core of anti-Semitism, wherever it comes from. Whether from Syria, Russia, France, Argentina, or Egypt.

Nor do I want to hear that Arabs, after all, are Semites, and also have Hittite noses. I read in the *Jew-York Times* the other day that in 2001 Mary Robinson, that extraordinary Irishwoman, as the UN High Commissioner for Human Rights, was presented with a book of such cartoons by representatives of the Arab Lawyers' Union and announced how deeply hurt she was, since, as she put it, *she* was a Jew. As an Arab, as a Jew, as a Pole, as a rat, as an American, and—for her dear sake—as an Irishwoman, I am also deeply hurt.

52 Marie Ponsot

Marie had her stroke a few weeks after I called her. I heard about it later than others, and when I asked it was assumed I had read the *Times* piece about her remembering the Lord's Prayer in Latin, then translating it into English, and thus beginning the long climb back; or that she was getting help from a rotating group of poets who came to her apartment to read and talk with her; and the fundamental importance, she says, of syntax, "a tool more important to human existence than the wheel." The article was dated June 25, 2010. I wrote about "Dancing Days II" (in her volume *Easy*) at the end of April or the very beginning of May.

53 Again Haiti

International donors, including the United States, have given only
a fraction of the money they promised for aid to Haiti, Bill Clinton
said. The billions they promised never came; though there are not
enough tarps for the rainy season.

54 Charlie and Elvira

Charlie, Elvira, and I met again early this morning, July 16, a Fri-
day. We sat on Anne Marie's front porch, on the swing and rocking
chairs. He actually loves talking about his life—this silent man—
and I have to slightly force my way in for my turn. Charlie was in
the Signal Corps in World War II and part of a sophisticated system
of predicting enemy activity in the Pacific. He goes in two disparate
directions—he is an engineer, a specialist in electronics, and he is,
at the same time, a wordsmith, the term he uses, and, as I said (see
section 48) he was an in-house editor for several large companies,
including Merrill Lynch. He went to Lafayette College, in Easton,
Pennsylvania, after the war, part of the huge G.I. onslaught, and
though he initially majored in engineering, he switched, to the
dismay of his teachers, he says, to English. He talks readily about
the work he did, but it came out only gradually about his marriages
and children. He met his first wife—a Spanish woman named Jose-
phine—in New York City, and they left America for Mexico dur-
ing the "suffocating" Eisenhower years. They had two sons. One
of them, who had epilepsy, fell in the shower, hit his head, and
died. He was only twenty-one. A horrible accident. The other
got into drugs and disappeared. The *disparu* is named Anthony. In
Mexico, Charlie fell in love with his best friend's wife and they ran
off, or came back, to New York and lived in Brooklyn Heights,

not upscale then as now. Her name was Millicent. She left him because he didn't get a divorce, but he explained to me how difficult that would be, with Mexican law and Mexican lawyers. His grandson lives in New York—with his mother, I think—and comes to visit Charlie in Lambertville. He is thirteen. I don't know the circumstances and don't want to press the issue as if I were cross-examining him.

Charlie worked for an electronics company whose headquarters was in northern New Jersey, maybe the Edison area, and whose factory was in Lambertville, which was once a small manufacturing city. Charlie moved to Lambertville in the early 1970s to manage the small factory, but when it moved down the river to Newtown, Pennsylvania, he quit but continued living in Lambertville. For a year or so he had a store where he repaired hi-fi equipment, but (he said) he only made a profit one month and that was for twelve dollars. I don't know what he did after that, but he now lives in a small apartment on Main Street.

He would have stayed with me another hour, or at least until Elvira got hungry for breakfast. I don't really know him but have taken to him already. I love the clarity of his mind and how he thinks through his response to a question and answers concisely and clearly. I am interested in the circumstances of his leaving America when he did; and that it was clearly political. I am interested in what his first dreams and ambitions were, and who and what his father and mother were. I am not altogether sure why I am drawn to him.

55 McChrystal

When it comes to things military, the last thing we should trust is the government, our own beautifully "elected" government, which seems actually to control that military from time to time. The McChrystal affair is a delightful little operetta that engaged, angered, amused, and even delighted those of us who knew about it for a week or so. It was an interlude, a distracted solo from the wrong score; at once a chaotic mass made personal and a kind of populist revenge on uncontrolled wildness, even as it was an indignant fight against faceless authority, itself populist, with touches of tea-partyism and whiskeyish rebellion about it as well as the good ending we love so well, reminiscent of Truman descending on MacArthur or a mob descending on Coriolanus.

McChrystal and his toads talked to *Rolling Stone*, itself the most unlikely, comic, and "irresponsible" event you could imagine, and he didn't come out looking too good. In fact, there was no way of saving his bad ass after that. Maybe he wanted out of Afghanistan and this was the only thing he could think of. Maybe he "couldn't help himself, poor thing." Maybe he was delusional and thought he ruled the U.S. as well as Afghanistan. Maybe he thought no one would read the article.

There is no question that he was a runaway general. That he was and is rebellious violent brilliant cocky insubordinate focused a braggart a patriot, and, as the head of Special Operations and as a commander in the Rangers, a specialized killer. But he was also cunning and political. He did theater. The fact that he ate only one meal a day and got by on four hours of sleep and did night duty with Seals is bullshit and irrelevant. The problem is, as I understand it, he was an impetuous "hero" who, as commander in Afghanistan, had to embrace a policy of what is stupidly called "counterinsurgency," which means building wells and lending out books, as if it were the Peace Corps, and restricting American troops from recklessness, say killing civilians. Actually, Obama got a great break when McChrystal opened his big mouth. Now he can fight his dumb war in peace.

My only issue, as I said in section 47, is that they retired him with four stars. That way he's still a millionaire player, eligible to "advise" the Pentagon on matters *militaires*. I would have demoted him, as I said earlier, to corporal. After all, I was sent back to first grade for a week for pushing Irv Molivar into Shirley Kruman, when we were all in the sixth grade—and breaking her arm—since he—Irv—was in love with her. But I didn't strangle anyone at three in the morning. And I didn't call the vice-president a wimp, and I didn't elevate the middle finger against the French or anybody else, with my fellow maniacs. As he did when he was wasting his share of the billions we throw into the shit-pile every year in our pursuit of peace and justice, American style, everywhere.

56 Bob Bernat

In the mid-1970s my friend Robert Bernat was appointed director of the Pennsylvania Arts Council by Milton Schapp, the feisty popular Pennsylvania governor, and asked me to take time off from teaching and run the literature sector for him for a year or two. Bob and I were close friends and had taught at Indiana University of Pennsylvania together for a number of years; he in music, I in English. Bob was from Johnstown, Pennsylvania, home of floods, steel, and steep hills. He started off as a jazz musician and was playing in bands by the age of twelve. While he was in college he directed a jazz quartet (sometimes a quintet) called either "The Bobby Bernat Quartet" or "Quintet," piano, bass, drums (or vibes), and clarinet (or sax). Bob was the wind. He studied composition at Carnegie Tech (later Carnegie Mellon), where he wrote music for the Shakespeare productions, and did his graduate work at Brandeis. He was born in 1931, so he had the classical early-1950s music education. He studied with Aaron Copland, whom he brought to Indiana in 1965 for a week. (I wrote a poem about Copland's "flirtation" with my mother—while he was in Indiana—called "Both of Them Were Sixty-Five.") I remember the lovely piece Bob wrote in the mid-

1960s, a passacaglia called "In Memoriam, JFK." It was performed at the Syria Mosque, in Pittsburgh.

He always had a deep interest in politics and did work (as I did) for the Kennedy campaign. His first wife, Edwina Bernat, told me today—July 19, 2010—that the two of them were in the audience for Kennedy's final TV campaign speech in Faneuil Hall in Boston. Bob was director of the Arts Council for about six years, probably from 1973 to 1978. It was the early days of federal funding and large grants were given to orchestras, ballet companies, and individuals in the arts. I was in charge of the Poetry-in-the-Schools program and also administered the program that gave money to journals that were housed in Pennsylvania and to colleges to underwrite their reading series. (And didn't read in any Pennsylvania college for five years after.) Bob, who was interested—obsessed—by English brass bands, created the River City Brass Band after he left the Arts Council, which had its headquarters in Pittsburgh and was an astounding success all through the States—and Canada. Bob wrote music for the band and always mixed in several classical pieces with the standards. It's still going strong, fifteen years after Bob's death.

I hired some forty poets for my program and paid them so well that we were receiving applications from all over the country. The going rate then was $50 to $100 a day, and I started off giving my poets (my teachers) $250. The head of the literature sector in D.C., Len Randolph, came down to Harrisburg to fight with me on the issue and I ended up paying $175 to $200, still the highest rate in the country (1974). I spent two or three days a week in Harrisburg (PA), used the Bucknell College summer high school institute as a training ground, and, like Yeats (a sixty-year-old smiling public man), visited schools in every county to negotiate with superintendents and principals and to observe my poets. A lot of crazy stuff— breakdowns, affairs, drunkenness, and in one case in southwestern Pennsylvania I had to fire the poet who brought his wife to class and discussed their own sex life. My warnings didn't work. There are sixty-three counties in Pennsylvania, and there was a lot of work and for a while a lot of money. One of my rules was a poet could not teach more than three (forty-five-minute) classes a day. When the principals complained I replied that their teachers shouldn't either. A poet, if he were a little careful, could live off the schools I gave him—or her. We used to meet, the whole body, in early September at a hotel in Harrisburg—me lecturing, lunch, group sessions, assignment-giving. I had a wonderful assistant, John Hesselbein, who did much of the legwork. John died in the late 1970s.

Bob, who was in his early forties, was having a few crises (the famous *crise de quarante*). He and Winnie got divorced and there were several other marriages. Two Nancys, as I recall. Bob lived on a farm about twenty or thirty miles south of Harrisburg. Near Boiling Springs. My memory is that there was a beautiful small brick house, a very large wooden barn, outbuildings, and countless acres. Southern Pennsylvania, close by York and Gettysburg. I used to occasionally go down there, in my '66 Volvo, at the end of the week and go back home (to Raubsville, near Easton) on Saturday or Sunday.

One evening Governor Schapp drove down for dinner in a state police car, accompanied by two staties. We invited the two over-armed, uncomfortable policemen in, but they said they would prefer to wait outside, a cool and lovely May or June evening. I remembered, suddenly, that there were long green plants hanging over the barn rafters drying at a perfect temperature and that they were in full sight. Bob's favorite plant, whose leaves he had been smoking since he was in his early teens, as many jazz players did. So, Bob, his wife, the governor, and I had a lovely dinner, talked about art matters, the war, family history, dreams, and the like—which you do—while the two state policemen strolled outside in the evening sun, Bob and I occasionally looking at each other with a certain anxiety and a certain insane knowledge of the utterly comic and perfectly horrible. If those cops had walked into the barn, and if they had anything of the dutiful and righteous in them, with their close-shaved heads, their comic boots, and their silly hats, we would all have been ruined, especially the governor, especially my dear friend Bob, whose mother died when he was four, whose father was a mailman, and who paid for his own keep by the time he was fourteen, including a college education. I could see the headline of the *Pittsburgh Post-Gazette*, the *Philadelphia Inquirer,* and the *Harrisburg Breeze:* "Governor Caught in Marijuana Tryst." Poor loveable Schapp developed Alzheimer's, I remember. Bob died at sixty-three or sixty-four of lung cancer. He and Winnie had three lovely daughters, Brenda, Becky, and Betsy, two of whom live near their mother—in West Virginia now—with their own children. I'll see some of them the end of July in Seaside Heights on the Jersey shore. Bob adored his daughters, and since his own mother died so early, he was always searching for the "feminine," as I see it in my crazy homegrown way. We drove to Hawk Mountain once for the view; and once while sitting at his dining room table in Indiana, my family and his, we heard barking under us, in the basement. Bob sheepishly admitted they had a dog but kept it housed "below," at his insistence; for four or five years I sat at that table and never knew it.

57 Montpellier

I think it was 1950—not 1949—when I took a Dutch freighter from Hoboken to Antwerp and a train to Paris for my first extended stay in Europe. And it was almost two months later that I realized that though I was attending lectures almost every day in the *Cours de civilisation française,* and training myself to hear a certain formal French, I wasn't really speaking it, except to waiters and bus drivers, since I was surrounded by American friends who lived in the small hotels near the river at the lowest end of Boul Mich. I was totally ignorant of the university system but got hold of a map showing the location of the French universities and identified the one farthest from Paris—Montpellier, near the Mediterranean—and carrying my heavy foot locker on my right shoulder I took a train there, probably the next day, and arrived at three or four o'clock in the morning. I slept on the bare floor of the train station and woke up in the light to make my way—however I did it—to the university offices and began, that day, attending classes.

I have various memories of my stay in Montpellier. The city was much smaller then and the psychological distance from Paris was greater than it is now. The accent was southern, the ends of words were more enunciated, more "Italianate," and the speech was slower, a great advantage for someone speaking American. There was much less distance between the foreign students and the *bureau*—it was more personal, even protective, quite different than it was at the Sorbonne. There was a special school for foreigners there, as there was in Paris, an *école pour étrangers*, and there were parties, dances and outings where we got to know each other. I was on the World War II G.I. Bill and I suppose I was only at school to get my seventy-five dollars a month, a kingly sum then in Europe, though it sounds now like a pittance. I went to the American Embassy every month for my check when I was in Paris and certainly to an equivalent office in Montpellier. All I had to do was show my stamped and dated registration card. I lived a few kilometers out of the city and bought a bicycle to ride back and forth. I don't remember about gears but I suspect there were none. I found myself speaking a lot more French there even though many of the foreign students spoke English. Of the French students who went to the university, many of them in law and medicine, there was an overwhelming sense that they were provincials from the small cities near Montpellier, Nîmes and Narbonne, for example, and the feeling I had then was that they were replicating the lives of their fathers and perhaps even grandfathers, and that the war was only a slight interruption. Except there were a number of Spanish students, probably from refugee families, as well as French-speaking North Africans from both sides of the political spectrum. It would be later that I would experience the student protests—in Paris—and watch them march by the hundreds and thousands chanting "France oui, Algiers non, France oui, Algiers non" or see them actually overturn long red Coca-Cola trucks while the drivers stood helplessly by in their orange striped shirts shrugging their shoulders or smiling sheepishly. The one thing I'll never forget is the names of the rectors—I think that's the word—of the medical school in Montpellier engraved on the wall above the W.C.; and a certain François Rabelais, early but by no means the earliest, among the others. The restaurants were amazingly cheap. You could buy a full meal, wine included, for about twenty-six cents American. Really a good deal cheaper if you counted the francs you got on the black market for American dollars.

The person I was closest to during my stay in Montpellier was a poet I had met originally a year or so earlier at Columbia University when we were both working for our master's degrees in comparative literature. Jim Lovett. I remember his poetry, and I know he spent his working years at Roberts College in Istanbul, and I know we had a friend in common in Philadelphia named Bill Basnight, who ended up teaching French literature at the University of Washington in Seattle, and died maybe fifteen years ago. I saw them together once, Bill and Jim (or Jim and Bill), in Philadelphia at the end of the 1950s. An evening that ended up with Basnight drunk, semiconscious, and sleeping in his bathtub—on Spruce Street near

Seventh. I saw Basnight in Seattle about two months before he died, depressed, withdrawn, and ironic, lying on a small cot in his living room, mostly silent. He worked for the American Friends Service Committee in Philadelphia, and it was he who introduced me to Dorothy Day.

Jim was sleeping with the chambermaid of the small hotel where he lived. She was short, with close-cropped hair, calloused hands, and big eyes. She reminded me of Edith Piaf, and I called her little sparrow, in English. One night we went to the opera, Lovett, the sparrow, the German girl I was seeing, and myself. *Carmen* was playing. It was my first opera—ever—and I bought a box in the ancient opera house, practically on the stage. The German girl, also a student, had blue eyes, blonde braided hair, and her name, hard to believe, was actually Marguerite. If she was twenty-three then, she would have been born in 1927, a perfect Nordic and, as likely as not, a former member of some youth corps or other, like Ratzinger. She said that her family hated the Nazis and that her father was a Socialist, but I always felt uncomfortable and wondered why I chose her instead of one of the Moroccans or Spanish, or even an American. The velour seats were faded and stained, the curtain was patched, and our knees pressed against the ornate box fronts, but we were—I was—overjoyed.

I knew nothing about Bizet, or the Opéra-Comique. Nor did I know Prosper Mérimée's novella or that Love is a rebellious bird that no one can tame. And though I knew the gypsy myths of wildness and freedom, I could barely understand the French. If it is comic and sentimental, the music is nonetheless great and the counterstroke of realism and irony help make it still moving. But I would love it no matter what. And if a thirty-five-year-old French musician, in the very heart of Europe, can realize his ideal of a woman who is independent and mistress of her own decisions, in 1875, then *my* heart goes out to him, especially when he died suddenly—after the thirtieth performance at the Opéra-Comique—without knowing that *Carmen* would be not only universally popular but applauded by Gounod, Massenet, and Offenbach and later by the three major European composers, Wagner, Brahms, and Tchaikovsky.

The guidebook tells us that the ornate opera house sits at the end of the huge square (shape of an egg) at the old center. Judah of Toledo, an indefatigable wandering Jew, writes about Montpellier (in the twelfth century) as a world center, with trade and diplomatic connections with Egypt, Persia, Spain, and Gaul. The university was founded in the thirteenth century and, though it had a much smaller population when I was there—in 1950—it now has sixty thousand students, though not all of them can study with Rabelais.

By Thanksgiving it was mostly cold and rainy, but we decided, three or four of us, to bicycle down to Sète, Montpellier's seaport, to visit two of the students who lived there and celebrate the holiday. It's twenty-eight kilometers from Montpellier to Sète, and my memory tells me we went down and back the same day, which makes it a bit of a trek. I know Lovett was there and an American from the New York area who came to Europe not to learn French or encounter the past or get a degree or open his mind but because it was cheap living and he could get laid there, which apparently he couldn't on the Hudson. I don't remember his name but we kept encountering each other in various places in France as he hopped from bed to bed. The McCarthy period was just getting started, and Eisenhower was somewhere fretting and hiding. He would continue to fret and hide until a lesser general and a journalist would take on the drunken pig from Wisconsin. But the hysterical McCarran Act had already passed, Russia was about to get the bomb, the Communists—by the millions—were storming Cleveland Heights and the South Bronx, and America was in deep paranoid shit. Nobody in Europe loved us anymore, and those of us who were this degree or that to the left were getting the bitters. It was the twenty-year itch. Yet Thanksgiving was Thanksgiving, and we spent several hours hunting for a turkey—to no avail. There probably was one in the zoo, if there was a zoo, but we didn't want to deprive the young of their exotic *oiseau* joy. At one point we went down to the water to talk about renting a boat for three or four months to visit cities on the Mediterranean. Sête, as far as I could figure, was a port since Phoenician days, and many of the ships had a look of the old Semitic, or so we thought. We made a deal with an owner at an astoundingly low price, him included, but we didn't follow through. We would have gone to Greece, Italy, Spain, Morocco, and Egypt. It was just one of the lost chances. I don't remember visiting Valéry's grave, but I am sure we recited what lines we could remember from "Le Cimetière Marin." Lovett knew whole stanzas. All I can remember now is "La mer, la mer, toujours la mer." But that might actually be Rimbaud.

There were maybe six of us. We ate what we could, told stories of home, sang songs, even wet our eyes—and cheeks. I remember, vividly, bicycling back, more than a little drunk, between the rows of poplars. We did some tricks on our wheels and sang together. I want to say it was a full moon, but I'm only being a sap. I had beaten everybody in arm wrestling, even the girls, and I had fallen in love with one of them, farewell Marguerite. It was my best Thanksgiving in years and I wouldn't remember another one till the great snowfall of 1951, coming across the Pennsylvania Turnpike in a '48 Chrysler coupe, two hundred books in the long trunk giving us leverage as we went past dozens of stranded cars, going from Pittsburgh east to Long Island with Pat and Willy Wallace, he a math teacher, me the newly installed high school principal—my first full-time job—in a corrupt, bankrupt private school near a lake with bottomless pits and monsters.

58 The Steel Pier

Another hour on NPR about the rejuvenation of Atlantic City. Similar to the ones I heard thirty, forty years ago. The main theme then was that the casinos would siphon off money to rebuild the city and help the poor. I didn't listen long enough to find out what the current bullshit is. I heard something about a steel pier—a new one I guess, if the old one burned down, or maybe it was the million-dollar pier that burned. I wonder how much the insurance was. *My bottom dollar that it was more than a million.* I can't remember if I ever wrote about watching and hearing Gene Krupa on the drums at the Steel Pier, and I don't know if I paid a dime or a quarter to get in or if I just used my daytime ticket. The Imperial Hotel packed lunches—for the "children"—and we ate inside at picnic tables. I never got over the white horse diving through the ring of fire into the giant tin tub. I know I wrote about swimming out into the ocean and through the huge waves around the Steel Pier when I was fifteen. In a wool bathing suit. Finally no top. In the 1940s. I caught a slight mention that the casinos were "islands" shut off from local restaurants and stores. And, as we all know, no windows to distract you from throwing your money away. There was also something about Charlemagne, Henry Adams, and some corrupt planners, but I was already putting on Leonard Cohen, the concert I heard in Boston.

59 Charlie III

I ran into Charlie Howard again today—his last name is Howard—and I almost didn't recognize him because he wasn't walking with Elvira but with another dog, smaller and more frisky. He told me he had to put Elvira down and a day later went to the pound to get a new dog. This one is half Chihuahua and half fox terrier, with a

beautiful tan coat. His name is Tre. He was in the midst of vacu-
uming in his apartment, he said, and told me how Tre attacked the
Hoover, mistaking its noise for growls. We agreed to meet an hour
later at City Market next door to his apartment and have a coffee
together. As I said before, he was quite comfortable talking about
himself and actually didn't ask me any questions at all about myself;
all he knew, or learned, about me was what I volunteered, and I
had to vigorously interrupt him to get a word in about my own life.

His mother, he told me, was from Barbados and was part of a
small Barbadian community on the far edge of Brooklyn. She came
to America to study nursing and took a job as the private nurse to
a physician—in his late forties at the time—who had heart prob-
lems. He—the doctor—was Charlie's father. Charlie was born in
1923. He wanted to adopt Charlie but his mother resisted. Charlie
was, he told me, a kind of orphan, raised by other members of the
community. The doctor's name was Beaugarde, an Irishman with a
French name, and his first son—Charlie's half brother—was Hum-
phrey Beaugarde or Bogart, the famous Bogey. I said, in section
54, that Charlie went to Lafayette College in Easton, Pennsylva-
nia, and today he told me he went there because of "Presbyterian
connections." When I talked to him a little about poetry he told
me that Milton was his favorite poet and that Hart Crane had gone
to Lafayette. He meant Stephen Crane, author of *Maggie, A Girl of
the Streets* and *The Red Badge of Courage*. He told me, again, about
Fina (Josephine), his first wife, and Millicent, his best friend's wife
he had "stolen" and fled with (back to New York and Brooklyn
Heights), and the horror again of the Eisenhower years. When
I asked him who his friends were in recent years, he mentioned
Suzanne Douglas, a painter who lives in Lambertville and is origi-
nally from Pittsburgh. Suzanne is legally blind and troubled now
with her legs. She and I often talk about our city over breakfast.
She told me how tall and handsome Charlie was in the early 1970s.

Since Tre is half Chihuahua, I told Charlie the story behind my recent poem "Save the Last Dance for Me," about rescuing a Chihuahua from a sewer when I was twelve. And he told me about someone in his company who, while installing an electrical cable in an apartment, was attacked and bitten on his heel by a Chihuahua and how he swung his hammer, instinctively, and hit the little dog on the head and killed him, while his mistress was in another room. He grabbed the dead dog and threw him down the incinerator and left. He could hear the owner calling, "Fifi, Fifi." I paid for the coffee (iced, $3.75), and he paid the tip ($1).

60 Libby

My mother was born in Bialystock—in 1900—in what was then, after the carving up of Poland, a part of Russia, and came to America in 1905. So she said, but I always thought there might be a slight error here and there, that she maybe was born in 1901 and came to America in 1904, say, for mistakes were notorious and memory was often strange. Anyhow, she never had a specific birthday—she was born "on the eve of Passover," and the dates for Pesach change every year. But in the census of 1920 it was definitely stated that Ida Barach was indeed born in Bialystock in 1900 and was twenty at the time the census was taken. Her mother was born in 1872 and her father in 1864, so Libby was forty-eight and Beryl was fifty-six in 1920. We found out, by accessing Ellis Island on the Internet, that they (all) sailed on the S.S. *Noordam*, a ship on the Holland America Line, and that it landed on December 27th. Simon, her older brother, was nine at the time, and Harry, her other brother, seven. That would have made Libby twenty-four when Simon was born, which was old for a first-time mother then, though there could have been a child who died earlier, and if not that, then it's indicative that she came from an urban, somewhat liberated middle-class family, far from the shtetl physically and especially psychologically, for shtetl brides were often—commonly—twelve or thirteen and by the time they were twenty-four they may have had five or six little ones, of all sizes, trailing after them the way you see them do now in Brooklyn and twenty or thirty other American cities, wearing seventeenth-century dress, the women demure, hidden, and bewigged.

I have a large photograph of Libby hanging over my dining room mantle. My house, in Lambertville, built in 1850 or '60, befits the photograph, which may have been taken in her early thirties before she came to America. She is, in the photo, an absolutely beautiful woman, with a broad face, calm, intelligent eyes, and long, soft, brown hair parted in the middle. The photo is not exactly in color, but I can tell the hair is brown. She has on a rich velvet dress, brocaded at the neck, with a watch hanging down from a long gold chain. I gave the watch and chain to my daughter, Rachael, ten or so years ago. On the back of the photograph there is writing in Russian, probably the name of the studio where the photo was taken. Bialystock, though an important Polish city, was, as I said, in the Russian zone and the Russian language was being forced on the Poles. In the 1920 census the country of birth was indicated as "Russia," not Poland. I don't know if Libby and Beryl, born in the 1860s and '70s, thought of themselves, or would describe themselves, in addition to Jewish, as Polish or Russian. I suspect Polish, given their ages. I know that Libby, in addition to Yiddish and Hebrew, knew Polish, Russian, and German, but I don't know the extent. I spent endless time with her alone, but I don't remember ever talking much to her about her family, what business her father was in, was it textiles, did she go to school, what were her friends like, where did she meet Beryl, was it an arranged marriage, what her brothers or sisters did and where they lived, what their house was like in

Bialystock and what was the relationship to the two women den-
tists, first cousins, who went to Paris rather than to New York, and
whether they studied in Poland or France? I forgot to ask the two
of *them* that when I saw them in Paris in 1950.

Beryl I don't remember well. I have written about him in sec-
tion 50, how strange he was to me when I was a small boy, how
remote as I now remember, certainly partly because of his lack of
English. He was sixty-six when I saw him at his son's house (Uncle
Harry's) in Wheeling. He may have hugged me or tried talking
to me in Yiddish, I don't remember. As I said earlier, he was a
ritual butcher—he killed chickens on Friday morning and taught
Hebrew, a Melamed. When he got home on Friday afternoon he
dropped his bloody apron on the floor and, after eating a little
chicken soup, he retired to his "study," the one large room in the
small apartment, that maybe had pocket doors. It was on the second
or third floor of what had once been a single residence. His wife,
dear Libby, had rolled Russian cigarettes for him and arranged the
lamps. When my mother and her two brothers made noise, Libby,
according to my mother, put her hand to her lips and said, "Quiet,
the father studies." In Yiddish. I don't know if he did religion or
literature—the two are the same finally in Judaism—but he worked
alone, which was itself suspect. My mother told me that once he
passed her by when she was reading a thick novel. "Vas redst du,
mein tokhter?" (What are you reading, my daughter?) "*Anna Kar-
enina*," she replied. "Ah," he said, in Yiddish, "I read it in Russian."
My theory is that he was some sort of literary critic, maybe an essay-
ist, certainly a moralist. Certainly he went to *schul*. Everyone did.
But I don't think it was religion that motivated him. A "Litvak,"
maybe his family was part of the tens of thousands who fled to
Poland from Lithuania and Belarus after the wave of pogroms fol-
lowing the assassination of Alexander II; he was probably Russian-

speaking, poor and orthodox. If he was touched by Haskala (Jewish enlightenment) in one way or other, which he probably was, that would account for his knowledge of Russian literature, of Tolstoy.

It is interesting that we had no connection with any of his relatives—no Baraches, Barreks, or Berschs, which the Ellis Island document seemed to highlight. His two sons went to public school, in Pittsburgh, and didn't continue their Jewish studies after they were bar-mitzvahed, though they certainly knew enough of the prayers and rituals to be leaders in their small-town communities. They went to work when they were thirteen or fourteen. Simon, in particular, was nonreligious; Harry was an angry "cultural" Jew who mistrusted goyim. He was the one who was in World War I and suffered his whole life from undiagnosed trauma. Beryl could have been from Bialystock itself, some Orthodox corner, or he could have come from a nearby shtetl. He probably was a learned young man who married a well-to-do urban girl—the way they did—Libby never told me. She treated him with a kind of reverence but I don't think it was a marriage of love. That would wait till she married her second husband, David Jacobson, who owned a huge dairy farm in Clinton, Pennsylvania, south of Pittsburgh. There she made breakfast for the "hands," six or seven of them, who lived in several low-lying wooden buildings on the farm. The foreman's name was Steve. He was Polish, had a pet skunk, and collected mushrooms. She probably married Jacobson in 1932 or '33. They ended up in one of his houses in Homestead, across the river from Pittsburgh, where he died one day lugging groceries up a hill. Maybe in 1940. I asked the four questions at his table, and once I drew a likeness of him that was superb and which made him very angry. His family resented the marriage; Libby signed a prenuptial and stuck to it, though he was quite rich. My Uncle Harry and my father supported her the last four or five years of her life. She could have come to live with us, as she had done fifteen years earlier, but

my mother was too depressed, exhausted, and incompetent to man-
age it. After we abandoned our "home," during the Depression, we
never had more than one small bedroom. Ida couldn't manage two,·
let alone three. Not to mention food and the rest. I adored Libby,
tall, brilliant, and deeply perceptive.

61 Bialystock, 1906

In 1906, the year after they came to America, there was a major
pogrom in Bialystock. By that time Bialystock had a population
of close to seventy thousand, the majority of whom were Jewish.
The Russian census of 1897 indicates that 65 percent were Jewish.
It was a major center of the textile industry, the owners—of the
factories and work spaces—were significantly Jewish and a huge
segment of the workers also were. Today Bialystock has a popula-
tion of two hundred fifty or three hundred thousand, and there are
no real memories of the Jews. There was a Pillar of Sorrow above
a mass grave where the victims of the 1906 pogrom were buried
together, a beautiful structure—in the old Jewish cemetery—with
a special epitaph, in Hebrew, by the poet Zalman Sznejur. It stood
for decades, even during the German onslaught, but after World
War II it was vandalized, cut into three pieces, and discarded near
the outskirts of the cemetery.

The Bialystock pogrom, ironically, was not organized by priests
or crazies, but by czarist murderers after the chief of the czarist
police force in Bialystock was assassinated. He was, it turns out, a
liberal, and loved by the whole populace, Jewish and Polish (if a
police chief can be loved). Jews and Poles alike belonged to revo-
lutionary parties, but this particular police chief had previously
restrained Russian soldiers in Bialystock who were targeting Jews
by actually saying "as long as I live, there will be no pogrom in
Bialystock."

The attack occurred on Green Thursday, a Christian holy day, when there were Catholic and Russian Orthodox processions on the main streets. At a given signal, "hooligans," armed with knives and axes and escorted by police and soldiers, fanned out into the center of the city, smashed doors and windows, and pillaged everything in sight. The killing and looting lasted for three days. The Jewish Self-Defense League saved many people, especially in Jewish working-class sections. When the Duma, the Russian parliament, learned of the pogrom, they immediately sent a delegation from St. Petersburg and the attacks ended. We are talking eighty, a hundred, people killed, twice that number wounded. It wasn't like the work of the Germans thirty-five, forty, years later, but what occurred did so in a modern city, in broad daylight, with the participation of thousands. One of my main witnesses, David Sohn, writes in the *Bialystocken Memorial Book* (1982) that "the vicious criminals gouged people's eyes out with their nails or stuffed their cut-open abdomens with feathers." "Some of the victims," he says, "included small children, whose hearts, and other organs, were removed."

There always was hatred, humiliation, and torture but seldom pogroms, which one of my dictionaries defines as "a massacre for the annihilation of any body or class, especially with governmental collusion, more specifically one directed against Jews." The word—a Russian one meaning destruction—seems to have been in use from the early 1880s onward, particularly after the assassination of Czar Alexander II, which was blamed—again—on the Jews. Those wild terrorists. There seems to be general agreement that the Russian secret police was the institution most responsible for government action, though there must have been collusion with politicians, priests, petty nobility, sickies, and God knows what and whom. They (the secret police) are given credit for writing the "Protocols of the Learned Elders of Zion," a document circulated in Russian official circles at the end of the nineteenth century purporting to reveal the covert Jewish motives of history, a "plan" made by a secret Jewish "government" for the overthrow of Christian society (ah, Adolf; ah, Ez). The Protocols, a ridiculous forgery, were wildly popular in western Europe and are discussed and broadcast on Egyptian and other Arab radio stations to this day. We are lucky in America, for the time being, that the right wing "likes" Jews, or God knows what the Father Coughlins, Lindberghs, Henry Fords, and America Firsters of our day would be doing. Though I abhor them—the right-wing philo-Semites—and their defense of the most arrogant Israeli actions and their stupid assumption that all American Jews approve of Israeli government policy.

I'm trying to resist the temptation to take on everything, poisoning wells (Black Death), blood libel (matzos), deicide (brother Yeshua), cosmopolitanism, hatred of Goyim (Barbarians), separation, lack of patriotism, weakness, super strength, host-eaters, shrewdness, swaying, chanting, exploiting, bastard language, Rothschildism, big-noseism (Hittites), Bolshevism, liberalism, secrecy, Nihilism, Zionism, internationalism, hypersexuality, secret drinking water, vegetarianism, dairyism, banking, usury, lack of flowers, horns, fins, tails, beards, hats, antitheism, financialism, supremacy, parasitism, hairiness.

62 Poland I

If Jews are, and were, "the other," in this country and that, they were so—sometimes—mystically and positively as well as sinisterly and negatively. Their long—and huge—presence in Poland is a case in point just as, at the opposite end, their cruel history in Germany. Jews settled in Poland as early as the ninth century. For hundreds of years it was home to the largest Jewish community in

the world, and it was, amazingly, one of the most tolerant coun-
tries in Europe. It was knows as Jewish paradise—Paradisus Judae-
orum—the Golden Age. By the middle of the sixteenth century
three-quarters of all Jews lived there. And it lasted for five hundred
years. Jews formed the middle class and came to form the backbone
of the Polish economy. They minted coins, engaged in trade, and,
in general, served the lesser nobility in their relations to the serfs,
sometimes sadly. But it was more than that—the whole economy
rested in their hands. In 1264 Boleslaus the Pious, with the consent
of the class representatives and higher officials, issued a General
Charter of Jewish Liberties that granted all Jews the freedom of
worship, trade, and travel; and in 1334 King Casimir III expanded
Boleslaus's charter, to make it a crime punishable by death to kid-
nap Jewish children for the purpose of enforced Christian baptism.
But the Black Death at the end of the fourteenth century, which
decimated the population of Europe, was blamed on the Jews, and
in 1347 the first blood libel accusation—in Poland—was recorded
and the "Jewish riots," in Poland, began. Jews and goats both have
beards, and though goats are not known to poison wells or make
unleavened bread from the blood of Christian children, they too
are guilty—of everything, and it is only just to throw them out of
windows.

The Polish rulers were able to resist the Roman Catholic Church
and the pressure from neighboring German states at first, but the
decline finally set in. The history is various and even confusing.
There always seemed to be some country waiting, and when the
Jews were expelled from Spain in 1492 and a little later from Aus-
tria, Hungary, and Germany, Poland became a haven for exiles
from western and central Europe, and the cultural and spiritual
center of European Jews. If you had to indicate a date for the
decline, it would have to be the middle of the seventeenth century
(1648) with the Chmielnicki Uprising in which the Cossacks and

their allies, the Crimean Tatars, killed hundreds of thousands of Christian and Jewish Poles in Ukraine, then a part of southern and eastern Poland. This was followed by the Swedish invasion, under Charles X, which overran the whole country, the Jews caught in between. The Jewish losses, from war and disease, may have been as high as five hundred thousand, but Poland lost three million in all, a foretaste of later things. The various partitions of Poland ended up with the Jews mostly under Russian control. *Their* official policy was limiting and mostly discriminatory.

63 Poland II

When an independent Poland was re-created at the end of World War I, there was an attempt to create a *Polish* state rather than a multicultural one, though the borders were always in doubt and there were wars between Poland and its neighbors—Russia, Ukraine, Belarus—which always involved Jews. Thousands of Jews entered Poland from Ukraine and Soviet Russia. They felt safer there. But there remained two cultures, almost two states, interpenetrating each other. It is true that urban Jews were increasingly attracted to Polish culture, though only about 10 percent were fully assimilated. What would have happened if there had been no war is hard to say. Certainly more and more assimilation. The *Free Encyclopedia* says that 73 percent of Jews lived in large and smaller cities, and 23 percent in villages, that a third of Warsaw was Jewish, and 10 percent of the whole population, three and a half million, were. That they worked in manufacturing and commerce. That the majority of retail businesses were owned by Jews. That 56 percent of the doctors and 43 percent of the teachers were Jewish. That they belonged to diverse political parties. That anti-Semitism was widespread in the new commonwealth and the influx of Russian Jews only exacerbated it. That Jews were often not identified as Polish nationals.

That there was enormous discrimination, exclusion, and violence at the universities and anti-Jewish squads developed on the right (though Piłsudski, the great patriot, was against ethnic assimilation and considered only loyalty to the state). That Jews made up 20 percent of the student population in 1928, but by 1937 their share was down to 7.5 percent. That there were ghetto benches. That there were "Aryan clauses" expelling Jews from professional unions, including those of lawyers and doctors. That there were separate Jewish trade unions. That Jews were virtually excluded from Polish government jobs. That anti-Jewish feeling was increasing more and more in the years before World War II—as, of course, it was elsewhere, everywhere, in Europe. That there were boycotts of Jewish businesses and the term "Christian shop" was promoted by the right (the Endecja Party). That a substantial portion of Polish Jews lived in grinding poverty. That "the religious-based anti-Semitism was sometimes joined with an ultra-nationalistic stereotype of Jews as disloyal to the Polish nation." That "hostility toward Jews was a mainstay of the right-wing political force and the Catholic Church." And that there was an "official Polish government desire to remove Jews from Poland and that it continued until the German invasion." Those with memories and those who read know this.

One could point out the ravages that Poland experienced; and its desperate desire for ethnic unity and how the Jews stubbornly resisted or interfered with that; or how Jews were not really Poles and the majority still spoke Yiddish and what the hell did they want anyway; or that they refused to become Catholic like the rest of us; or that there was a high degree of dwarfism, redheadedness, and left-handedness anyhow among them; or that they did, indeed, if not desecrate, then certainly not respect, the Host; or look what we've done for them, for God's sake; or they call us Goyim; and spit; and what do they say about us in their Hebrew; or they want to fuck our women; or so many of them learned Russian and anyhow they're leftists; and communists; and they never hunt; and they hardly drink; and what good are they at weddings, except to play their violins; and they all want to go to America anyhow; and not one of them knows Latin; and they don't like blood soup; or lard sandwiches; that the Polish past and the suffering means shit to them; and all they want to do is go to their stupid Palestine; and they hide in their cellars on Easter; and who cares about the Red Sea; and they don't know anything about wild mushrooms; and they speak too many languages; and why should they have cars; and Poland is for the Poles; and fuck autonomy; and how rich they grow at our expense; they're parasites; saprophytes; a surplus population; they should go live in Madagascar; or float in the Dead Sea; and don't get me started.

And what am I doing, and why am I doing it? For reasons beyond sense I love Poland. In spite. And Polish food and its poetry and its countryside and its beauty. And I wish there had been some way. I don't love Russia, or Ukraine, or the Baltics. And I know too much. And I am weary of Romanian anti-Semitism. In *2010*. I am weary of Europe. I am weary of Judaism itself. For me to be obsessed about the period before the war, when the trap was already set, has to do with my own life and the age I was, and am, and the maps I drew and the books I read and the libraries I plundered, and the things I knew—when I was thirteen, fourteen, fifteen. Poland was not alone. The other central and eastern European countries were the same—and worse. It would take fifty pages to describe what was going on in Romania. After Versailles—and Wilson— Romania found itself a multination state, like the new Poland, but it didn't want to accommodate ethnic diversity within its borders, Hungarians, Ukrainians, Gypsies, Slovaks, Jews. The Romanians were actually ahead of the Germans. Their government attacked the Jews as a "bastard race and the source of degeneration." Their first goal, like the Germans', was wholesale expulsion. One fascist ideologue (Alexandru Razmerita) proposed imprisoning the whole Jewish population in concentration camps and working them to death. "This plan seemed more practical than a rival proposal by an Orthodox priest to drown all the Jews in the Black Sea." (I am quoting from a book called *Holocaust* by Debórah Dwork and Robert Jan van Pelt.) Romania had its own version of the Nuremberg laws, and Codreanu's Iron Guard took over the government in 1937. This is what he said: "The Jews, the Jews, they are our curse. They poison our state, our life, our people. They demoralize our nation. They destroy our youth. They are the arch-enemies. We shall destroy the Jews before they can destroy us. . . . Every single Jew must leave this country. You ask where they should go? That is not my business."

But what I'm most ashamed of, as a person of Polish descent, is the anti-Semitism, the Jew-hatred, *after* World War II. Some ninety thousand to one hundred thousand Polish Jews survived the war and the Holocaust by hiding or by joining with Polish or Soviet Partisans. Others were repatriated from the Soviet Union and elsewhere. There were, in the late 1940s, up to a quarter-million Jews in Poland. Many came from Hungary, Romania, Czechoslovakia, and Yugoslavia. But there was a wave of emigration in the 1950s, and after the Six-Day War (in 1967), the Polish Communist Party adopted an anti-Jewish course of action, called anti-Zionism, which in the years 1968–69 provoked the last mass migration of Jews from Poland, leaving about thirty thousand Polish Jews in all.

64 Neighbors I

The issue of Jews and Poles (or Jewish Poles and Christian Poles) as "neighbors," to use the code word, is difficult to understand or explain. There was a spate of books written in the early years of this century on the subject of neighbors, and the book called *Neigh-*

bors, by Jan Gross, tells of the murder of the entire Jewish half of a population—1,600 people—by the Christian half in a small town in northeastern Poland, called Jedwabne. The event occurred on July 10, 1941, and was overseen by the German occupiers who gave the Poles a period of time—eight hours—to accomplish the deed. These were people who had lived together for hundreds of years, were integrated economically and culturally, and knew each other—everyone—on a first-name basis. The ring leaders—in Jedwabne—were a carpenter, a small farmer, a town hall receptionist, a letter carrier, and a shoemaker, some of them family men with five or six children, one as old as sixty-four, one twenty-seven. Jews were killed by axes, hatchets, knives, crowbars, and studded clubs—or were drowned. The remnants were locked in a barn and burned to death. The same thing occurred in the nearby (neighboring) villages of Radziłów, Wąsosz, Wizna, also in the first months of the German occupation. There were explanations and justifications of course, but by and large Poland was shocked when it learned—sixty years after the fact—of these horrors. They are more or less in denial, in spite of overwhelming evidence. Always the Germans are blamed, or the Russians.

Another book, *Imaginary Neighbors*, is a collection of essays—by Geoffrey Hartman, Zev Garber, Joanna Zylinska, and others—on the events of Jedwabne, the suppression of the past, and the issue of redemption. Garber, who writes about Auschwitz, does take on church leaders, for example the Primate of Poland, Cardinal Hlond, who—in 1936—said "a Jewish problem exists and will continue to exist as long as Jews remain Jews"; and Bishop Wyszyński, who did not condemn the Kielce pogrom on the grounds that the Jews engaged in ritual murder. 1946. Or Cardinal Józef Glemp's sermon on the fiftieth anniversary of World War II (1989) where he condemned Jewish elitism, international media power, and propensity (by Jews) to kill. "Anti-Polonism," he said, "is the cause of

Polish anti-Semitism." And Glemp again, at the sixtieth anniversary of Jedwabne, 2001, where the president of Poland, Aleksander Kwaśniewski, apologized for the Polish action: "I don't want politicians to tell the Church how it should express its sorrow for crimes committed by some group of its believers." Neither did he come to the memorial service, thus sending a strong message.

How hard it is for Poles, martyrs themselves in competition with Jewish martyrs, to hear and accept the denigration, especially if they were themselves helpless. I just reread the interview with Miłosz on Polish-Jewish relations, published in *Tikkun* in 1988, and I am struck by, what seems to me, how weary and bored he is by the questions, perhaps the questioner. Sometimes even desperate; as if Miłosz had not endlessly agonized over Europe and its horrors. He who wrote "A Poor Christian Looks at the Ghetto" and "Campo dei Fiori" and "A Song on the End of the World" and "Child of Europe." Though I have to say that—in the interview—the mutual resentment Czesław refers to implies equal strength (of Jews and Poles), which was clearly never the case; and I have to disagree when he says that the Holocaust was "pagan" and the result of "half-baked scientific ideas" and had neither roots nor connections with Christianity and its history. I say this while deeply loving him and his poetry. Here is his great poem "A Poor Christian Looks at the Ghetto":

> Bees build around red liver,
> Ants build around black bone.
> It has begun: the tearing, the trampling on silks,
> It has begun: the breaking of glass, wood, copper, nickel,
>   silver, foam
> Of gypsum, iron sheets, violin strings, trumpets, leaves, balls,
>   crystals.
> Poof! Phosphorescent fire from yellow walls
> Engulfs animal and human hair.

Bees build around the honeycomb of lungs,
Ants build around white bone.
Torn is paper, rubber, linen, leather, flax,
Fiber, fabrics, cellulose, snakeskin, wire.
The roof and the wall collapse in flame and heat seizes the
 foundations.
Now there is only the earth, sandy, trodden down,
With one leafless tree.

Slowly, boring a tunnel, a guardian mole makes his way,
With a small red lamp fastened to his forehead.
He touches buried bodies, counts them, pushes on,
He distinguishes human ashes by their luminous vapor,
The ashes of each man by a different part of the spectrum.
Bees build around a red trace.
Ants build around the place left by my body.

I am afraid, so afraid of the guardian mole.
He has swollen eyelids, like a Patriarch
Who has sat much in the light of candles
Reading the great book of the species.

What will I tell him, I, a Jew of the New Testament,
Waiting two thousand years for the second coming of Jesus?
My broken body will deliver me to his sight
And he will count me among the helpers of death:
The uncircumcised.

— WARSAW, 1943

My own book of poems—in Polish—is called *Podziemny Taniec,
Underground Dancing.* There's a mole there too, though mine is danc-
ing. I read from this book in 1999, in Kraków. I danced with Czesław
on an outdoor dance floor in Napa one night in the mid-1980s. His
severe side suddenly changed as he broke into a loving smile—I
remember the cool, dry weather, the noisy writers and the happiness.

I sometimes imagine that there was no war, and Jews didn't die,
and Poles. And I go back to Warsaw and Bialystock, and Kraków,

but not with a heavy heart. I am sure the shtetls would be gone
under any circumstances and the Jewboys and Jewgirls would be
writing their poems in Polish, as well as Yiddish, and we could
scream at each other poetic truths without the hideous memory.
I'd probably have to learn that crazy language. I'd probably have to
kiss the ground—or at least a tree or two.

What "neighbors" are I will think about for the rest of my life.
And I will remember the admonitions. And what Hillel said, and
Jesus.

I will, alas, also remember the gouged-out eyes, the burned
beards, the desecrated Torahs, the iron bars, the studded clubs, the
bashed heads, the forced singing and dancing, the accordion and
flute music to drown out the screams, insults, babies on pitchforks,
whipping, stabbing, beheading, kitchen knives, drowning—and
burning; as well as robbery, expropriation, plunder, extortion, kid-
napping, and bribery. I have to.

Christmas Sticks

Before I leave I'll put two sticks on the porch
so they can talk to each other about poor Poland
and wrap themselves around each other the way sticks
do when most of life is gone. They will lie
a little about Wałesa, one will dance
and shake his dried-out leaves as if to threaten
the other, one will lean against the wall
as if there were boots to give him courage, as if
there was a moustache somewhere there among the scars
and a thin sword and a thin tear. I'd make them flower
again, I'd make them drive through Warsaw
on the back of trucks, I'd have them reach their wooden
hands through the flimsy slats and take the gifts
and live out the dream of 1830 and the dream
of 1863, the Russians gone,
the Germans gone, the life remade, the flags
flying over the factories, workers dancing

above the trees, a wedding under a walnut,
the food amazing, the last memory the bride's
father in white showing his empty pockets,
his beard a little white to match his suit,
his eyes all wet, his shirt half open –
all that sweetness, all that golden fat –
the fat I love, the sweetness I love – and the two of them
walking home at night after the wedding
talking to each other again about Pulaski
and Casimir the Great and Copernicus
and what it could have been if only sticks
had ruled the vicious world, remembering again
the Jews arriving from Spain, the scholars of Europe
descending on Cracow, half the Italian painters,
living in Poland, the gentry reading books,
the women drawing and playing flutes –
forgetting the dream-crushers out there in the swamps,
forgetting the liars, forgetting the murderers –
two sticks in the moonlight carrying on
after the wedding, lifting their empty bottles
for the last time, one of them heaving his over
a sycamore – a buttonwood tree – one of them
heaving his across a frozen river
and listening with his hands on his bent knees
for the old crash, slow in coming, the impact
a half a minute later than he expected,
both of them laughing at the stupidity;
both of them weeping for the huge carp
frozen in mud, and both of them toasting the bride
with broken hands, with nothing this time, with fingers
ruined and shredded, kissing the dear one good-bye
before they go off like wounded soldiers, home
from fighting the Turks at Vienna, home from fighting
the Deutschers a hundred times and the Rooskies two
     hundred,
home from fighting the Swedes and the Austrians,
two great masters of suffering and sadness
singing songs about love and regeneration.

– GERALD STERN

Underground Dancing

There's a bird pecking at the fat;
there's a dead tree covered with snow;
there's a truck dropping cinders on the slippery highway.

There's life in my backyard –
black wings beating on the branches,
greedy eyes watching,
mouths screaming and fighting over the greasy ball.

There's a mole singing hallelujah.
Close the rotten doors!
Let everyone go blind!
Let everyone be buried in his own litter. ·

— GERALD STERN

65 Lev Going

Tomorrow, Wednesday, August 11, Stephanie Smith, my long-time assistant, and I are driving to Brooklyn to meet my second or so cousin, much removed, in a real estate office on Coney Island Avenue—either Kensington or Borough Park—in Brooklyn, to talk about my father's side of the family. His name is Lev Dolgo-pyatov, and he's the grandson of my father's oldest brother, Eliazer, who stayed back in Ruzhin, in Ukraine, when the rest of the family came to America, from 1901 on. My grandfather, who died when my own father was twelve or thirteen, ran a small sawmill and had modest holdings in real estate, a fishery, and grew some tobacco (before he came to America), all of which Lazer presumably held onto. Lazer had two children, one a son who was a high-ranking officer in the Soviet army, and Lev was, as I understand it, *his* son. Lazer—in his sixties—was in hiding with a Christian family during the onslaught and was shot by a German soldier when he walked out one day. Lev's father died in the Battle of Budapest. Lev is in his early seventies, has been in America a couple of years, and speaks no English. I gather, from my cousin Norman (Stern), son of the second oldest brother, George, that Lev came over as the result of a second marriage, or third. I thought the family name was Dol-giapiat, not Dolgopyatov. Another removed cousin, Ronald M. Grossman, M.D., I think from Cincinnati, wrote a family history and spelt the name Duglepiet—changed to Stern at Ellis Island. *His* history centered on his grandmother, Della, my father's sister, and his grandfather, Samuel Grossman, a paper hanger from Pittsburgh who had eleven children, ten boys and one girl, one of whom, Isaac, was Ronald's father. We're supposed to meet at two o'clock. It's a seventy-two-mile drive, according to AAA, and I called Norman a while ago to double-check. He reached Lev's wife, who speaks some Yiddish, in addition to Russian, and I'm waiting for confirma-tion. I have no idea what Lev did—or is doing—in this life, whether he has children and what his memories are. And I've never been on Coney Island Avenue. I'm going to take a few pictures, and some of my books, with me.

66 Lev Not There

Lev didn't show up—which didn't surprise me. Norman—who is ninety-three—called the evening before and informed me that we were meeting at one o'clock, not two. Lev, he said, preferred the new time since he had appointments later in the day. So I rear-ranged my schedule—and Stephanie, hers—so we could be there on time. We left at 10:30 in the morning and got there a little after 12:30. There were accidents, tie-ups, traffic, detours, new routes, and creative driving, but we reached our destination and parked at a meter near the real estate office, the Advocate, at 874 Coney Island

Avenue. We were in the middle of an intensely urban, somewhat crumbling, neighborhood, small factories, businesses, chain restaurants, broken sidewalks, small ugly houses, large ugly apartment buildings, and endless side streets, some of which were tree-lined and had large houses, built, it looked like, in the first twenty years of the twentieth century. The neighborhood, Mr. Fleischman, the owner of the Advocate, told us, was Jewish, Palestinian, African, African American, Russian, Chinese, and Italian. I saw covered women, tall thin black-clad bearded young men walking by with their eyes glued to books, and dozens of children, half of them wearing yarmulkes.

We walked into the office about a quarter to one. Norman was the only one there. He goes to the office two half-days a week to answer the phone. During his working life he had a small real estate business—in Pittsburgh—called "Stern Realty." I don't think he ever made much money. He lives now, with his wife, in a lower East Side apartment a floor up from his daughter Rachel and her husband, Michael, and their eight children. Orthodox, to this degree or that. I knew Norman well back in Pittsburgh, on Miller Street in the Hill, and later on Uncle George's farm in Mars, Pennsylvania, site of the Twin Willows swimming pool, two-thirds of the way to Butler, up Route 8. There were eighty acres, an old farmhouse, a large barn, dairy cows, goats, dogs, apple trees, corn, woods, and a long twisting narrow dirt road to get into or onto the farm, from Route 8. We used to go there every few weeks; my father adored the country but my mother was more or less horrified. Norman had eight brothers and sisters; his mother, Aunt Anna, had Parkinson's from an early age. George divorced her in his sixties and married a young widow who worked in a bakery. But he moved Anna to a house in Pittsburgh, brought her groceries, cooked for her, and took her to the bathroom. I remember my mother, in the early fifties, asking George why he didn't just take a mistress. He was shocked; he said it was a violation of one of the 612 commandments.

We waited for almost two hours. It was Norman, Rachel, Stephanie, and later, Mr. Fleischman, no customers. Stephanie was fascinated by Jewish Orthodoxy and the woman's place in it, and she and Rachel talked all the time we were there. Later we went to a marvelous kosher Pakistani restaurant and afterward I phoned Lev, who answered, but I couldn't communicate with him. Norman, who was back home by this time, called Lev and then called me, on my cell phone. Lev told him he was sick and wasn't able to come. Norman apparently informed Lev we had traveled eighty miles to get there and gave up the whole day, but it didn't seem to matter. I kept wondering if Norman had given Lev the phone number of Advocate Realty so he could call if something went wrong, or if Lev truly understood that we were driving through two states to get there, or if he thought all of America was in Flatbush, or knew I was his cousin (much removed); or if he was too terrified or too anxious to leave his house and street and whether I should be angry at Lev—or Norman, or Mr. Fleischman—and I realized I was in the hands of others and they were enacting my destiny and I had little to say. Rachel, whom I love, was the sane one. She thought, lovingly, that her father had maybe gotten the time of the day or the number of the Advocate wrong. She also thought Lev was a frightened and fearful man, maybe afraid to travel (one-half mile). At one point, when I asked Norman whether he gave Lev the right number, he said "866," which was not the "874" he told me. Norman then showed me stationery which said 866 on the envelope and 874 on the pages. It made me realize I was in the midst of a huge Jewish vision, conundrum, or joke. Columbus, blessed be him, was supposed to be a Jew, which explains why he went west to go east and why he screwed up on India and the rest. Though wrong-way Corrigan wasn't Jewish, either because he was Irish or his head was too big.

Lev seemed to show no remorse or guilt. Maybe he was too self-absorbed for that. So, unless I contact him again, there are a few things I won't find out, such as where was he during the war (born in 1938 or '39), what was his mother's name, what town he actually lived in—or city; did he know his grandfather and grandmother; or father, even; what language, aside from Yiddish, he spoke; where he went to school; what happened to the family holdings; did he have children; why he came to America when he was seventy—or why did he wait so long; what occupation did he have; did he have a Jewish education; was he "observant"; what was his attitude to Ukraine; to Israel; what was the situation of the Jews in Ukraine; what he's "doing" now; and where has he traveled. I may give these questions to Norman. I might fax him—to *ask* Lev. I may not.

In a large family like my father's you have closer connections to one brother or sister than to another. My father's closest siblings were Della (Grossman), mother of eleven, and George (Stern), father of seven—eight. George, Norman's father, was the oldest of the children (of Jacob) to come to America. His real name was, according to Norman, Joseph. The name of the Ukrainian shtetl, according to Norman, was not Ruzhin, but Jetamor. The family tree (which Rachel gave me) lists me—incorrectly—as a twin to Sylvia. It lists my David and Rachael but not their mother, Patricia Miller. Chmielnicki's real name was Khmelnytsky. He destroyed three hundred Jewish communities in the middle of the seventeenth century. In 1918 five hundred Jews were killed at Odessa in a single day by counterrevolutionary groups. Lenin said the Jews did not constitute a "nation," but Stalin changed his mind. I am exhausted from eastern European history. It was such a joy to drive west over the Verrazano Narrows Bridge, though it cost eleven dollars.

67 Neighbors II

I still have some more to say about "neighbors." It won't let me alone. *They* won't. I suspect every writer has a single passion that, if he's not careful, will consume him and, worse, irritate the reader. But this thing about neighbors might, after all, be the secret text of this book.

At any rate, there was an article by a Leo Stein, published in the *National Jewish Monthly* of May 1941 (I found God knows where), in which Stein claimed that he shared a cell with Martin Niemöller, the famous German pastor, at Moabit Prison in Berlin in the mid-1930s, and that later they were together again at Sachsenhausen, a German concentration camp, and talked endlessly as they walked in the "small circle," given over to the old and sick, during "recreation." Stein, a year later, with some significant help, I'm sure, wrote a book called *I Was in Hell with Niemöller,* which spells out in more detail their "friendship." Stein, apparently, was released and came to America in 1939 or 1940—he doesn't tell us when—and wrote the article, and a book that followed shortly thereafter.

Stein is a little slippery in talking about himself. He—apparently—taught at a university in Berlin. He was a doctor of jurisprudence and church law, though whether he was baptized or not he doesn't say. I was struck by the fact that, according to the *Jewish Monthly* article, he "shared a cell" with Niemöller, which made them very close neighbors, and I began writing on the intriguing issue, though after I read the book (in an hour or two) I realized that they weren't cell mates but "cell-block neighbors" since the cells, Stein says, had only one bed and a second person would have had to sleep on the cement floor. If they *had* been cell mates they would certainly have been "neighbors," and fairly close ones at that. As it turned out, they were more distant neighbors. I wondered, in my first ignorance, whether they talked about their wives or what books they once loved or who was the angrier and complained the louder and who was hungrier and which one missed cigarettes the most—or wine—or did they talk of escaping and whose feet were bigger. And I'm wondering if the good pastor, who was indignant that baptized Jews were still persecuted as *Jews* by the Nazis, ever reminded Stein about a famous sermon he gave in 1935 in which he said that the reason for the Jews' punishment is that they "brought the Christ of God to the Cross." And if they saw the irony of their situation, the two of them. And which one had the softer pillow and which of them loved his (more distant) neighbor the more, and which one of the Golden Rules (or copper) did each of them follow, and what did each of them think of the Bahai's rule, or Islam's, or Ancient Egypt's (late period)? And did either of them mention Hillel the Elder and, in his memory, did either of them become a stork?

I was confused by how Stein could have gotten out of Sachsenhausen, but he was sent there in the first place not because he was a Jew as such, for it would be a year or two before the Germans did that, but on the charge of high treason for something he presumably said in class; but the case was so poor against him (apparently) that he wasn't found guilty. He was released (a few months? a few years?) later and, along with eighty other Jews, was allowed to leave Germany. When, in one of their talks, Stein asked Niemöller why he was an early supporter of the Nazi Party, Niemöller, Stein says, said he thought that Hitler would save Germany from the excesses of the Weimar Republic and restore honor and religion (read law and order) to the Reich. Niemöller had had an audience with Hitler—in 1932—before Hitler became chancellor—and Hitler promised, on his word of honor, that the Nazis would protect the Church and not issue any anti-Church laws. He also said, according to Niemöller according to Stein, "that he wouldn't allow pogroms against the Jews though there would be restrictions."

I at first thought the whole thing was a fabrication, the article *and* the book, but I think there was some kind of Stein and that he did share space in both Moabit (the Berlin prison) and later, in Sachsenhausen, though I doubt the twenty-two months he claimed. I tried desperately to swallow the bad writing, the absurd melodrama, and the treatment of Niemöller as a saint, almost a redeemer. I guess I'm not that interested in the silly propaganda but got caught up in the weird character of Stein.

As far as neighbors, there's nothing like a prison, and the more or less uniform treatment, to promote close identity, as well as jealousy, love, and hate; and the keepers of the gate exploit that *in extremis* for their own needs, as they see them. My own neighbors, here in Lambertville, are a loving sort and I'm very happy to be among them. The city is small enough that almost everyone is a neighbor, though some are more so—if that is possible—than others. If there were only eighty people here instead of four thousand, we would be more "intense" neighbors, if I can put it that way. If we were all gay or nudist or Hasidic it would be very intense, or too intense. Jedwabne was, by the way, about a third smaller than Lambertville. Across the river is New Hope. Lambertville and New Hope are *near* neighbors, though seen in relation to the rest of the state they are closer than *near*. People in Trenton or Princeton would then be "near."

Today we sat on steel folding chairs at faux tables eating lobster dinners and drinking wine in front of the city park on York Street—the street itself blocked off from traffic—at fifty dollars a head, to raise money for another park, one side of the elementary school playground. The food was donated by local restaurants: corn, potatoes, sausage, lobster, mussels, clams, shrimp, wine (red and white), and there were maybe 100 people there, 125. Six, seven thousand dollars. A band, and a singer, on the nearby bandstand. I knew at least half of them by sight. We were neighbors. Though we were cut off from the many other 125s who maybe couldn't afford

the fifty dollars, the hundred dollars a couple. *Less* than neighbors
in this case; or *other* neighbors. But I live in two houses here in
Lambertville, one mine and one Anne Marie's, so I have two sets
of neighbors, or immediate neighbors, and I only ignore one of my
(immediate) neighbors, although not his dog.

68 Neighbors III

Chase—not Chase Bank, just Chase—sent me a $200 gift card
today, which is mine if I open a Chase checking account, and which
I can redeem in person or online. They promise that when I have
$36,000 in my account they will pay me 23 cents, but no minimum
balance is required, and I can pay my bills online, and I have free
access to over 15,000 Chase ATMs, and I get a free debit card with
built-in security and free voice and email alerts. The gift card was
addressed to "Our Neighbor," and where the stamp should have
been it said the gift card was paid by JP Morgan.

In Romania, I suppose, the Roma are not neighbors, so why
should they go to school and get medical assistance? I talk to Linda
Gregg every week, and when I mentioned the Roma she said that
they were a tight-knit group, separate and exclusionary, but I
pointed out the obvious, that they, the Romas, are the more perse-
cuted; and loving your neighbor might be more the responsibility
of the Romanians and she immediately agreed. She was reading *The
Master of Lucid Dreams,* and I liked the title so much that I ordered it
that afternoon. Now I only have about thirty books waiting to be
read. Linda, an original and moving lyric poet, has been my friend
for forty-five years. We are neighbors but more by phone now. We
shared an apartment once on St. Mark's, and I guess we were some-
thing other than neighbors, though I hate the word "roommates."
The six months *I* was locked up, while in the army, I had thirty-
nine roommates—they were neighbors—and we were forced to

sleep with the light on, a bare bulb. I was directly under it. They were all African American—to a man—in there for AWOL and drunkenness. Like Leo and Martin we hated Hitler but, at the same time, more the provost-sergeant, a kind of Nazi bastard himself. But I can't remember his name. I write about that in my book of essays, *What I Can't Bear Losing.*

The question remains always who, and what, are neighbors. In many cases people nearby, or among us, are ignored, or invisible; not counted because of race, illness, age, or economic status. They are not "neighbors" and we don't have to "love" them. I am on a train now, going from Trenton to New York, and my neighbor—that is the person sharing my small, uncomfortable bench—is wearing a baseball cap and reading a golf magazine. He's been at it for over an hour and I have a feeling I don't love him. It is Saturday morning of Labor Day weekend, and the train is packed, and noisy. I closed my eyes a while ago and listened to the sounds, babies screaming, passengers talking in four or five languages. After a while the talking got louder; there was a general hum—no, more than a hum, more than a clucking, a roar really—and I felt I was a soon-to-be dead chicken, my beak gone, squeezed into a box, a cage, and crying for help. My neighbors were all fat feathered force-fed birds, my own grandfather waiting with his flat razor-sharp knife before the throat was opened and the dead heart skipped away from the blind and foolish body. The day will come when we either will lift our sharpened hatchets against our fellow humans or—the whole other way—we will retreat in horror, even in the killing of the blooded other animals we now call poultry, cattle, and game, and kill, or murder, by number, by belt, by hammer, by hook, in one Chicago after another.

I carry around my small book of *Extraordinary Chickens* Anne Marie bought for me on Madison Avenue near 92nd Street years ago and stare at the Lakenvelder, who stares back at me, or the magnificent Red Shoulder Cockerel from Yokohama. On page 178 is the Cornish Bantam Dark Hen, encased in pure black, a living creature with a huge sad eye that, if I cover up the horrendous beak, I see as a human eye, which, combined with the other features, shows fear and wonder in an eternity of ignorance and helplessness. I stare longingly at the eye, huge and round, a black pupil, or very dark brown, surrounded first with a slightly reddish circle and then with a tan or light-brown rim punctuated in the center—of the pupil—with a small bright dot of light as if an eye doctor were shining his invisible instrument into the eye or as if the feathered soul were trying to assert itself, or pleading through its tiny brilliance for the killer to reconsider before he lifted his hatchet or, in the case of my grandfather, his razor-sharp knife. It was Stanley Kunitz's eye, especially when I covered the cruel beak, for Stanley had no such beak, its brown, horny mass arrayed there for catching worms or dead flesh or a piece of an egg itself, with the blue shell, if it was blue, hanging like a flower from the long, narrow opening before the beak curved or the upper part did, and clamped itself tight over the flat and extended lower part. The hair around Stanley's eyes was short and bristly, the isolated black ones separated sharply from each other over a lighter (tan) skin and the complicated nostrils and what I would call a forehead distracting me from the overwhelming presence of the yearning eye into which I had invested so much emotion. And if I too was in that book, would I be a Cochin Black or a Dark Brahma; and what poet twenty years younger than me, and already retired, would stare me down? And would his meat be white or dark? And would he erase my beak as I did Stanley's? And would he describe my feathers? And would we talk, or not, as Stanley and I did, at the cape or at the apartment on 12th Street, given it was 5:30 or even 5:00 and we were ready to drink our afternoon martinis very dry and poke with our swizzle sticks into the life and

times, oh 1940 to 1990, or even 2000, such gossip, the moustache
of his youth still showing, still bristling in his old man's face, or on
it—and mine as well—or was I rather not a giant frog squeezed into
a largemouth jar with "Bass" embossed on the glass, my great and
tasty legs caught helplessly, my own eye staring, my throat like a bel-
lows going out and in with fear at this unforeseen trap or prison, the
dead fly now of no use to me? There for his—or her—pity. There
for their love, those poets. For we all can't be chickens.

In Jedwabne the Jews and the Christians were clear-cut neigh-
bors but they were *separated* and only some had studded clubs. Par-
ents and children and cousins and friends aren't neighbors but are
something more—or something else—and lovers most of all. It's
a strange word—*neighbors*—ambiguous, ironic, culturally and his-
torically and geographically determined. Those of us who were
neighbors in 1946, and the five years before, wore dog tags around
our necks with either the letters *C*, *P*, or *H* on them—for burial's
sake—(no *J*'s—we were "Hebrews"). There were no *A*'s either,
which could have stood for agnostic or atheist or alcoholic. Nor
B's either, nor *J*'s—no Buddhists or Jains—and for all I knew the *H*
could have stood for Hindu. I don't know if it's changed or not—
the dog tags—though, as we all know, there are no *A*'s in foxholes.
It may be that in earlier time "neighbor" only referred to members
of one's group, be it ethnic, religious, or covered in blue grease.
The biblical prophets had the double role of affirming nationhood
and extending the beliefs of "the nation" by making God univer-
sal; a peculiar and weird trap. We may have had to wait for Jewless
Christians to extend the Jewish ideas even if they radically changed
them, though I don't want to argue with my neighbors. Nation-
ality, nationalism, is surely an extension of ethnicity, though the
absolute identification of the two is a perversion, whoever claims
it. I delight in the fact that ethnicity is not possible in American

nationalism, which makes "our" patriotism something other. What we have instead is the two-flag solution, which is good for the soul and also the belly. It's also good for neighborliness and for street fairs. I used to always eat a sausage sandwich, with onion and pepper, on a large shtick of Italian bread at the San Gennaro street fair, wandering among the T-shirts. I'm sorry for all the Jewish stuff, but I'm trying, while I write this, to understand the connections between Jewish nationhood and religion and all the endless permutations, what with secularism, assimilation, tri-culturalism, Orthodoxy, Israel, the murdered Europeans, the exiled African and Arab Jews, Jewish gypsies, and the lost tribes of New Mexico and Mongolia.

In my *Standard Jewish Encyclopedia* (1959), I read in an article titled "Nationalism" (pages 1396–99) about the complexity. Ironically, the article on "National Socialism" immediately precedes the one on "Nationalism," and the article on "Natore Karta" (Guardians of the City) immediately follows. Neighborly. The "Guardians," a small group, refuse (on religious grounds) to recognize the state of Israel (or they did in 1959). I love the picture (on page 1398) of the twenty-six attendees at the Kattowitz Conference of 1884, which was dominated by the spirit of nationalism. Twenty-three have beards, seventeen are not wearing headpieces. Their clothing varies, especially the length of the frock coats. I believe in the mystery of leaping, as I do in the one of flipping. Montaigne's mother was a member of a Marrano family from Saragossa. Montefiore was the name of a hugely wealthy English family of Italian origin, which gave itself over to philanthropy and scholarship. Sir Moses Montefiore was born in 1784 and died in 1885. He negotiated with czars, kings, and sultans, in Russia, Romania, Turkey, and Morocco. His family opposed Zionism. (My Libby died in Montefiore hospital in Pittsburgh. I was the first one to see her dead.) Montpellier was an important Jewish center until it was annexed by France in

1293 and the murderous French took over. The Jews were expelled in 1306. In Morocco there were Jews hundreds of years before the common era. Some Berber tribes converted to Judaism. Over and over the Jewish communities were destroyed, then prospered again. Under Byzantine rule (seventh century), all synagogues were destroyed. Under the Arabs, Fez and Sigilmassa became famous seats of learning. From time to time the fundamentalist Arab governments promulgated anti-Jewish measures. After the expulsion from Spain in 1492, when there was a large influx of Spanish Jews into Morocco, they were ill-treated, confined to mellahs, forced to wear distinctive black clothing, and periodically subjected to fanatical attacks of violence. Under the French (1912–55) the Jewish status improved, but after 1948 over 100,000 Jews migrated to Israel (1959) and 160,000 remained (1959). I don't know if there are a hundred or a thousand left. My dear friend, Ruth Setton, a Moroccan Jew living now in Allentown, Pennsylvania, and teaching at Lehigh University in Bethlehem, left when she was five. France first, then Israel, then the U.S. Her first novel, *The Road to Fez*, centers on Arabic and Jewish mysticism, a commonality that intrigues her. She and her father went back to Morocco fifteen, twenty years ago and visited their house in Casablanca. They were invited in for tea by their Arab hosts and sat on the same sofa her father had bought decades before. Bizarre neighborliness. I notice, in the *Ms*, that Moravia, where the Jews were massacred in 1337 and again at the time of the Black Death (which they caused) in 1349, was a center of rabbinic learning and had a population of 50,000 Jews in 1938, most of whom were killed by the Germans. All this in the neighborly *Ms*.

The Cherokees were the good Samaritans in the South; in the eastern Mediterranean it's the Palestinians. They are the *neighbors* and nothing can justify their exclusion, elimination, entrapment, dispossession, eviction, or persecution; neither opportunity, nor realpolitik nor European oppression nor Arab fascism nor rockets nor rage nor murder nor stupidity nor French nightclubs nor Iran nor Syria nor Libya nor Islam nor Christian fundamentalism nor Jewish orthodoxy nor false memory nor true. Neither Polish peasants nor Slovak nor sexual anxiety nor the Hebron massacre nor the Damascus; neither slander nor the German Olympics nor the general anxiety nor the exhaustion nor the ghettos nor the mellahs nor vengeance nor nationhood nor comparisons nor the Dream; neither cattle cars nor the Greater Thumb nor Yahooism nor pickles nor myth nor scripture nor archaeology nor longing nor arrogance. Buber said, "Tear down this wall, Mr. President"; Reagan, who dyed his hair black, only stole it. From a movie of the same name. Hillel himself stood on one leg.

It's the *border*, isn't it? Inviting; or excluding. Sometimes formidable, made of piled-up stone, or cemented; or barbed wire; sometimes—given what we are as humans—mythical, psychological, invisible. Or the in-between, racial, ethnic, and religious. I think of all the fences in Asia, America, Europe, Africa, Australia. I read endlessly of the exclusions, the barriers, the hatred—and fear. I see the images of Central Americans and Mexicans sneaking under or over. I read about them being suffocated in sealed trucks; I listen— for a few agonizing seconds—to the baboons in Arizona and California making their ugly speeches while exposing their red asses.

It's exhausting to take up another country or another corner of a country or a new continent or an unheard-of river or mountain or language. Maybe it's a permanent part of human history, only we read about it constantly now, though we didn't a century ago, total exposure, even if it's always only partly. I should free myself from the *New York Times* and *The Nation*. I am drowning. Let me pick up a *New York Post* that's left on the seat of a slow, uncomfortable train to Trenton. It's late at night and I'm the last one out. I make it onto the platform just as the train is about to pull out for its night's sleep. Something about China and the Uighurs. Han and Muslim.

I'm deeply ashamed of Bosnia and Darfur and Rwanda. I'm bored by reconciliation. Once or twice was all right, but we now have the ritual. I had a dream—though I didn't—of Henry Miller driving his old Hudson into the rear of a BMW that had a Free Tibet sticker on the bumper. I'm giving up meat, sugar, cream—but not cheese; never cheese. And never eggs.

They were neighbors, weren't they, on Flight 93? September 11th. Sometimes we are temporary neighbors while in the air, soul mates, lovers even. Then strangers again. There was no chance for them ever again to be strangers. We will never know exactly what they did, we who know and record everything. One idiot Congressman opposed a projected memorial. He didn't like sugar maples; or he didn't like the name "Shanksville."

69 Neighbors IV

I am lying now on my back in my dark bedroom and my left hand is caressing the smooth, cool cover of the book that's been there for several years, John Cage's *X*, a collection of prose and poetry, brought out by Wesleyan in 1983. It's full of chance writing, but not much silence, since you can't have that in either prose or poetry, at least as you can in music. Even a book of empty pages is not the same as absent musical notes.

I open (by chance) to page 119 and there is a poem there called "B. W. 1916–1979," which turns out to be an elegy (a memory) of Ben Weber, of about eighty lines, the letters *B, E, N*, then *W, E, B, E, R*, in a straight line directly down the pages with the text at both sides so that BEN WEBER is the formal organizing principle; an affectionate memory, including their differences in music theory as well as the strange world of Weber, but—amazingly—at the heart of the poem a central concern with *boundaries*, so that the issue is, of all things, "neighbors" and, as I say, *by chance;* though I called it *borders,* not boundaries. With the different implications, the limit, as opposed to that lying along the limit:

> the Boundary
> bEtween us
> is a liNe
>
> right doWn
>   thE middle of the master   janus
>   he looked Both back
> and towards what joycE calls
>   the footuRe   mujik of the footure

I remembered in *X* a meditation of sorts on *meadows,* which caused me a year or so ago to remember a meadow one hundred miles north of Pittsburgh, near Clarion, Pennsylvania, where I lay down one afternoon in absolute peace among two groups of intertwining flowers, black-eyed Susans and cornflowers maybe, though I'm not sure—maybe one of them was marguerite—two *neighbors*—that's what I was thinking—and I decided to govern the whole afternoon by chance, in homage to John Cage.

Though there is nothing more chance-ridden than the U.S. mail. Anything can happen—to ruin your day, or your life, or make you dance with joy, or just sigh over the general onslaught, or go through it again, only more slowly, to see if the check is there, or the apology. I got three pieces of mail, only three, two appeals for money and one, a notice of a talk and an art opening. There was a desperate request from Sharon Angle, the Republican nominee running against Harry Reid for the U.S. Senate. It was "personal," to me, in script, very carefully crafted, asking for $28, $50, $100, $500, $1,000, $2,400 to defeat Reid, since I am a "party activist" and "a patriotic American who loves this great country enough to deliver a knockdown blow to Obama," a strange communication to a lifetime leftist, about a mile or so to the west of the party. The second appeal was a request from the Southern Poverty Law Center—for $25; I gave $100. And there was the notice from Lafayette College of an exhibition of quilts and a lecture in honor of the anniversary of the arrival of Lafayette's first women students in the fall of 1970. There was also something hand-delivered—stampless—from Elaine Restifo, a near neighbor.

There is no word in the language that I love more than "meadow." And I never found a meadow anywhere that I loved more than the one near Clarion. There was a slight climb, a small rise, so when I laid my head down, probably on a sweater or hat, it was as if I had a pillow, nor did the sky move in slow circles as it would have if I were lying flat, or even—God forbid—with my head *lowered*. I guess I slept, maybe only for a minute or so, though, naturally, it seemed much longer. I may have been wakened by the sun showing through a cloud, or by a sudden burst of unbearable happiness, the same thing I guess. No dumb armies had ever stood in that meadow wearing ridiculous clothes and facing each other, as the wildflowers did, only thirty, forty, paces apart, their own guns exploding in their faces or the bullets, or balls, smashing knees and making cripples of those dumb boys forever; though there may have been football or even the strange warfare—when we were twelve—that we conducted with weapons we fabricated ourselves an hour and a half south (of Clarion); smooth, small, varnished boards that served as barrels; and clothespins that triggered the rubber bands, cut from old inner tubes (as bullets) that once even blinded one of us guarding a hill above the apartment houses. We learned to make war then, and some of us—even then—made love instead, long before the T-shirts and the strong leaves. Did I not say in a poem once, "the world at last a meadow"?

The quilts I'll go see, or the talk on quilts, or is it a lecture on books *about* quilts since, after all, it's a seat of *higher* learning. I tried calling the lecturer, or *presenter*, since it turns out she is a near neighbor, with a New Hope (PA) address, but it wasn't a shop, it was a computer site, so there was no place, evidently, to feel, fold, smell, and see the quilts at different angles. What I have instead is the invitation with a *picture* of a quilt and the *illusion* of folded cloth.

I started to collect quilts in Iowa in the early 1980s, although there were certainly plenty of quilts in Pennsylvania and, for that matter, New Jersey. I *suddenly* discovered them, the rich colors, the designs, the mystery of the aesthetic, given it was often a group effort, and I was taken by the *craft*, that it was a practical item, a blanket, and that it was also an art object—as so many other things are, from silverware to sinks to airplanes and automobiles. But there was something so *comforting* about a quilt, and so *hamish*, and motherly and peaceful. I tend to learn slowly, so I was going on sixty when I discovered them.

I bought five or six from a dealer in Iowa City and started to make greedy forays into nearby towns. I was very late on the scene—decades, for that matter—but I wasn't looking for a magic purchase, I was rather eager not so much to *learn* but to enjoy, to delight in, what I saw—I would say "swim in the joy" if I were Swinburne wandering through the Amana Colonies in Iowa—and I couldn't wait for the shows that showed up every late spring in Iowa City, especially the 1930s quilts, which I particularly loved. I think I paid about one hundred dollars apiece for my quilts, dark blues and purples, bright reds and whites, checkerboards, stripes, bars, roads to nowhere. Michael Orick, a former art student at the university who lives in Little Italy (New York) made a living, of sorts, collecting and selling quilts, and when he came to Iowa City, usually at Thanksgiving, he brought a large cache with him and once he spread a few out in the downstairs rooms of my house on Governor Street. And someone from the English department, eighteenth century I think, who was in my house with a friend of hers, proceeded to bid against me (for the quilts) as if it were an auction house and not my living room and as if Michael was an auctioneer, not a friend. My "boss" at Iowa (Frank Conroy) criticized my quilts, hanging then on my walls, for being imitative (he said) of Matisse and for being "craft" and not "art," and I thought of roomfuls of farm women, whether in eastern Pennsylvania or Alabama or Ohio, stuffing the batting and discussing minimalism or neo-neo-expressionism, certainly before they collected the eggs or peeled the potatoes. In my black and purple quilt, eloquent, clear, melancholy, almost tragic, there is a block of squares that is of a slightly lighter blue than the others. It may have been the only scrap around that seemed to fit or it may have been whimsy, or it may have represented one of the lost sons or daughters, off to Philadelphia or St. Louis, or it may have been all that but also a crafty, artistic move reminiscent of some Province-town, New York, or Parisian madman making his wild move under his black beret, much too small for his swollen head. My worn-out daemon warns me not to read things into where they don't belong. Unlike me, she is horrified at sentimentality—but I tell her that some neighbors *do* work together and even love each other; and there are many places where the women are not raped and the chil-dren are not buried alive or have their heads bashed against trees and walls; and their limbs sliced off; and because of their color, or their accents, or their dress, or where their sacred places are, are impaled or burned alive or have their organs removed—and sold. For which my daemon threatens to leave me altogether and pounds against my tympanum, struggling to get out through my ear, as I'm sure Athena did to her wise and ferocious old father, the left ear being particularly amenable to such strategy.

There is a quilt whose top was made by Missouri Pettway (of Gee's Bend) whose dates are 1902 to 1981, consisting of blocks and stripes made out of her dead husband's work clothes, cotton and corduroy. Its designs and its color remind me more of one of my own quilts than anything else of the famous Gee's Bend quilt mak-ers, the African American women living southwest of Selma, Alabama, who have been quilting for six generations and whose quilts, which they once hung up on lines by the road for passers-by to purchase, have been recognized as major—and priceless—American art work. This from an isolated all-black community nestled into a curve of the Alabama River and, ironically, near Selma where the murders occurred. What Missouri Pettway said, according to her daughter Arlonzia, was: "I going to take his work clothes, shape them into a quilt to remember him, and cover up under it for love." No statement of art more wise—and beautiful.

Love your neighbor as yourself is the dearest of all admonishments. It comes out of a culture that also honored "strangers," where even, through hospitality, they became neighbors. Those of us who lived a while in New York City, or other such places, knew and hated and were horrified or disgusted by or frightened of the little roach, our unwanted and intimate neighbor. One of my relatives made a living through their "extermination." Yet Muriel Rukeyser, one of the great American poets of the last century, wrote a poem about the clean little insect, called "St. Roach," where she turns horror into love. It is a simple poem, yet shocking when it was written, and shocking now. It is not just the Jain refusing to breathe in "other life" by accident; it is not just the monk honoring filth; it is a statement of love absolute and beyond measure; and it puts to shame the others. Was it a metaphor for "other killing," human and otherwise? Of course it was, but it is more. She was—and she will be—cursed for her foolish love, ridiculed and made fun of. But it is one of the two, three, great poems of that insane century. One should say St. Muriel.

St. Roach

For that I never knew you, I only learned to dread you,
for that I never touched you, they told me you are filth,
they showed me by every action to despise your kind;

for that I saw my people making war on you,
I could not tell you apart, one from another,
for that in childhood I lived in places clear of you,
for that all the people I knew met you by
crushing you, stamping you to death, they poured boiling
    water on you, they flushed you down,
for that I could not tell one from another
only that you were dark, fast on your feet, and slender.
    Not like me.
For that I did not know your poems
And that I do not know any of your sayings
And that I cannot speak or read your language
And that I do not sing your songs
And that I do not teach our children
        to eat your food
        or know your poems
        or sing your songs
But that we say you are filthing our food
But that we know you not at all.

Yesterday I looked at one of you for the first time.
You were lighter that the others in color, that was
    neither good nor bad.
I was really looking for the first time.
You seemed troubled and witty.

Today I touched one of you for the first time.
You were startled, you ran, you fled away
Fast as a dancer, light, strange and lovely to the touch.
I reach, I touch, I begin to know you.

— MURIEL RUKEYSER

70 Saltwater Pools

Atlantic City has always been a focal point for me—long before the ocean-hating casinos arrived. I adored the old hotels on the board-walk, and when I was sixteen, seventeen, I used to wander into one or the other huge low-lying buildings, sit down in one of the wicker

chairs inside—as if I belonged there—and even, occasionally, order
a pot of coffee or tea from one of the judgmental waiters, and spend
hours reading Farrell or Hemingway, or my heavy Spengler, dur-
ing a long afternoon, the boards outside maybe spotted with rain,
the sand, as the drops hit it, popping a little, as if there were some
jumping beans out there, or some nervous marine insects.

When the Marlboro-Blenheim imploded at the beginning of the
movie *Atlantic City*, I was already a little more than bitter, for I had
stayed there a number of times and was, insanely, loyal to the build-
ing itself. When, in the film, the young couple arrives in the city, to
destroy and be destroyed, my mind refused to wholly engage for I
was thinking of the auctions on the boardwalk and the time when
my father, a born salesman and sucker, bought a watch there that
kept time for two hours; and I was thinking of the Million-Dollar
Pier where, as late as the late 1930s, you could see silent movies
again, with a live piano accompanying the action. And when it was
advertised that Scorsese (in 2010, for God's sake) was doing his take
on "old" Atlantic City, I was more than ready for the black sedans,
the tommy guns, the short-skirted blondes, the boughten mayors,
the crime bosses, and the tilted fedoras. Soulless, dull, and by the
book. Except a forced touch here and there.

It was a hot summer in 2010 and I had the crazy idea of merging
with the salt, only what I was thinking about were the saltwater
swimming pools that once were everywhere on the shore. As late as
the mid-1980s I know there was an Olympic-size saltwater swim-
ming pool in Ocean Grove, the "Methodist" community imme-
diately south of Asbury Park, down the street from the Quaker
Inn, the hotel that Diane, an old girlfriend, managed—living there
maybe four months a year, including the times she got ready and
the times she closed up, four weeks of which—every summer—we
spent in that tiny apartment behind the front desk. But the only
saltwater pool Stephanie and I could locate on the shore was in

the Chelsea Hotel—in Atlantic City, it turned out—between the Boardwalk and Pacific Avenue.

I must say I was excited when we drove down to look at the hotel and the pool. I knew that the city was hideous but I thought I'd take refuge in the Chelsea, maybe spending four or five days there, writing, reading, swimming (in the salt pool), sipping my coffee—or my wine—and taking long naps. When we got to Atlantic City we had to drive four abreast through huge casino-driven passageways under enormous parking garages to find the entrance to the small hotel and stand in a long line at the desk to get information and to—hopefully—see one of the rooms. We made our way first to the coffee shop where we sat at the counter questioning the manager, a thin redheaded freckled smiling thirty-something, and the lovely young waitress, a college student in Warsaw, over to make some money in the *goldene medina* to help support her and her family in Poland. The coffee shop, which also faced the street, was called Teplitzski's, the name of the hotel that once stood there before Howard Johnson, or whoever it was that owned the Chelsea now, took over. Teplitzski's, I learned from the manager, burned down in 1968, and when I asked him if it was "Jewish Lightning" he looked startled, while Stephanie hurriedly explained that *I* was Jewish lest he think I was delivering a slur. The waitress spoke almost perfect English (and I'm sure German, French, Italian, and Spanish as well). She told us she was half-Polish, half-Belarusian, and spoke Polish, Russian, and Belarusian, making distinctions in grammar, morphology, vocabulary, and pronunciation for us. I did not bring up Jedwabne, but I thought of it. Her field is international relations. The salt pool, right next to the coffee shop, was deserted that day because of the rain, but certainly too small to swim lengths in and, undoubtedly, when the sun shone, overrun with small, noisy dippers. In the lobby we spoke to an incoming guest who was a DJ and in Atlantic City for a conference of DJs. I asked her if she knew what the Taj Mahal was since her conference was being held at that piece of shit. She said she certainly did—it was "one of the six wonders of the world." An upscale bellhop showed us a room upstairs, which was surprisingly large, with a desk, a view, and a bathroom with a marvelous showerhead. But the room was decorated with odd scrollwork, and corporate paintings; and we saw, through open doors, that all the other rooms were identical. Furthermore, the piped-in music was loud—and horrible—and we got out of there pretty quick. I know there was plenty of salt in the huge stretch of ocean the other side of the thin gray strip of filthy sand, but that's not what I wanted—so I gave up that dream. Though we bought delicious small peaches and a perfect eggplant on the way home just off Route 539, in the Pine Barrens.

71 Childhood in New York

I said earlier that I first experienced New York when I was thirteen, or close to it, but I think I was only nine or ten when I went there with my father on his buying trips. We left the grand brick-laden Pennsylvania Station in Pittsburgh at eleven or twelve at night, slept in our cozy sleepers, and woke up somewhere in New Jersey, traveling through a swamp or acres of weeds, or by oil storage tanks and empty brick buildings standing alone by abandoned tracks, as we made our way into the city, descending into the dark or emerging into the light for a second or two before we made the final push into the huge railroad station on 34th Street.

Mostly we stayed across the street at the Pennsylvania Hotel and—as I said earlier—I spent the day alone, walking through Times Square, eating lunch at Paddy's Clam House on 34th, riding the buses and subways. Though I was big for my age and might have looked eleven or twelve, decent enough in those days of comparative trust, and safety.

I think that though I later spent year after year in New York, and went to school there, and gave fifty or more readings there, and walked from end to end—both ways—and haunted the bookstores and wasted hours on 42nd Street, and grew bitter over the changes, it was in my earliest years, when half unbeknownst to me, I was actually, in E.B. White's words, "in quest of something." I didn't yet have a manuscript in my suitcase, and there was no pain in my heart, not that I knew of, but I was already in love, and this was long before I read Hart (or Stephen) Crane, and Dickens and Whitman and Jacob Riis and Abraham Cahan and Henry James and Marianne Moore. Or Céline or Thomas Wolfe or Damon Runyon or Malamud or Kazin or Langston Hughes or Singer. Or Baldwin or Paley or Auden or Delmore Schwartz.

I think the years I'm most passionate about are the first decade of the twentieth, the immigrants and the theaters, or the five or ten years after World War II, though every decade, and every quinquennium, had its excitement. And I'm bitter now, mostly about the artists being forced out, the stupidity of crowded mindless Soho and the loss of neighborhoods, and I strongly dislike the rich and arrogant current mayor (2010).

I was looking forward to rereading Henry James's *The American Scene,* published in 1904, and his rediscovery, disappointment—and delight—in visiting America again after decades of living in Europe, especially the New York sections; and I was looking forward to searching through Henry Miller's *Air-Conditioned Nightmare,* which I first read when I was twenty-one years old, at the end of World War II, sixty-five years ago. That book was published by New Directions in 1945, but it must have been written before the war, judging from Miller's preface, probably in 1939 or '40. Though as it turned out, except for very brief references, the only mention of New York was *in* the preface, and we have to go to another "text," a long, seventy-five-page letter Miller wrote in 1935 to his

friend Alfred Perlès and published later as a book called *Aller Retour
New York*, to get his take on New York. But it was Simone de Beau-
voir's book, which I discovered in a bookcase in one of my back
rooms next to the facsimile edition of Whitman's *Leaves of Grass*,
that I treasured most. It was published in 1948 and is called *America
Day by Day*. On the dust jacket there is a photograph of the endless
towers, cloud-ridden and enveloped in fog, with the Empire State
Building in the very center, the red and blue beacon of empire dark
in the early dawn mist.

72 Henry James in New York

Henry James's New York centered on old Trinity Church and
lower Fifth Avenue. He was horrified at the new New York and
sought out the oases of his youth and tried to understand what New
York had become, and what its spirit was—if it had one. There was
a certain terror, a fatalism, in his voice. The city was a "monster"
that would continue willy-nilly its mad rush, even as it perceived
its new forms as provisional, as it destroyed, annihilated, its older
forms. So that its "actual work" it sees as the "merest of stop-
gaps." He was shocked at the height of the skyscrapers (fifty floors
in 1904) and used the word as if to torture himself over and over.
He saw New York as a "vision of energy," "big and insolent" and
went out of his way to describe "some colossal set of clockworks,
some steel-souled machine room of brandished arms and hammer-
ing fists and opening and closing jaws." It was as if, in some weird
way, he was anticipating some of Hart Crane's later writing for
The Bridge, only from a negative rather than a positive viewpoint.
And he bemoans the fact that the Trinity Church spire can no lon-
ger be seen from a distance, this only a quarter of a century before
the Chrysler Building and the Empire State Building were built.
He goes back—for refuge—to the Church of the Ascension and

John LaFarge—on Fifth Avenue; and the blocks between Washington Square and 14th, and ends up inveighing against *vulgarity* and *money,* juxtaposing—opposing—this money with beauty, as if we were talking about ugly window-obsessed Trump-ets a century later. I'm afraid it's classical and even at times ordinary; though it's a critical part of James's view. But his incredible spirit always relocates and transforms.

He doesn't inveigh at all against "foreigners"—aliens, he calls them; there is nothing at all derogatory in his language, but rather a kind of wonder at their huge presence, the Italians, the Jews, the Armenians, a deep understanding of who they are and why they're here, and a deep sympathy—and fascination—with their economic, and domestic, lives. Given his English love of Italy, he relates strongly to "the dense Italian neighborhoods of the Lower East side," and interests himself in the geographic origin; and he is absolutely obsessed with the Jews of eastern Europe, living as they did (1904) in the most crowded conditions in the world, Bombay included. He is delighted by the babel of voices in Central Park of a Sunday, and he investigates, as it were philosophically, "who and what an alien is," as if migration were his subject, referring to the Croatian, the Lusitanian, and the Calabrian influx; and like a good modern, pays service, in his late, complex, and abstract style to the notion of the *eternal* alien, making only the slightest reference, as I understand his prose, to the loss of "colour" in the new place and— given it's James—the lack of the *manners* he so espoused.

He writes about a summer evening spent in the "Yiddish" quarter by invitation of a high public functionary "who was to prove one of the most liberal of hosts and most luminous of guides." It was—the notes tell us—the playwright and thinker Jacob Gordin who accompanied James throughout the Lower East Side, showing him theaters, cafés, and houses, I'm sure taking him to Jewish restaurants and synagogues and explaining the rituals and languages.

Gordin, born in Russia, wrote eighty plays and tried to establish Jewish farming, both in Russia and America. He believed in physical labor and helped establish many colonies. He was a proponent of "Ethical Judaism" and a follower of Tolstoy. He—Gordin—was born in 1853 and died in 1909. James talks of a great "swarming" as soon as they crossed Rutgers Street and entered the East Side. "There is no swarming like that of Israel," James says, "when once Israel has got a start, and the scene here bristled, at every step, with the signs and sounds, immitigable, unmistakable, of a Jewry that had burst all bounds." He—playfully—wrote about "the bottom of some vast sallow aquarium in which innumerable fish, of over-developed proboscis [*le nez*], were to bump together, forever, amid heaped spoils of the sea." James writes about the very old and the very young, and about the reverence for intellect. He compares *this* ghetto, with its hopes and ambitions, to the "dark, foul, stifling ghettos" of Europe, and he particularly admires the endless fire escapes of the "New Jerusalem." He called it "a city of redemption," that philo-Semite.

James recognizes, and praises, public things, buildings, vistas, parks. He remembers the old NYU building on Washington Place and is delighted by the Columbia University buildings in the Upper West Side. He accounts for the provisional, even the Ugly, and looks forward to the future. He sees New York as an upturned broken hair comb and imagines new teeth. He writes about the perspective of the river, Grant's tomb, the sea light, even American shoes—and hats. He grieves over the vulgarization of the clubs, and says "it takes an endless amount of history to make even a little tradition." He loves, as I said, Central Park, the smiling valleys, bosky nooks, and wild woodlands, and adores the polyglot crowd of pedestrians. He uses the word "swarming" endlessly. He is amazed at American teeth. And elevators. And the Metropolitan Museum. And he ends up, this part of the book, in the restaurants on Third, Second, and the "fabulous unattempted First," and praises the Yiddish actors and actresses who crossed over to Broadway, anticipating our Paul Munis and our Edward G. Robinsons, the adorable intermarriages.

73 *Air-Conditioned Nightmare*

Henry Miller, in the preface to *The Air-Conditioned Nightmare*, starts out by talking about a reconciliation with his native land, but though, as he says, or said, his journey was more in the way of having a last look. He writes, on page 10, "I was confident for the first time in my life I would look upon New York and what lay beyond it without a trace of loathing or disgust."

But the boat he was on—originating in Greece—stopped at Boston first, thus interfering with the famous dramatic entry. And barely in New York harbor, he had changed his mind and was—already—attacking the bridges and skyscrapers. Still on the boat, he said, "I felt as I had always felt about New York—that it is the most horrible place on God's earth. No matter how many times I escape I am brought back, like a runaway slave each time detesting it, loathing it, more and more." In a sense he was just being irascible, stubborn, and cantankerous, maybe even comic—but he also meant it. He was having his cake and gobbling it.

Reading *The Nightmare* is a good preparation for reading the long letter to Perlès, even if the letter—and the book—come five years earlier. It's part rage and part *ressentiment*, and it's about being cheated—of life—and taking revenge, or it's just one long boring sermon. Miller was standing on a fault line and didn't know whether to go forward or back; and the book's single greatest stupidity was its defense of slavery (hard to believe) in the name of some kind of aristocracy that never truly existed anyhow. Only an imitation of an imitation.

There is a quaintness, and a deadliness, to the book in his fierce rejection of things American, more particularly the industrial north and its "inhuman" life. He praises the South, its climate, landscape, manners, customs, and soft speech. "The world of the South," he says, "corresponds more nearly to the dream life which the poet imagines than do other sections of the country." "Little by little," he says, "this dream world is being penetrated and poisoned by the spirit of the North." And referring to the Civil War, he says: "I see no results of this great conflict which justify the tremendous sacrifice that we as a nation were called upon to make. I see only an enormous waste of life and property, the vindication of right by might, and the substitution of one form of injustice for another." I don't know if he carried a Confederate flag on the back of his rented car. I don't know how he felt about strange fruit.

Though I did enjoy his visit to New Hope, Pennsylvania—across the Delaware—and the attack on Pittsburgh and the Ohio valley southwest to Youngstown. Endless steel mills, slag heaps, filthy rivers, and railway cars. "We begin here then," Miller says, "in the very quick of the nightmare, in the crucible where all values are reduced to slag." Writing about his hotel room he says, "If I were to occupy this room for any length of time I would go mad—or commit suicide. The spirit of the place, the spirit of the men who made it, the hideous city it is, seeps through the walls. There is murder in the air. It suffocates me." I think I recognize the Fort Pitt Hotel, no longer there, or the Roosevelt. Miller calls it an inferno worse than anything Dante imagined, and refers to the "hideous grandeur" of a steel mill on the railway line: "Wherever there is industry," he says, "there is ugliness, misery, oppression, gloom, and despair." It was these flames of the night and those mills lit up twenty-four hours a day that we, the Pittsburghers, loved. My father used to take visitors to a high point—Mt. Washington—to see the scene: the rivers, the tall buildings, the sky lit up. A true Pittsburgher hates what happened, the factories and mills removed, train stations turned into playgrounds. We prefer the clean air, yes, but we are nostalgic for the hideous grandeur. I think it was at the Fort Pitt that Miller confessed that the only important experience in the whole trip—from New York to California—was his reading of Romain Rolland's two volumes on Ramakrishna and Vivekananda.

In addition to the South, Miller loved the Southwest (the enormous rectangular area found within the four states of Utah, Arizona, Colorado, and New Mexico) and revered only the artist. He had contempt for the ordinary citizen, gullible and stupid, especially in the face of Nature. "Nowhere else in the world is the divorce between man and nature so complete. Nowhere else have I encountered such a dull, monotonous fabric of life as here in America. Here boredom reaches its peak." And he bemoans the fact that he—and his friend Barry Ratner—were turned down for Guggenheim fellowships and makes a hilarious list of those who got the fellowships and what their "projects" were. Himself, like a good American, he heads west and settles in southern California. He had, over a period of time, six wives.

I have to tell this story: I came back from my first trip to Europe with the lining of my raincoat loaded with copies of his *Tropic of Cancer* and *Tropic of Capricorn*, the two famous banned books. It was 1950—they were all the rage then but only available in the nether world. I had about fifteen. I bought them for the equivalent of fifty cents each and expected to sell them for fifteen, twenty dollars apiece. I had made the mistake, I thought, of reading from the books on the long trip back (on the *Edam*), and when we landed in Hoboken I felt a little dread. When my name was announced on the loudspeaker and I was asked to report to the captain's cabin, the raincoat grew heavy as stone. It turned out—after we had all talked a little—that a Canadian smuggler was using my name—the same name as me—for one of his aliases, and when it was ascertained that I wasn't he but a college student home after a year abroad I was given special entrée, with no questions asked. I could have had thirty books if the lining would have held them! But just a little later, the ban was lifted, Grove Press released the American edition, and my books were worth hardly what I paid for them. I ended up giving them away, though at least I had a large bag of 50-centime pieces, each the exact size of a dime and good for a ride on the New York subway. I calculated 1/700th of a dollar; I sold them for a nickel apiece. Hundreds.

74   Henry Miller's New York

Aller Retour, Henry Miller's book on New York, is, as an introduction by George Wickes says, "disjointed, episodic and improvised," almost entirely Miller's personal reactions to New York, "expressing his disgust with all things American: food, drink, women, advertising, skyscrapers, and Alka-Seltzer." It is an interesting record of America at the tail end of the Great Depression, as seen by a Sensitive, and the (limited) few-months' history of a selfish, narcissistic bohemian, full of hatred for his country and its people. It is playful and irreverent, "more like a journal," as Wickes says, "recording Miller's moods and impressions as they occurred to him." It is, more than anything else, an attack on any kind of social action, even on hope, and, particularly, a diatribe against women, whom he mostly refers to as "cunts"; an attack on "intellectuals," whom he scorns; and an endless, brutal rant against Jews, of all sizes and sorts. Like Pound, he dilutes and confuses this hatred with his profession of friendship with the many Jews (five?) he knows in New York and Paris. Perlès himself is probably Jewish and certainly Walter Lowenfels (Cronstad in *Tropic of Cancer*) is, one of the many who fed him one or two nights a week, since Miller was a *schnorer*—a leech, as we say—of the first order. I knew Lowenfels, by the way, born at the turn of the (twentieth) century, a fine lyric poet, a communist, and wealthy, hounded in the 1950s by the Federal Bureau of Idiocy. Miller was uncomfortable with, or despised, Jews for their belief in social justice and their efforts, intellectually, politically, communally, in trying to achieve it. That was the *nominal* reason, but it was really more basic. He resented their huge presence in New York—Hymietown—and he was a carrier of the disease of anti-Semitism. It wasn't that Jews murdered Christian babies for their blood, or poisoned wells—he probably would have liked that—it just was that they were there—interlopers, modifiers. I'm sure he thought they were greedy, and pushing and disgusting—what else? On one interesting page (14) he writes about his father's tailor shop on 31st Street, across from the Hotel Wolcott, near Fifth Avenue, one of *my* hotels. He refers to his father's (defunct) cronies, Chucky Morton, Tom Ogden, *et alia*, and sitting in McElroy's, a bar on 31st, he looks across the street at the Hebrew National Restaurant where there is an enlarged photo—in the window—of a dinner "given by Lou Siegel to his playmates Eddie Cantor, George Jessel, Al Jolson and the other well-known comedians of Jewish vintage." "This is what has happened to good old 31st Street in the space of a generation," he says. I suppose a person can be an asshole in a private letter, but Miller chose to publish it as a book. I wonder how he'd feel today to discover that 31st (and 32nd and 33rd) is mostly Korean. Marvelous restaurants; dozens of them; no Eddie Cantor or Al Jolson.

The bigotry is outrageous—I know how the 1930s, '40s, and '50s were; but Miller is special. He seems actually to hate everything or really not to *love* anything except one or two lost souls he bumps into. "The poverty of New York is on a grand scale, as is everything else. Behind this dire poverty stand the hope and courage of 120,000,000 morons and idiots tattooed with the N.R.A. double eagle." The whole country. But special attention to Jews: "all New York owned and run by pushing, grabbing Jews." "The intellectuals are in my hair—and the artists and the communists and the Jews"; preceded by, "If ever I come back to this country I will skip New York and go straight to the sticks where there are nothing but ignorant and adorable people"; or "a Jew can read a fat book while walking the street, especially if it's a learned work"; though there was also a hit on "chinks, wops, polaks, litvaks, mocks, croats, and finns" (I don't know what mocks are).

God knows that the Jew here is a pure thing, a symbol, something unearthed and horrible; and God knows that it's boring, and distasteful of me to push the point; and Jews are anyhow now loved—and women too—*n'est-ce pas?*—his second main object of vitriol; and anyhow he's a *comic* writer.

The book actually takes place in a few bars, mostly around Times Square and one trip to the suburbs, wherever those were. He particularly hates skyscrapers. It seems that the future, the "dream" in our novels and films, in our imagination, is identified with them, particularly in the early days (the 1920s through the '50s) and you have to take sides. New York is the *presence*, but it's really America he writes about. "America is a dung-hill," he says (in a letter to William Carlos Williams that he included); and when he finally gets back to France, at the end of the book, he has a vision of America as something lost, like a timeless clock.

I don't know where all his hatred comes from—it is certainly self-hatred—and envy. His Paris, his France, is timeless too—how long was he there and where and how was he a part of the culture; and which culture? He was in a park, he was in a Disneyland where romantic anarchists walk freely about and call themselves artists. And he lived off of that for the rest of his life. He had a Brooklyn accent and he punctuated every sentence with the ridiculous phrase: "Don't choo know?" He was a lost German. He spoke Deutsche and hid it. He was homeless. And pontificated. A flawed genius. And a lowlife.

75 Simone de Beauvoir's New York

De Beauvoir landed in New York in January 1947. The exact date was the 26th, a Sunday morning, and it was that very night, twelve hours or so later, that I arrived at the B&O Railroad station in Pittsburgh, after a six-hour ride from D.C., just discharged from the army. And while she was walking with her American friends through the Bowery looking for a restaurant that was still open, I was walking across the pedestrian bridge that connected the station with Second Avenue, where I would take a streetcar home and where—on the bridge, late at night—I tossed my barracks bag, full of khaki, into the Monongahela River.

It was a critical time in American history. Women had lost their wartime jobs and were sent back to the kitchens and bedrooms. Industry would move south and west, the cities would die, the interstates would take over, the suburbs would be built—with a vengeance—malls, on a grand scale, would enter our lives, prices would double, we would be *consumed* by buying, and we would lose whatever radicalism we had before the war. The bomb would enter our bloodstream, we would build holes in the ground and stock them with cornflakes and tuna fish, we would become (even) more alike, except those of us that didn't, or couldn't, belong. We would become frightened, we would become madly ambitious— and obedient—and stupid—and put boxes in our front rooms with images to amuse, educate, and control us.

I knew none of this, though, and lived increasingly in a world of books. And for years to come I would be living only in cheap rooms and eating very simply and not feeling in the least deprived; nor was I, hugging the east coast of America and the west coast of Europe, ever truly a part of the new arrangement; and came to it reluctantly and, I think, strangely, as if I finally had to come in, not join but come in, partly out of sheer curiosity.

De Beauvoir's book records her trips to Washington, Chicago, and across America to the Southwest, Texas, Los Angeles, San Francisco, New Orleans, the South, and back to New York. It was an extraordinary visit. She wandered the streets, lectured at colleges, met writers, and went to movies, bars, and theaters. She loved America as only a Frenchman could (or a Frenchwoman). She held it up for scrutiny, and praised it and grieved over it. While in Berkeley someone gave her a record of Henry Miller, reciting from *Tropic of Cancer*, but she didn't have much to say about him, that Parisian. She did write about the Congressional debate over Greece and George Marshall's intention to "intervene," calling it "aid"; and she wrote, unhappily, about Truman preparing an address to Congress calling for loyalty oaths and the (sad) destruction of the left wing in the name of fighting "communism." The periodic hysteria that America goes through. And she bemoaned the lack of interest, on the part of students, in politics, and causes, of any sort. Though there were a few dung beetles still teaching Socrates and Thoreau.

I learned a lot about my country from reading de Beauvoir's book, even if some observations seemed slightly wrong and the matters she discussed were undergoing enormous change even as she wrote. She was incredibly gifted, and loving. I particularly like her visit to Chicago and the beginning of her long affair, her "marriage," to Nelson Algren, the mad visits to "sordid" bars and their dinners in Polish restaurants. I don't know why no one has made a film about the threesome, Sartre, de Beauvoir, and Algren, and the complex relationships, ending with her wearing the silver ring Algren gave her after her hurried second trip to Chicago just before she left for France, the ring she wore to her grave.

As far as her time in New York—my subject—it was in some ways like that of Henry James, though in plain English, albeit in French. She delighted in the city, walked endlessly, and was astonished by how it was identical with the New York of her imagination, which she learned from books, films, conversations—and myth—and yet how different it was; and how she had to create it anew, as every new visitor to New York must, in her mind and heart. Emotion overwhelmed her. Here she is just taking off from the airport in Paris: "It seemed as though I were about to step out of my life altogether; I did not know if I should feel anger or hope, but something surely would reveal itself to me—a world so full of interest, so rich, so unforeseen, that I myself would experience the extraordinary adventure of becoming someone else." And "I closed my eyes; when I opened them again all the stars in the sky had rolled over on to the ground"; and "now I could make out the houses lining an avenue and I thought: I shall walk on those streets." I would almost have to literally reproduce the pages of the book to explain her feeling. "In the restaurant, decorated with red and gold palm trees, dinner was a feast of initiation; the martini and the lobster had a holy taste." From what she describes, I think she stayed at the New Yorker Hotel, where I sometimes used to go as a boy with my father on his buying trips, and which is now owned by Reverend Moon.

Like Miller, she wanted to go to Broadway first. It was *her* Statue of Liberty. But, unlike Miller, she roams endlessly, and doesn't get stuck in one or two downtrodden bars. In a minute she is by the Hudson, then Washington Square, then on a boat circling the island. And "the Chinese quarter," as she calls it. And the Bowery. "I look and look," she says, "with the astonishment of a blind man who has just got back his sight." And, "New York belongs to me, and I to it."

Everything surprised her, and as it did, we saw New York through her eyes, green canvas awnings bearing huge numbers, the elevators, the doorbells, the letter boxes, the overheated interiors, the dominance of automobiles, the smell of the East River. "Paris has lost its power," she says. She loves having breakfast in drugstores. But, it must be said, she was saddened by the plight of the poor and unknown artists and intellectuals and the omnivorous recourse to *publicity*. And by the universal (fake) optimism and by the eternal smile in the ads—toothpaste, Ex-Lax, whatnot. But she is moved by the warmth, the lack of suspicion, and the generosity. Mostly, though, she walks. Lexington Avenue, the Empire State Building, Rockefeller Center, the skating rink, 57th Street, Columbus Circle, and, in fact, to Harlem and the Savoy (with Richard Wright and his wife).

Most of all she was moved—or horrified—by the people she met at parties, in restaurants, houses, universities, and magazine offices. It was refreshing to encounter her honesty, her kindness, her sanity, and her full-throated opinions, whether about American racism, window art, shoes, art galleries, sunsets, subways, sexual relations, alcohol, Stalinism, war psychosis, "red terror," antilabor laws, the luxury of drugstores, fruit juice, self-assurance, 52nd Street, or the Cloisters.

She was going on forty and already well known as Sartre's colleague—and *amie*—and as a famous writer. She was met at the airport, taken here and there, set up with a series of talks—probably by the French Embassy—at major universities. She met with the *Partisan Review* editors, she went out to dinner with well-known writers; she was a famous guest in New York and elsewhere. At one point she went to a "big party" at Erwin Piscator's house. Le Corbusier was there, Kurt Weil, and Connolly—who wrote *Green Pastures*, that strange novel, then film, about African American heaven—and dozens of famous critics, musicians, writers, and actors. Charlie Chaplin—Charlot—arrived and addressed and entertained the crowd. There were, de Beauvoir says, only two women there: Chaplin's wife (very beautiful, in a violet dress with golden earrings) and a friend (I guess she wasn't counting herself). Oona was *enceinte* again, and very quiet in Chaplin's presence; de Beauvoir describes her as an "Arab" wife.

She is brilliant on subject after subject, American adolescence,

American women, Frenchmen in America, intellectual trends (in 1947), the search for happiness, goodwill, Times Square, freethinkers, the circus, publishing, muzak, the novel. And it is moving—and sad—to read her on American democracy, in 1947. She is smart and accurate, as she writes about the ideals, and the realities. She is not cynical; on the contrary, like a loyal European, she praises what she sees and shows the unique differences between the old and the new civilizations. What is "sad" is how far—in 2010—we have abandoned so much of the dignity and the generosity we had then. Nor, though she herself has a kind of reverence for her America, perhaps deepened by America's part in the war, she is not naïve—about economic inequality, ruthlessness, bigotry, racism, and self-deceit. I only would say that she doesn't address herself deeply enough to the rift, the cruelty, the complicated half-truths, the ignorance, maybe the madness, close to the heart of things; something that used to erupt from time to time but, it seems to me, is becoming almost a permanent condition now. Auden (partly) addressed it in 1940:

> Some think they're strong, some think they're smart,
> Like butterflies they're pulled apart,
> America can break your heart;
> You don't know all, sir, you don't know all.

I wish I had the sense, when I went to Paris for the first time—two years after she came to America—to try to find *her*, but I was twenty-four and ill-schooled—and somewhat ignorant and didn't know, at the time (fall 1949), even who she was, though I had read Sartre, on the heated floor, as I recall, in the stacks of the Carnegie Library on Forbes Street, now called Forbes Avenue and going only one way when it then went two. And what would she have done anyhow with me, one of the thousands of Americans taking classes (more or less) on the G.I. Bill, collecting my seventy-five dollars each month at the American Embassy? Should I have walked over to her, say, at the Flore or the Deux Magots or at the basement bar in the Hôtel Pont Royal where she was seated with Sartre and one or two others—Violette Leduc, Merleau-Ponty, Arthur Koestler—and just started talking in my miserable French? Or, should I have bumped into her in front of 11 rue de la Bûcherie where she moved into a three-room apartment (on the fifth floor) facing Notre Dame (I just discovered today in Deirdre Bair's biography), across the street from the Hôtel du Centre where *I* was living (on the second floor facing the court) when she went off to shop with her net bag and I went down to Boulevard St. Michel for my first coffee? A piece of *exposte* or *poste-poste*. I having nothing to show, living up there with my Milton and my unpainted "Bound Slave" with his (stone) undershirt pulled up over his chest. I'm just loving her for her mind—and heart—though Algren finally called her a "bitter spinster," and she was, not uncommonly, perceived as cold or arrogant. Though she may have only been protecting herself.

She visited America several more times and had many friends here. She took everything in, absolutely everything. She was almost obsessed. The last thing she says (speaking of America) is: "All human problems are set forth on a gigantic scale." That is what moved me strongly when I took my leave. "America is a pivotal point in the world where the future of man is at stake." "Here is a battlefield, and one can only follow with excitement the struggle she carries on within herself, the stakes of which are beyond measure." She died, world-famous, in 1986.

76 Atlantic City

As far as Atlantic City, I know that James—and Miller—never got there, and I rather doubt that de Beauvoir did. I hope she got to Coney Island and I imagine—with delight—how she struggled over the French word for *coney*, absent at least from my dictionary. Miller, I'm sure, took a subway to the playground a few times, and either held his breath on the Cyclone or ate a hot dog at Nathan's, a little yellow mustard, a little sauerkraut, sour Kraut that he was. I'm sure that his excuse was the saltwater, for a romantic can't resist the ocean. I can even hear him weeping—dropping bitter tears—that it wasn't Greece, that America once again ruined another ocean. Ah, Steel Pier, ah Million Dollar.

77 Turkish Restaurant in Paris

There was an inexpensive Turkish restaurant in Paris where I got in the habit of eating night after night, usually a meal of roast meat, carrots, and thick gravy over rice, with a piece of bread and a small carafe of red wine (*très domestique!*). I always sat at the same table, and, moreover, I always had the same three neighbors, a large—and loud—North African Jew who for dessert always ordered a large pear, on a dish, which he peeled with his own pen-knife, in dexterous, perfectly aligned sections, the skin removed, making sure he got no juice on or under the enormous ring on his second finger (left). His wife, dark-skinned like her husband, sat opposite, a bemused smile on her face, her hands supporting her chin. They were in their thirties. Beside her sat a rather small Frenchman in a slightly greasy brown suit with safety pins on the inside of the lapel (left). His gray hair was thinning and he was constantly shocked by the North African, his deep voice, his wild neckties, and his flashing knife. The Frenchman was studying English and—endlessly—asked me the names of things and tried, hopelessly, to pronounce the strange words. He was particularly interested in the word "chipmunk" and asked me what it was in French. We ended up calling him Monsieur Chipmunk, which he rather liked. To make matters worse, or better, his two front teeth extended out more than a little, which gave him the look of a rodent. The North African, in his deep voice, constantly asked me about vice in America and was absolutely in love with Chicago and its corpses. *His* name, I'm afraid, was M. le Vice. He adored it. They each had their own napkins, hanging from pegs.

I came back four years later, with Pat this time, and they were there sitting at the same table, in the same chairs. M. Vice was still mad for Chicago and M. Chipmunk wore the same suit, the same safety pins, and still inquired about the quick nervous ground squirrel. Vice sold neckties on the sidewalk of Boulevard St. Michel. Chipmunk came to our apartment one night for supper. He brought flowers and candy, but was very judgmental about the order of our dishes. An obsessive Frenchman. He made little sounds of disapproval with his tongue and teeth when Vice asked about the raunchy and the murderous. And simultaneously shook his little head. I don't think we ever spoke a word to the wife, nor did she ask any questions or say anything. They were probably from Casablanca. I guess their people (my people) were there when it was the bread-basket for Rome, and when it was salted over.

78   Paul McCartney

Sir Paul published one book of poetry, with Norton, my publisher. It was probably for that reason and that I was a friend of his editor that I was invited—along with Robert Pinsky—to a lunch at a posh restaurant, in a private room, to celebrate the book. He was there with his new wife—she may have still been his fiancée—and there were maybe ten or twelve reviewers, editors, or reporters from most of the major magazines and newspapers in New York. I think it was 1999. I can't find the book in my library, but Stephanie says it was uncorrected proofs we had and that we gave them to Pitt along with my other papers. Sold it, not "gave" it. Anne Marie was there too, sitting at the other end of the table. That's three poets, unless we count McCartney as well, though Anne Marie insists she was there as my driver, not as a writer. Pinsky and I sat at either side of McCartney—and Heather sat next to Pinsky, to his left. The food was vegetarian, and it was extremely good. The journalists were all in ties and jackets but McCartney had on a T-shirt and sneakers. Most of the time, Paul spoke to *us* and, as I recall, there were very few questions from the suits and ties. I feel bad that we dominated things, but all they had to do was speak up. For me the high point was when McCartney turned to me and asked what kind of music I liked. I said jazz, blues, classical, ballads—all of it. He asked me who my favorite singer was, and I said Jimmy Durante. I remember singing a few bars from "Try a Little Tenderness," in the Schnozzola's style, replete with *his* tenderness and sentimentality. I remember Paul singing with me, but memory has odd twists—strange turns, as the Possum said. The other time I met him after that he assured me I was his favorite poet, but I forgive him if he also said it to Pinsky and one or two others. I have a couple of photographs of him, Billy Collins, and myself at George Plimpton's house at a book party for one of Billy's books. It was the night before September 11th. We were all a little drunk, but they more than me since they had arrived earlier. I'm not sure now if Durante is still my favorite singer. Maybe Rudy Vallee. The truth is I get in a different state when I listen to Bach's *Suites for Unaccompanied Cello*, particularly if it's Casals playing; though I for one don't see anything unusual about loving both, one of the suites and "My Time Is Your Time." Anyhow, that's what I did with my life, wandering between the "high" and the "low," forgetting there were such distinctions. The last few days I've been reading and rereading Miłosz's beautiful paragraph on "Pity" published as a short piece in *To Begin Where I Am*. I'm glad he didn't seem to know that "pity" has such a bad name in many critical circles or that he chose to ignore it. I'm with him.

79 Yom Kippur Pear

What I remember about a certain Yom Kippur, in 1940 or a year or so earlier, was the horrific experience with the juicy pear. It was a very warm day, sometime in September, but we were wearing wool suits, white shirts, and striped or flowery neckties. And new shoes. Come to think of it, it was actually still summer. I remember there were two sanctuaries full of people and one was more sumptuous than the other, and one even had folding chairs in the rear that embarrassed me with the air of poverty it seemed to register, though when I sat there I enjoyed resting the bottom of my shoes on the steel crosspiece and feeling the gray coldness of the metal seat where I placed my hands and rocked a little. I was amused, I remember, or at least occupied, by the different sizes of the print in the prayer book, as I was by the English, and tried, as if it were a game, to keep up with the turning of the pages and the sudden wild leaps forward and the clear abandonment of twenty or thirty pages of text, as if it were disposable or no longer viable. Most of the day, though, we stood outside, talking and shielding ourselves from the sun; and moving up or down the steep steps, overwhelmed by boredom and lassitude.

I may have been fourteen, the day I remember. I had driven our four-year-old Pontiac—early that morning—slowly around the block, shifting the stiff gears effortlessly and parking easily, in the very same place, in front of our apartment building. A few days before I had secretly gone to the hardware store to have the ignition key duplicated, and put it on a key ring along with the house key and, I remember, a spare key that opened nothing I knew but which I used to give my ring a little more weight and complexity than it might otherwise have had by one bare key rubbing against another. We had finished supper early the evening before so we could walk together to the synagogue for Kol Nidre, so, though it was only 8 or 8:30 in the morning, the hunger pangs were already setting in and I had my suit and tie on and it was going to be a very long day.

One of the things we did was walk down the streets, past two other synagogues, onto the main thoroughfare with most of the businesses closed and up the next street and around to where we had started. A fast of one day is no big thing, especially when it's really not the *whole* day since you break the fast at supper; it's really just being a little hungry, and certainly good for the body; and the feeling of emptiness in the belly and a certain light-headedness is a delicious feeling, combined as it was with the sense of satisfaction, even righteousness, you got from spending those boring hours reading out loud what you barely could understand, or humming it really and faking it, especially leading up to the ending of one of the long narratives or prayers, which you punctuated by a final—graceful—bowing and a deliberate and long "Amen," leading to an extended, almost-silent reading with considerable swaying and rocking this time; and combined as it also was with the knowledge that the long day would be over in a matter of a few hours and you would break the fast with some cheese and crackers and a little fruit before you sat down to the main dishes.

At around 3 p.m. I left *schul*—it was Beth Shalom at the corner of Beacon and Shady—and turned *left* on the main street—Murray Avenue—and headed for our apartment, to rest, to recover, alone, before the final fatal hour. My mother and grandmother, Ida and Libby, had set the table, even ironed the cloth napkins, and piled fruit high in the fruit bowl. The beautiful small plums and the sweet summer apples gave off a lovely mild fragrance, but most of all it was the Bartlett pears that attracted me. They were deep yellow, rosy in part, and speckled, so that you didn't even have to apply any pressure to see which were the ripest; and, carefully of course, my mother and grandmother had—earlier—covered the pears in brown paper bags to speed their ripening, almost magically preparing them so that they would be at their very best when the fast was broken at sundown, or thereabouts, when everyone came home.

I fingered one of the pears, I held it in my palm as if to weigh it, and I smelled it, with my eyes open and my eyes closed, before I pulled off the stem; and I placed my tongue on the skin and pressed my teeth as if on the exact rosy spot before the saliva came and I bit into it—with my eyes open or closed, I can't remember—nor can I remember whether I was sitting in a chair or standing over the sink or lying on the sofa with one foot on the floor, my shoes still on, the digestive juices hardly beginning. *Hocht* purple prose to describe the simple act of forgetting atonement and giving up to animal hunger, symbol as it was of greed, disobedience, and, for those who believed in it, sin of the highest order.

I didn't know, at the time, about Augustine and the shaking of the pear tree—a different recklessness but one also involving the same fruit. It has always been my favorite, and I treasure the gift in a painting that Sheba Sharrow did for me of three pears, heavy yet floating in a dark-blue sky, touches of pale blue on the horizon, two of the pears yellowish-brown, one of them purple, the one inverted with its stem hanging down, the two others upright, a version of paradise from a painter of harsh justice, who left a teaching job in Pennsylvania early and bought a 1950s house in Cherry Hill outside of Camden—because she couldn't afford a loft in Philadelphia—and converted the whole building to a studio eight, ten years before she died of cancer, an artist I loved and respected and, to my relief, had the opportunity of telling her so—many times.

But that was almost sixty years after I ate the pear and hid the core, like the crazy boy I was, under the sink, as I recall, on a tin dish containing two pieces of much-used Brillo, the hard core there to keep the Brillo company for a while till I quietly, a day or so later, retrieved it and put it in the garbage. And though I am finally confessing, in a manner of speaking, I must also confess that the confession is *exceptional* in that I am wearing no prayer shawl, nor am I assembled, nor is it because I am ashamed or fearful—I don't think so—and though I wish with all my heart that Existence itself had a consciousness, I am too far gone, too ruined, too free, for that, even though I am wearing my straw hat; and if I am not written in the Book of Life it will not be because I ate a piece of fruit on Yom Kippur, for the truth is I have suffered enough from that, but for my joking and mockery in the face of holy Existence. Maybe this is enough of *Teshuvah*, this realization. For I am the goat.

80 The Engineers' Club

When I go to my dentist in New York City, I walk from the bus station east on 40th Street, past the south side of the library, to just the other side of Fifth Avenue. Across the street from Bryant Park, really across the street from the fancy restaurant at the western end of the library, there is a fourteen-story building, in stone and brick, with a brass plaque by the huge door announcing that the building was built to house the Engineers' Club, that it was completed in 1907, that it was one of the first skyscrapers in midtown Manhattan, and that it was designed by the architects Whitfield and King. The building was started in 1903, the plaque says, when Andrew Carnegie presented the Professional Association of Engineers with an initial, certainly generous, contribution. The club's renowned membership included Carnegie, President Herbert Hoover, Thomas Edison, Brigadier General Charles Lindbergh, Cornelius Vanderbilt, Henry Clay Frick, H. H. Westinghouse, and Nicola Tesla—an inventor, electrical engineer, and mystic, best known for his many revolutionary ideas in the field of electromagnetism.

I think Tesla is the only one I wouldn't put on my enemy list— if I were a Russian anarchist and not a mournful poet, making those noises from time to time you hear from the doves flapping down on the birdbaths or resting a bit in the maples. It was a little gift to my bad side, that plaque. There certainly were others in the club, but I couldn't, for the life of me, construct a more ideal set of brilliant oppressors. Nor did you have to do more than just say the names—it was so musical. At least it was to someone with my interests and knowledge; nor do I want to look too hard and have some perplexed fool respond, "Mussolini who?" Or didn't Carnegie give us the libraries? And didn't Westinghouse invent the air brake? And, for God's sake, Frick again? The next thing you know, you'll be lecturing on the Homestead Strike of 1892, which took place probably before your Grandmother Libby even conceived her first son, in Poland, for God's sake, and eight years before her first daughter, your mother, was born. Well, that strike and others are, to me, what your Civil War, if you are a buff, is to you, whoever "you" are. Although we're so used to corporations doing their dirty work and so used to—or indifferent to—union-bashing, unemployment, and poverty that we hardly blink and rarely sigh. But I have to point out, whether you like it or not, and whether you are bored or not, that Carnegie Steel was the absolute bellwether in the industry, and that Henry Frick, the partner and managing director, arbitrarily sought to lower the wages of the steelworkers and laborers in Homestead, Pennsylvania, as they were doing in the other plants they owned; and when the skilled workers tried to negotiate through their union (Amalgamated Iron and Steel) as they had done in the past, Frick, whose main purpose, it became clear, was to bust the union, refused to negotiate, even though the steelworkers saw themselves as partners and were willing—fair or not—to take a moderate cut.

Carnegie, of course, was "away"—giving dimes to pigeons, building little libraries in Scottish towns, and basking in the gratitude the Scots in Ayrshire and elsewhere displayed to the benevolent philanthropist. Frick, who stayed home, pigeons or no pigeons, erected an eight-foot wooden fence around the whole property. It was a lockout, not a strike, even though it is known as the Homestead Strike of 1892. In addition, Frick hired hundreds of Pinkerton detectives, transported them secretly up the Monongahela, and began to place them in strategic places, as if a war were about to erupt. He also, by the way, had holes cut in the fence for sharpshooters, though he claimed it was for spotlights. I suspect Frick knew who he was dealing with, for the workers, almost all of German, English, Irish, and Scots descent, outwitted the Pinkertons, fired on the barges (where the invading army was trapped) with cannon and rifle, almost set the barges on fire, and terrorized and physically beat the Pinkertons when they landed with their white flags and were forced to go through a gauntlet.

Frick's methods were always the same. Make no concession. Use the coal and iron police—a private army—or the Pinkertons; and, as a last resort, with his political connections, press the state militia into service. It is interesting, and amusing, to note that Carnegie, in writing, called the right of workers to unionize a "sacred" right. It is also interesting that he stayed in Scotland, in his baronial castle, during the Homestead war. Nor did he let the news interfere with his pleasures, shooting birds, I think. He also said that "the handling of the case on the part of the company has my full approval and sanction." I think the workers had a fuller sense of the nature of power and the uses of propaganda then than workers do now. The city of Homestead even refused the "gift" of a library at first, as several other river towns had done. It would be refreshing if our "consumers" had the same good sense now, say, toward the corporations, the media, or the government.

The lockout, by the way, was successful. Scabs were hired to replace the steelworkers; the spirit of the workers was broken, and many spent the rest of their lives in poverty. It wouldn't be until the 1930s that industrial unions were federally sanctioned and univer-

sally accepted. But I think I'll do everybody a favor and let Hubert
Heever and the rest alone. Even Lindbergh we used to call Colo-
nel. Hitler's friend. After all, he lived in the next town over from
Lambertville.

81 Betty Kray

I am full of strange feelings now, for an hour ago I passed the place
on Lexington Avenue where I last saw Betty Kray, someone, aside
from friends and family, only poets would know and for that mat-
ter only poets of a certain age, or those who take a special interest.
Betty—Elizabeth—came to New York with her husband, Vladimir
Ussachevsky, who taught music composition at Columbia. I believe
they lived on Claremont Avenue, with the other academics. I don't
know what she did before, but she began work for the Academy of
American Poets in the early 1960s and was, for twenty or twenty-
five years, the executive director and, as such, put poetry on the
cultural map through readings, programs, and prizes, including the
Poets-in-the-Schools program in New York and the Walt Whit-
man Award. She cofounded, with Stanley Kunitz, the Poets House
and organized walking tours in lower Manhattan in memory and
celebration of Poe, Melville, and Whitman. She had a plan to put
metal engravings of poems that took place in New York City at
their locations, and was going to place "Straus Park," which I wrote
in 1975, on the back of a park bench in that little park on 107th
between Broadway and West End Avenue. With her support, Phil
Levine and I organized the first poetry walk across the Brooklyn
Bridge as part of the huge centennial celebration in 1985 (while
eating dinner at the Grand Ticino on Thompson). There is a room
named for her in Poets House.

She had left a restaurant on Lexington—it was 1986, I think—
and was searching on the crowded sidewalk for one of her gloves.

I saw her—from a bus window—and got off immediately to help. We found the glove in the street by the curb and went back to the restaurant to recover with a cup of tea. The glove, a pale red, was covered in dirt, but she felt relieved she had found it and, I'm sure, would reclaim it. That was the last time I saw her—she died in 1987, seventy-four or seventy-five years old.

There was a group of us who sat in a restaurant somewhere holding a small memorial for her. My memory is that Galway Kinnell organized it, and it was originally only friends gathering for a pleasurable evening, and that it took the shape it did only gradually. I am content that, for me, it's in a fog, or a white cloud. It was a very small group, I remember, for such a "celebration." There may have been ten of us at the most. It would be foolish to try to guess if Jane Cooper were there, or Howard Moss, say. I want to let it be as it was, as it is. The only real memory is that we sat on leather or cushion-like seats, around a few tables in the form of a horseshoe. Galway was opposite me, four or five feet away; and he was eloquent, loving, and deliberate, as always. Or was it earlier and the occasion was something else, and we seized the moment? In memory, the issue is always to have the right combination to the lock. The most joyous thing is when the tumblers relent and the lock opens.

82 Hole in Forehead

In the middle of my forehead there was a gaping hole once where they had extracted something that made me less—or more—than I should have been. The extraction also surprisingly gave me the cynical power to dismiss what I fatuously called a vestigial or useless organ. It wasn't only that we didn't need it, we clearly did not need our own teeth, or our hair, or especially the heart that we had been born with, for there were chicken hearts and pig hearts and calf hearts lined up for miles on the wet planks of some

beloved seaside town, say Charleston; for unless we built a build-
ing for them, a factory or storehouse, there was no place else to put
them. But to say that "they" had extracted something smacks too
much of a malicious and sinister force, some government or secret
brotherhood, a corporation perhaps, or a tiny arm of an otherwise
benevolent society, hardly known and never advertised, innocent,
even motherly on the surface, so present in the narratives of the
late 1930s and '40s, even earlier in central Europe. Cognate with
mystical—or mythic—presences in fairy and folktales, or operas or
plays derived from them; or in the malicious grip of the cruel God
or the Obstacle; or in our great and domineering religions where
hugely educated (and learned) men tremble, starve themselves, lash
their own limbs, or appeal mutely or madly to that which can steer
them through or ignore or bless them, for it is good to be blessed,
as Mel Brooks says.

Though it was a poet's mouth, or his (or her) tongue that did the
dirty work, that put the meat-eating lamb on a throne or gave the
Lord his beard and his frown, and his stone tablets, to begin with,
who even provided the extraction; I'm sure of it. It was a way of
speaking, it was—here, there, everywhere—an act—it was acts—
of imagination, spells, bursts, that were accepted, finally, not as
metaphors, but oy, literally; and there was a direct line from the
poet to the *believer,* the *crude* believer, for, believe it or not, the poet
herself became a believer since she was caught in her own trap, for-
getting sanity for a second, and thus remained in perfect sync with
the repressive narrow-minded fundamentalist, even if her goal was
otherwise and her heart was elsewhere, and she was already into
another creation. I think this is obvious to poets, and to a few crit-
ics; it is even, as they said in Mother Russia, beating a dead horse.
So that, given Hanukkah, 2010, the festival of lights, Jews every-
where remember the miracle of the oil, how during the rededica-
tion of the Temple and the lighting of the eternal flame, there was

only enough (oil) for one day, but, miraculously, it lasted for eight days, just the length of time it took to press, prepare, and consecrate fresh olive oil. Or maybe the consecration itself took eight days. Something involving eight, for the Hanukkah menorah contains eight candles and one extra to light the other eight, called the *shammash*, the sexton—or janitor. Certainly, the shammash himself was a poet. Certainly it had to be a poet, not a priest, who invented the idea. In the Jewish joke, "Look who's being a nobody" (fortieth telling), it is the shammash who is the tenth man for the minyan. He wears secondhand clothes, has long hair and a heavy growth, and is more or less humble and apologetic. The others—doctors, dentists, lawyers, stockbrokers, who *provide* for the shammash—are upset; they nudge each other, when he—like the others—bows deeply, maybe the deepest, at early morning prayer in front of the ark and exclaims, like the others: "Good morning, Lord, forgive me, a nobody." "Look who's being a nobody," the stockbroker says to the dentist, nudging him. A poet invented the tale. He tied together the victory of the Maccabees over the Seleucid Empire (Antiochus IV Epiphanes) with the ever-burning oil, pure metaphor. It's a political holiday mostly, a Fourth of July, forced into the same time frame as Christmas and thus celebrated with it. Though, unlike Christmas, it's a relatively minor holiday; and it pushes fried food.

I don't think that a poet invented the dietary laws—Leviticus, Deuteronomy, and elsewhere—no poet is *that* boring—but a poet may have been attracted to, or created, the mystery of the pig. I like the idea, though I think it all came from the distant past, and poets just loved the mystery. I prefer to believe that the dictate against *eating* that animal was not, as such, because it does not ruminate, for though it may not chew the cud, it may indeed meditate, or at least it *considers*. High Criticism often thought of the pig as a god or referred to pig-worship in the Near East and elsewhere and suggested that the origin arose for that reason, though, as we all know,

one could just as well have *eaten* god as to have desisted, and, as a
matter of fact, pigs *were* sacrificed in Egypt, Greece, and southern
and western Europe, centuries before the common era. I used to
totally doubt the hygienic reason, but I'm not so sure now.

In addition to the drawings and cartoons I do, I write a little
doggerel, though I usually tear it up before anyone can see it. Here
is a little piece of bad poetry I was going to attribute to a former
student of mine. Then I realized how unkind it would be, even if
no one knows him. I gave him the name Solomon Levy, but that
was not his true name, though his initials were S. L. I wrote it or
he wrote it, while we were thinking about and listening to Delta
Blues, so there may be a very slight connection:

> I was eating pig before you was born
> so no sense in being succinct and forlorn
> for up in Chicago there's Muslim and Jew
> eating chicken and meatloaf too,
> but there's two main reasons they don't eat pork
> one in Detroit and one in New York,
> first it's the worm that everyone knows,
> gets into your stomach and there it grows
> and second the beast that Jesus called 'swine'
> was once in the desert revered and divine,
> but mainly because He said it was so
> and wrote it in Hebrew for us down below
> who hated that mountain and wanted a calf
> And hated His beard and hated His staff
> and didn't want to moan but wanted to laugh
> eating unclean pig or Kosher giraffe.

I liked that we had two sets of dishes and two more for Pesach.
I liked the fierce arguments among the three women in our house.
And I got used to drinking a glass of milk *before* the meat, for some-
how that was all right, digestive processes be damned. When my
former wife made pork and sauerkraut, once every three weeks
maybe, I would automatically have a stomachache for a couple of

hours after the meal, not severe but disturbing enough for me to loosen my belt or undo the top button. I thought it was from eating pig, I thought it was my punishment, and I thought it was psychosomatic, emotional—until, after some serious experimentation, I discovered it was from too much sauerkraut, especially the juice. But I don't like Chinese food, at least the kind I was exposed to, so I never knew what, as a Jew, I should do on Sunday night, till I remembered Hebrew National hot dogs. I even turned on the radio, hoping against hope that Jack Benny would be there again arguing with Rochester.

As far as First Paradise and the Fall and the snake and Adam and his missing rib, I feel that that, or those, in particular, were a poet's invention. When poets were into big things; and Genesis—may Moses and the Lord forgive me—as beautiful, and spare, as the writing is, may be a summary, or compendium, of a longer richer stranger more detailed more mysterious work. I suspect we would be surprised; I suspect there would be elements we can't understand. My main guess is that originally there was more of a closeness to the animals, and that they were more equal, more sovereign; that Eve was significantly different, more original and powerful, and the snake too, may he forgive us. We lost something that we may never have again. The secret text in Genesis may be that what we lost is not "innocence," but the Great Poem that describes it. Making Genesis a cunning work of criticism. To project the ideas of disobedience, nakedness, pain through childbirth, the destruction or reduction of the original abundance is, to my eyes (and ears) a little mad. Although those ideas could have come from a poet, maybe a bitter one or one with a sour stomach. The weird one here is Augustine, not just repressive, but weird; though let the saints enjoy themselves by watching us snakes burn endlessly. After all, we have some extra skins up our sleeves.

It may be presumptuous, or delightful, to say that all poetry, or all great poetry, is about love or death or God or war or various combinations thereof; or a fight with the father—or sister—or the dragonfly—or the self—or what being is; or what being human is; or fear, love of perfection, deep memory, dreams, and rose bushes; but just comparing love poetry with war poetry you can say that, though death is present in both, and even God may be, there's very little murder (in love), though there can be warfare of one sort or the other as a daughter, or son, chooses the other side or even a queen does, as in *Romeo and Juliet* and *Antony and Cleopatra*. And, to confuse things, poets are in the habit of using warfare itself as a convenient metaphor for lovemaking. John Donne did it, and Shakespeare, lovingly as it were, and in our time e. e. cummings is most famous for it. Though it has to be a war with cardboard swords, and no one should truly die from it. I am remembering some lines from Byron, but Keats was too deadly serious. What he gave us instead was "This Living Hand," written in the margin of another poem:

> This living hand, now warm and capable
> Of earnest grasping, would, if it were cold
> And in the icy silence of the tomb,
> So haunt thy days and chill thy dreaming nights
> That thou wouldst wish thine own heart dry of blood,
> So in my veins red life might stream again,
> And thou be conscience-calm'd. See, here it is—
> I hold it towards you.

"Love and War" doesn't interest me much, but I do love the tearful love songs of the war to end wars and the one to begin them, sentimental, nostalgic, even banal; but if throaty enough, very seductive.

Anne Marie and I saw *Brief Encounter* on Broadway a week or two ago, so I'm especially interested in adultery now; I mean, I don't want to be adulterous, I just want to think about it, or think about what Noël Coward, in a serious moment, did with it. I recognize that it's not *Madame Bovary* or *Othello* and that Coward is, by a very long shot, neither Flaubert nor Shakespeare, but it's his thoughts that, good or ill, I'm interested in now. I could only remember the 1945 movie version as I was watching the play, and I grew irritated and distracted by the acrobatics (on 47th Street) and especially by the enthusiastic applause. We were mainly watching juggling and horseplay, and I wanted to mount the stage and remind them of the simplicity, purity, and good acting of the film. As I understand it, the film, directed by David Lean, was a longer version of *Still Life*, a one-act play, written for Phoenix Theater's production of *Tonight at 8:30*—in 1936—and converted to a screenplay by Coward in the mid-1940s. It starred Celia Johnson and Trevor Howard and is, today, not only one of the most celebrated of all British films but, for most, ironically, the only thing of Noël Coward's they know. Ironically because the suave world-weary fashionable witty disenchanted entertainer, actor, songwriter, dancer, dramatist, and producer ends up defending, more or less, if his heart is in it or not, the "enduring value of sound English character and decent middle-class values" against cheap adultery and promiscuity. Though the play—and especially the movie—is about something else; namely the powerful, almost superhuman conflict within the mind and the heart of two driven souls irremediably lost. There is no way of explaining altogether what is happening nor why it has so affected so many generations of viewers. For a brief moment, for an hour, we—they—struggle with their love in the face of ridiculous circumstances, their deep feelings, their pain, played out against the trivial antics of an uncaring world, that is both a reminder of their tender and ridiculous situation and an expression of the chaos they have entered into.

Remember the plot: there is a chance meeting between Laura Jesson and Alec Harvey in the refreshment room of a railway station. She gets a piece of coal dust in her eye and he—a young doctor—removes it. It turns out they both go every Thursday to

Milford Junction, she to shop, visit the library, and break up the monotony of domestic life, he to work at the local hospital.

Laura is disturbed that she is looking forward to seeing Alec again, and not only do they begin to see each other every week, but it becomes the focal point of their lives. She (the narrator) is essentially conventional, she loves her two children and is very fond of Fred, her husband, who smokes a pipe and does crossword puzzles, and she is appalled by her own feelings. Alec, who is also married, but now deeply in love, persuades Laura to meet him in the borrowed flat of a friend, who surprises them by returning home earlier than expected, deeply humiliating Laura. Alec, after great hesitation, tells Laura he has accepted a post in South Africa, and they have their final meeting the next week in the refreshment room against the background of ham sandwiches, sweets, and a flirtation between the barmaid and the ticket collector. They are finally interrupted in their sad farewells by a garrulous friend of Laura's who sits at their table and prevents anything but a brief farewell, a touch on the shoulder. At the end Laura hears Alec's train pull out of the station and out of her life.

It is amazing how close we are throughout to the banal. Is it the depth of the acting, almost beyond the screen, that saves us? Is it the secret text, Coward's homosexuality and the deep and honest feelings that that engenders? Is it nostalgia for the past, a simple, more coded time? Is it pity for those two entrapped lovers? Is it, indeed, a still life? Out of my own ruthlessness I asked Anne Marie if she thought the two of them had actually made love somewhere, on a bridge, in a boat, a car, a field, lying down, standing up. Had they kissed—passionately? Had they touched each other? Did they have—oy—oral sex? I think now, how absurd their reticence. Is that the theme—respectability, duty, a stiff upper lip? If adultery is the subject, did they commit it? Didn't they go even one step further than Jimmy Carter, the guilty Christian? Why would *I*—

of all people—be moved? Can I confess, at this late date, that I smoked one Fred or another's pipe from time to time, and suffered very little? What did Rachmaninoff's second piano concerto and the express trains rushing by have to do with unbridled passion and with terror? What in the world was Noël Coward doing, who preached promiscuity, aristocratic loving, chain-smoking, drinking, talking, singing, dressing smartly, degeneracy, decadence, indifference, gossip, raised eyebrows, winking, and going upstairs with one and downstairs with another? Had he become decent respectable stable hardworking dutiful patriotic—at forty-five? Was he always, and the other was just an actor a charmer a creation a persona a schmuck? Can you believe he was critical of Edward VIII for preferring Wally Simpson to the throne? Didn't he know that was all front and Edward was an admirer of Hitler and *that* was the reason? In the Eyes of God wasn't Wally committing adultery? Did the Ears hear them moan? I forgive Coward his nauseating conservatism because he wrote—and sang—"I'll See You Again" and "Someday I'll Find You." If he had Shaw's mind or Ibsen's or Wilde's or Chekhov's he may not have had six or so *métiers*. I'm a little worried about *my* many. Can adultery contend with murder? What is the difference when love is present, or not? What is the worst element, or factor, in betrayal? Aren't there, in fact, two betrayals? The more I think about it, the more puerile the movie becomes. Forgive me or not, I think it was a great failure *not* to fuck, if that's what happened. Let's say England could have refrained from occupying India, in spite of the temptation. Let's say one hundred thousand Haitians have died of cholera and two young Christians are agonizing over their genitals, or two Jews.

Does this mean I'm on Edward VIII's side, that minor fool who gave up the throne for love, or so told a nation in order to keep the royal family in power? Ah, if Montaigne is my master I should be more forgiving. When did Edward, or for that matter Coward, ever trespass against me? I'm writing about myself as Montaigne did—even if my (his) subject is (was) something else. Anything that crosses my mind. Adding things in the middle of something else. Changing his (my) mind, my (his) heart. I know for a fact that there once was a gaping hole in the middle of his forehead. Something was stolen, something was given—everybody's favorite fairy tale. You spend eighty-five years trying to get it back.

83   The Stages of Life

Shakespeare, and a few others, have written about the "Stages of Life," youth, old age, and such. It was a favorite topic of the humanists, Italian and others; Shakespeare may have picked it up from Montaigne, an absolutely appropriate subject for that wise and sane master, stretching his mind a little and smiling at the foolish mortals he lived among. I think, by and large, the "Stages" is a happier subject for the wise under fifty than for those over seventy, not to mention those in the next decade after that. For the old, it's not the dearest of subjects, for very few—if any—enjoy contemplating the last stage. And, although there are several cowboy tunes about the last round-up, I think the spurred crooners might have been all of thirty, in some cases an ancient forty.

For me, at eighty-six, lying on my back on my art dreco sofa, it is a little like drowning, as it's imagined—and described—your whole life passing before you in a few seconds, though to tell you the truth—not to disappoint you—it's not really that much different from stage three, your twenties, or five, if that is the number, your sixties, although there are some things I can't tell you.

I have to admit that I like this drowning, although I'm very different from that little bird, the Piaf, who said (who sang) that she "regretted nothing," for I regret a lot of things, though I'm somehow less bitter about it than I was a while ago.

I actually adore the drowning—it's a joyous time for me—
though I can hear someone in stage two, or three and a half, saying,
"I guess that's all you have, that drowning you talk about; I prefer
living over remembering"; though this drowning, this is life too,
and anyhow I do other things besides drown. And sometimes you
linger, you slow down instead of speeding up; if I were to develop
the metaphor, I would call it floating, the mind doing that, the
mind at peace—or *removed*—I would call it removed. Disembodied.
I would say it's a kind of contemplation, something sweet beyond
measure. A gift given probably only to humans.

Today the lingering was different from what it was yesterday; and
there was less wildness—fewer women. I thought for a long time
about our last four months in Europe—Pat and I—in 1953 I guess,
and how we lived in Vienna because it was one of the two (unbe-
lievably) cheap places to live then, before we returned to America,
on the *Liberté*, with twenty-three dollars to our name. And how we
hated Vienna, the rain, the bitterness, the gloom, and stayed mostly
in our room, playing homemade board games I had devised, on rot-
ten cardboard. And how, when we first arrived and took a broken-
down pre-war streetcar, a tram, to the youth hostel, replete with
a conductor *and* a motorman, medals on their shiny black coats,
seven or eight customers aboard, I inadvertently brushed—really
just touched—the long overcoat of the passenger sitting opposite
me as I crossed my leg in the cramped space, and how he scolded
us, me, my wife, our suitcases, and how I exploded—in 1953—and
stood up screaming, in German and English, that I was a Jew and
I would kill every fucking Nazi in the car, and how the motor-
man stopped the tram and everyone ran off, motorman and con-
ductor included, thus terminating our plan to "make peace with
the Germans"—that Austria I am giving a reading in in a month at
the Sprachsalz Festival, my poems beautifully translated, on a few
shelves now in the bookstores in Berlin and Hamburg. And just

before I fell asleep I remembered, I lingered on, how—at twenty-two, in 1947—I almost became Librarian of the Commonwealth of Pennsylvania, an unfilled, purely political, undescribed position, through the help of some well-placed local politicians of the Democratic persuasion, fathers, uncles of my friends, including Poopdeck Tucker, a rival—in the party—of David Lawrence, then mayor of Pittsburgh and later governor of Pennsylvania; and Ziggy Kahn, who played football, and baseball, opposite the great Jim Thorpe, Ziggy—then an alderman, I think it was called—with an office on Forbes near Murray, land of my living. And how I thought mostly of what I would wear as librarian, what kind of hat, what boots; and how when I went to Harrisburg for my "interview" I was sadly informed by the state representative I was told to visit that power had shifted, and I was one day too late, and the job would be going to someone else. Probably, I realized, lying on my sofa—in August 2011—I was being lied to, that I didn't have enough "influence" or the right patronage, and I would have to wear a different hat, and other boots.

But the main thing—at this stage—is the memory, not the job in Harrisburg, Pennsylvania, and not the anger in occupied Vienna, not as such. And I have to be forgiven for writing—at times—without irony, cuteness, triple-think, avoidance, self-pity, and stealth, as simply as I can, with the same speed and the same "first-thoughts" I would in a letter.

84 Port Authority

I don't know if it is nothing or something, but I'm sitting here in the Port Authority Bus Terminal for the first time in months, really in years. Though I used to come here regularly, first to make my way to Easton, then later to Lambertville.

I'm in the main downstairs hall of the terminal. Outside it's 40th and Eighth, and the lifelike statue of Jackie Gleason, the slightly overweight bus driver from *The Honeymooners*, is at the entrance, Alice nowhere in sight; and up the six steps where you line up to buy your tickets, in the center of the room, is the George Segal group, in plaster, ready to walk through a door and onto a bus, but looking not like casts of real people as we thought they did in 1980, and thus literal facile and unimaginative, but—already— like ghosts, waiting to walk onto the boat—or into the bus—that crosses over, dead for years, as Segal himself is, their eyes oddly closed; nor is it their whiteness that makes this so, but their still- ness, their resignation, their *suspension*, their lives not a replica but a mere imitation of ours, since they were obedient to other laws. For, after all, he was—can you believe it?—a great sculptor after all. I should mention that the group contains three figures in a line, two women in front and a man behind them. I stood in line with them, as many hundreds already have, and I was struck by the obvi- ous, that they had the hairdos and the clothes of the late 1970s and that they were patient, as Americans—then *and* now—have to be, since they trust, and are not consulted. They were an inch or two taller than us, and their pants—bell bottoms—were almost drag- ging on the floor. The women were carrying heavy shopping bags and overstuffed shoulder bags, but the man only had a coat loosely covering his left arm.

I don't know what the architects thought of the huge building when it was being built and, finally, when it was finished. A very little research shows you that the original building, built in 1950, had beautiful Moderne and late-deco lines, a classic "new" bus sta- tion, with an almost noble entrance; but it was added to over and over again, in 1963 and in 1979, and a north wing was extended to 42nd Street. But I was—over the years—more or less happy with it because it was serviceable and convenient to my needs; even if it seemed disorganized and chaotic, as though certain parts were built *after* the fact (which they were) since the choices were slim and you really needed an hour, maybe two, of orientation and explanation. There are, for example, *two* entrances and endless faraway pockets of life and even of business—restaurants and the like. How would a Frenchman, or a Uzbekistani, get to Scranton, Pennsylvania, or Sandusky, Ohio, or Northampton, Massachusetts? Not to mention Roanoke, or just Newark. I was familiar with *my* buses, in one case, oh, thirty years ago, in one of those faraway pockets in the upper reaches, and—more recently, the downstairs gates—eight, nine, ten, twelve, for my relatively short journeys west and southwest. As far as beauty, I think that's not the right word, and as far as mystery, awe, and holiness, whatever it once had in 1950 is now gone. I don't think those things were ever considered in the expansion. In the pre-ruined Pennsylvania and in the Grand Central, there was, there is, transcendence and monumentality, but not in the Port Authority. I particularly dislike the façade, with the red diagonal girders. Maybe a new pile of bricks will be amassed in one of the decades to come, and there will be true plans for a long future, but I don't have a vote, nor a dollar to spare. I wish only that the weird six-inch seats, installed to discourage the shelterless, would be enlarged so that tired—or injured—travelers don't have to lean against the wall for twenty or thirty minutes like half-dead crows. Waiting there I sometimes forget that I am at the center of existence and that the gate will open in a minute to inconceivable emancipation, I who did have an abode and clung to it tenaciously, holding my unspent ticket in my hand, throwing my bag underneath, climbing up the enormous steps, taking my seat, pressing a lever so as to lean back, falling asleep almost before we left one dark place and, after a second or two of brilliance, entered another, call it a pleasant journey to Clinton, New Jersey, call it a bumpy preparation for the life to come.

It was as if, like Segal's patient white figures, I was also becoming obedient to other laws, for something else sometimes enters the mind as it did mine that day, October 23, 2010, at 40th Street and Eighth Avenue; for I was, for a few minutes, seeing things without delusion or entanglement (I ridiculously thought), and even making the world (I believed that morning) à little less foolish—and brutal—at least for a while. Though moving, as I was, by intuition and chance where my feet, my fingers, my mind, and my car took me, what was I following? And did I or did I not have faith?

Permissions

GERALD STERN's recent books of poetry are *Save the Last Dance*, *Everything Is Burning*, *American Sonnets*, *Last Blue*, *This Time: New and Selected Poems*, which won the National Book Award, *Odd Mercy*, and *Bread without Sugar*. His essay collection *What I Can't Bear Losing* is available from Trinity University Press. His honors include the Ruth Lilly Prize, four National Endowment for the Arts grants, the American Academy of Arts and Letters Award of Merit for Poetry, the Pennsylvania Governor's Award for Excellence in the Arts, and fellowships from the Academy of American Poets, the Guggenheim Foundation, and the Pennsylvania Council on the Arts. In 2005 Stern received the Wallace Stevens Award for mastery in the art of poetry and the National Jewish Book Award for Poetry. He is currently a chancellor of the Academy of American Poets. For many years a teacher at the University of Iowa Writers' Workshop, Stern now lives in Lambertville, New Jersey.